Fruitful Lessons

FRUITFUL LESSONS

upon the Passion, Burial, Resurrection, Ascension,
and of the Sending of the Holy Ghost

Myles Coverdale

A facsimile version of Bishop Myles Coverdale's book, first published circa 1540. This is the Parker Society edition, edited by George Pearson, B.D., and printed in 1844 at The University Press in Cambridge, England.

The mission of Baruch House Publishing, founded by editor Ruth Magnusson (Davis), is to bring to the world again the lost works of the early English Reformation. Our main focus is the 1537 Matthew Bible, and our ongoing work is to gently update it for readers today, with reference to the editor's own 1549 edition. The Matthew Bible was the joint work of William Tyndale (c.1491-1536), Myles Coverdale (c.1487-1569), and John Rogers (c.1500-1555). It is the only English Bible that was bought with blood: both Tyndale and Rogers were burned at the stake for their work.

Baruch House also plans to re-publish individually the best of Myles Coverdale's treatises and small books in attractive, easy-to-read format. This volume is the second such publication. The first was *The Hope of the Faithful*, published in 2020.

The publications of Baruch House Publishing include:

The October Testament. The New Testament of the New Matthew Bible (NMB). This is the New Testament translation of William Tyndale, with also the Reformation notes of John Rogers, gently and faithfully updated.

The Story of the Matthew Bible: Part 1, That Which We First Received. The true story of the making of the Matthew Bible.

The Story of the Matthew Bible: Part 2, The Scriptures Then and Now. Part 2 of *The Story* tracks the startling changes made to the Matthew Bible since the Reformation and reveals the motivations behind some of them.

Hope of the Faithful. Coverdale's essay setting forth the traditional doctrine of heaven and hell, written to refute those who deny that there is an eternal life and an eternal retribution. An appendix shows how the change from "hell" to "Sheol" and "Hades" in the 1894 Revised Version of the Bible defeated the traditional doctrine.

More information is on our websites:
www.baruchhousepublishing.com
www.newmatthewbible.org

FRUITFUL LESSONS

upon the

Passion, Burial, Resurrection, Ascension,
and of
the Sending of the Holy Ghost

By Myles Coverdale

From *Writings and Translations of Myles Coverdale,* published by the Parker Society. The Society was "Instituted A.D. M.DCCC.XL for the publication of the Works of the Fathers and Early Writers of the Reformed English Church."

EDITED FOR

The Parker Society,

BY THE

REV. GEORGE PEARSON, B.D.

RECTOR OF CASTLE CAMPS,

AND LATE CHRISTIAN ADVOCATE IN THE UNIVERSITY OF CAMBRIDGE.

CAMBRIDGE:

PRINTED AT

THE UNIVERSITY PRESS.

M.DCCC.XLIV.

Copyright © 2021 Ruth Magnusson Davis (Baruch House Publishing)

This facsimile edition of "Fruitful Lessons upon the Passion, Burial, Resurrection, Ascension and of the Sending of the Holy Ghost" is taken with gratitude from an original printing of the 1844 edition of the Parker Society volume *Writings and Translations of Myles Coverdale*. The original is in the public domain; however, a considerable amount of work has been invested in preparation of this facsimile. All rights are reserved. No part of this publication may be reproduced, stored in a retrieval system, or transmitted, in any form or by any means, electronic, mechanical, photocopying, recording, or otherwise, without the prior permission of the publisher.

Contact publisher through the website at www.baruchhousepublishing.com

Cover design by Iryna Spica

Canada CIP ISBNs: Paperback 978-1-7771987-3-2; Hardcover 978-1-7771987-4-9.

About the cover

The cover art is a detail from the *Last Judgement*, a large 15th-century triptych (three-panelled painting) by Hans Memling. The centre panel of the triptych shows angels hovering above Christ, who is seated for the Judgement. The angels are presenting the *Arma Christi* or instruments of the Passion, such as the nails and the crown of thorns, by which Christ saved his people from the Judgement and was crowned their king.

Publisher's Foreword

Myles Coverdale's treatise *Fruitful Lessons* was published circa 1540, early in the English Reformation. Coverdale's English was remarkably contemporary compared to other writers of his period, so readers will be pleased by how well they can understand him. However, Baruch House has added at the end of this book a glossary of words and expressions likely to cause difficulty in this and his other works.

In the 19th century, the Parker Society in England undertook to reprint in modern spelling some of the works of the Reformation. It is from their volume *Writings and Translations of Myles Coverdale* that this facsimile of *Fruitful Lessons* is taken. The editor, George Pearson, said in a foreword, "The idea and plan of this treatise are borrowed from one by Huldric Zuingle [Zwingli] … but the learned writer [i.e. Coverdale] has so far improved upon his model, that it is justly entitled to the character of an original work." Pearson added,

> There is no table of contents in the original work, nor are the different passages of the Evangelists mentioned, from which the extracts are taken. It has been thought right, for the sake of clearness and the convenience of the reader, to supply both these omissions in the present edition. In all other respects it is exactly conformable to the original copy.

We in turn also thought it right, for the sake of clearness and the convenience of the reader, to amend Pearson's table of contents to show the new page numbers for this edition and, also, to refer to our glossary at the end. Our amendments to the table of contents are shown within square brackets.

Fruitful Lessons is a work that lives up to its name. Its instruction about Jesus is fruitful for building in faith, and is worthy oft to be read. It pulls mind and heart from the world, exhorts to the godly hope that prepares for eternity, and develops the desire for righteousness that draws a man closer to God. Coverdale proceeds chronologically, expounding the sequence of events as set forth in the four Gospels, from the Lord's Passion to Pentecost, in short sections that are perfect for daily devotional reading. They would also serve well for a series of sermons.

The first part of each section is a Bible reading comprised of a passage or combination of passages from the Gospels. The readings follow the 1539/1540 Great Bible closely, but not exactly. For example, in the Great Bible, John 14:27 reads "Let not your hearts be grieved"; however, in *Fruitful Lessons* Coverdale put "Let not your heart be troubled," as he also had it in his 1535 Bible. The second part of each section, entitled "Doctrine and Fruit," expounds the Gospel passages and concludes with a prayer.

An appealing feature of *Fruitful Lessons* is Coverdale's use of the historic appellative "Jesu," either simply or, more commonly, in the collocations "Christ Jesu" and "Lord Jesu." This follows the Latin, which changes the form "Jesus" to "Jesu" in certain grammatical cases. This form was familiar to 16th-century English speakers from the Latin Vulgate Bible, and was also commonly used in German at the time, reflecting the Latin influence. Coverdale used "Jesu" more often in the Scripture passages quoted in *Fruitful Lessons* than he had done in the Great Bible. For example, John 19:38 in the Great Bible describes Joseph of Arimathea as "a disciple of *Jesus*, but secretly for fear of the Jews"; however, in *Fruitful Lessons* (see page 129), this becomes "a disciple of *Jesu*." Assuming that Coverdale was guided by Zwingli's collection of

PUBLISHER'S FOREWORD

Bible passages here and elsewhere, he was probably following Zwingli's form. This would be the case whether he worked from a Latin or German edition of Zwingli's work, since this usage characterized both Latin and the German of the time. He then carried this form over into his own expositions of the Scripture.

In his discussions of Scripture passages, Coverdale frequently – especially concerning the Passion of Christ – refers to the Lord Jesus as our "foregoer." Jesus is our foregoer in the path of suffering, death, and resurrection unto eternal life, and we bear good fruit when we follow his example:

> By the example of our foregoer, we must learn to forgive our neighbor, to pray also for our enemies, and for those that do us harm. If we gladly forgive that little, God will forgive us the great. If we so do, we find grace and are the children of the heavenly Father. As for the recompensing of all despite, and taking of vengeance, we must commit and refer that unto our Father, who judges righteously.

The sweet gentleness of the divine foregoer is evident in the work of his servant Coverdale, and spills over into the reader's cup to nourish him up in Christlikeness.

In his lessons, Coverdale explains the significance of many events of the Passion, including Christ drinking vinegar upon the cross, the tearing of the veil when he died, what he meant when he said that he would drink wine anew with his disciples in the kingdom of God, and much more besides. He applies the Scriptures to daily life with practical advice, such as how we show our love for God:

> If we will declare our love towards God, it must not be done only with word and tongue, but with keeping of his precepts. "The eyes of the Lord behold the righteous, and his

ears consider their prayers." God wills not that we, whom he through his grace hath admitted for his own children, and purified through faith, should go idle. Faith, which God giveth us in our heart, standeth not idle: we have for this purpose received it, even to keep his commandments.

Now is it his commandment that we deny and mortify ourselves, hate and despise the world, take up our cross upon us, and follow him, stoutly and manfully confessing and acknowledging him before the wicked world, loving one another as he hath loved us; innocently and godly leading our lives, whereby we may daily receive the more gifts at his hand. For if we keep not his grace that he giveth us, if we do not continually and daily reform ourselves and with all diligence fashion our lives after his life, it is but right that we lose again what we have received.

It is necessary to qualify something that Coverdale said a few times in *Fruitful Lessons.* He wrote this treatise during a hopeful time in the English Reformation, and urged upon his readers the importance of gathering for fellowship in the church – especially, to receive Holy Communion. However, in a work written shortly after Queen Mary had ascended the throne, he urged readers to flee the church because believers must not partake with the wicked. Therefore, this work must be understood in the context of its time. Further, Coverdale used the word 'church' ambiguously, at one time signifying the visible body and at other times the mystical body that is in Christ; the latter, for truth's sake, must sometimes separate from the former.

A final issue is the Parker Society editor's footnote at page 143. Here Pearson casts doubt on Coverdale's opinion that Mary Magdalene was the woman who anointed the Lord's head and feet as he sat at supper in the Pharisee's house (Lu. 7:36-50). Coverdale's is the traditional view, and is the view also taught in the

PUBLISHER'S FOREWORD

1537 Matthew Bible. It is my impression that, in recent centuries, scholars have too far laboured with their enquiries to cast doubt on the traditional views, with no benefit but only harm to the integrity of the faith. I, for one, dismiss the note as unhelpful and unnecessary. Nonetheless, the Parker Society performed an excellent service to Christendom by bringing Coverdale's writings to light again, and Pearson's annotations generally enhance the work.

The Parker Society's collections of Coverdale's works were contained in two large, heavy volumes that are not comfortable to read. Baruch House intends to publish the best treatises individually, in the same attractive and handy format as this book, so that readers may be encouraged to take them oft in hand. *Hope of the Faithful* was published in 2020, and *Fruitful Lessons* is the second in the series. Future projects include *Exhortation to the Carrying of Christ's Cross, Treatise on Death, Exposition on the Twenty-second Psalm* (i.e. Twenty-third Psalm, which Coverdale translated from Martin Luther), and his *Abridgement of the Enchiridion of Erasmus*.

RMD, Baruch House Publishing, 2021

This facsimile book has been carefully prepared from a publication that is now almost 180 years old. There are no missing pages, and each page has received close attention to correct imperfections due to age or damage, which might impair a good reading experience.

FRUITFUL LESSONS

UPON THE

PASSION, BURIAL, RESURRECTION, ASCENSION,

AND OF

THE SENDING OF THE HOLY GHOST.

Fruitfull Lessons
VPON THE
PASSION, BV-
RIALL, RESVRRECTION,

Ascension, and of the sending of

the holy Ghost.

GATHERED OVT OF THE FOVRE

Euangelists: with a plaine exposition

of the same.

By MILES COVERDALL.

JOHN 14. 6.

I am the waie, the truth, and the life, no man commeth vnto the Father but by me.

TABLE OF CONTENTS

	[NEW] PAGE
The Author to the Reader	[13]

CHAPTER I.
The Passion of Jesus Christ out of the holy Evangelists . [23]

CHAPTER II.
The Burial of Jesus Christ out of the holy Evangelists . . [129]

CHAPTER III.
The Resurrection of Jesus Christ out of the holy Evangelists [136]

CHAPTER IV.
The Ascension of Jesus Christ out of the holy Evangelists . [193]

CHAPTER V.
The sending of the Holy Ghost . . . . . . [201]

[Glossary . . . . 237]

THE AUTHOR TO THE READER.

SINCE our human imperfections are such, as one sin driveth out another, and the frailty of our natures is so great, as having touched the brim of the ocean thereof, we never cease till we are overwhelmed and drowned in the bottom of the same; since of ourselves we are but grafts of a corruptious tree, children of eternal darkness, infidels who bow the knee to Baal, having uncircumcised hearts and lying lips, whose minds are fixed on the world and fastened on mammon; I thought good, christian reader, considering the self-love in us, which have converted the angels into devils,—which, as Augustine witnesseth, hath builded the very Babylon of contempt of God[1],—to level out a way for all men to tread, a glass for all men to see, an adamant, wherewith all souls may be drawn to the beholding of their vices, the loathing of the same, and finally the amendment and hearty conversion for their misdeeds. And for that it most evidently appeareth, that the justest man falleth oftentimes a-day, and they that discern errors in themselves; and seeing then that they are in the next step to amendment, it behoveth us to consider the weakness which is in us, how far we are fallen and do fall from the protection of the just; so that in the end we

[[1] The following passage seems to be that referred to: Videte nomina duarum istarum civitatum, Babylonis et Hierusalem. Babylon *confusio* interpretatur, Hierusalem *visio pacis* . . . . Possumus tamen et aliquid afferre, quantum Dominus donat, unde distinguantur pii fideles, etiam hoc tempore cives Hierusalem a civibus Babyloniæ. Duas istas civitates faciunt duo amores. Hierusalem facit amor Dei, Babyloniam facit amor seculi. Interroget ergo se quisque, quid amet, et inveniet unde sit civis; et si se invenerit civem Babyloniæ, extirpet cupiditatem, plantet caritatem. Enarratio in Psalmum LXXIV. Opera, Vol. VIII. p. 144, A. B. Ed. 1541. See also Expos. in Apocalypsim Joannis. Hom. XVI. Opera, Vol. IX. p. 148, E. F.]

may in the spring of repentance wash away original and successive sins, which have defiled our souls, and cleaving to the true corner-stone, whereon our faith should be builded, withstand the perils of perdition, which our ghostly enemy hath raised against us.

And for that truth is never known but by his contrary, and our nakedness is not disclosed, unless our eyes be opened; let us examine ourselves, and we shall find that these are inseparable errors in us, from which the justest are not exempted, namely, blindness and corruptness of judgment, pride in spirit, mistrust in God, to be slack and weary in God's service, defacing of God's truth, not to have God before the eyes, surmising, vanity of heart, curiosity and niceness, grudging in our hearts against the enemy, bitterness, desire of vengeance, a man's good intent, greediness to be seen and praised, vain-glory, ambition, proper election, maintaining of our own evil, a disdainful, false, unfaithful, wicked eye, and such like pharisaical points and feats, wherewith the devil tempteth the good men that keep themselves from the gross vices. These and other innumerable vices shall every one, how good soever he be, find in himself, if he search himself uprightly and throughly to the bottom.

Seeing then, that we find ourselves so vicious, altogether sick, poisoned, and wounded unto death, we ought day and night without ceasing to complain and lament before God, to watch and pray unto God for remission of our sins; yet should we not despair of life. The true Physician of our souls came down from heaven, and through his passion hath he made us a plaister for our wounds; only let us use it and lay it to the sore. The faithful Samaritan poureth oil and wine into our wounds, taketh us up to cure and to heal us; only let us follow him, and fashion ourselves after his image. He is the brasen serpent without sin, whom with the eyes of faith we must behold hanging and lift up upon the cross for us: he taking our sins upon himself, giveth us his own innocency.

If the burden of sin now oppresseth and grieveth us, we ought to run unto him: he shall ease us and give us rest; for his blood washeth away our sins. Him hath the Father given unto us to be our righteousness and redemption.

Besides this great treasure that God hath given us in

Christ, he is set forth unto us, especially in his passion, for a pattern or example, whereby we may learn to die from sin, and find a preservative against vices to come. For self-love and high esteeming of a man's own self is the well-spring of all vice. Consider that Christ was not proud himself of his own highness, but took upon him the shape of a servant, and came to serve us, humbled him most lowly, loved not himself, sought not his own, desired not his honour, but the honour of his Father; all despite and reproach fell upon him. If we ponder this by faith, all greedy love of ourselves shall fall away.

The obedience of Jesu in true belief considered expelleth and healeth our disobedience, and the idolatry of our own carnal heart. With his obedience covereth he the disobedience of all men, so far as we abide in the obedience of faith, that Christ be dearer unto us than the whole world; for the which cause we freely give over ourselves into his obedience, suffering all things for his sake. Pride and vain-glory is healed through Christ's humility and contempt, which he suffered for us manifold. "Learn of me," saith he; "for I am meek and lowly of heart." Why are we so greedy of temporal things, when Christ, the Lord of heaven and earth, became for us so poor, hanging bare and naked upon the cross? The chaste pure life of Jesus Christ expelleth in us all uncleanness of the flesh. Also his martyrdom, anguish, and trouble, which in his flesh he suffered for us, quencheth the lust and concupiscence of the flesh.

Oh, how evil doth it become a believer to be ireful and greedy of vengeance, when his forerunner, being in most humility like unto a sheep, prayed for his enemies!

Envy and hatred is highly expelled, if we consider the excellent deep love of Jesu towards us. Gluttony and excess of life shall fall away from us, if we well remember that Christ for us drank vinegar mixed with gall.

As it is here shewed in certain points, even so against all vices and blemishes of the soul there may remedy be found in the passion of Christ, if it be rightly used in the contemplation of faith. The old Adam ought we to lay aside, to mortify the members upon earth, and to put on Christ the Lord, as the new wedding-garment. In the cross ought to be our exercise, our joy, comfort, and life.

Hereunto also helpeth us our heavenly Father, who unto us his children, whom he most entirely loveth, suffereth manifold passions, afflictions, troubles, and anguishes, sickness, poverty, and persecution to come, to keep us upon the cross, lest we as negligent people gape for temporal earthy things. And if we will needs follow our own lusts, he hedgeth our way with thorns, nurturing and humbling us through trouble; that we, being tried and purified as the gold in the fire, may cry and call unto him, and that we may give our earthly things, seeing we find no quietness in them. He bringeth us into the land of promise, howbeit through the wilderness, through much travail and labour. Blessed are they that in patience, without murmuring, suffer the Lord to work, and do faithfully follow him.

All this, and more than I can say, ought to be the consideration and exercise, when we celebrate the supper of the Lord Jesu, that we so sprinkle the blood of Christ in our hearts, and drink it into us, that it may work in us, and bring forth fruit. Our eyes and hearts we ought to lift up into heaven, and consider what the bread and wine pointeth us unto, namely, unto the body of Christ, that was offered up upon the cross for our sins, and to his blood, that was shed for the washing away of our offences; and that we fashion ourselves unto his image, and practise also such love one towards another. This is the proof that Paul speaketh of, with the which a faithful believer ought to exercise himself before and in the Lord's supper, examining well his faith and love, which out of the love of God towards us is kindled and increased. First, ought a man to consider the excellent love of our Lord Jesus Christ, who so loved us, that he died for us. And seeing that he biddeth us to so high a feast of his grace, we ought also to ponder the same in such sort, that we be thankful unto him, and prepare ourselves thereafter.

St Paul saith, that there is a feeding with milk, and a feeding with strong meat, which is to be observed according to the nature and property of those that receive the meat. And in the church of God there be three sorts of men, as the same by the high illuminated good wise teacher Augustine and by others is written[1].

[[1] This classification of the members of the christian church does not appear in any single part of the works of Augustine, although it

First, there be men, which having spent their former time past in pastime and wantonness of the world, and con-

agrees with his general opinions on the subject. 1. With regard to the first class (who are described under the character of *Penitents*), the opinions of Coverdale will be found to harmonize in general with those of Augustine, as they are detailed in his general works, where he treats on the subject of repentance. 2. With regard to the second, who are described by him under the character of *Reformers*, the doctrine of Augustine is contained in his Treatise De Trinitate, c. 16, 17. Opera. Vol. III. p. 99, I. p. 100, A. B. Ed. Par. 1541. 3. Of the third class of persons, namely, those who are called *Perfect*, Augustine speaks in different parts of his writings, but more especially in his discourse, " De perfectione justitiæ contra Celestium;" and in the following remarks on those passages of the old and new Testament, which speak of the attainment of holiness, and contain exhortations to it; e. g. Deut. xviii. 13; Matt. v. 48, &c.: " Horum testimoniorum aliqua currentes exhortantur, ut perfecte currant, aliqua ipsum finem commemorant quo currendo pertendant. Ingredi autem sine macula non absurde ille dicatur, non qui jam perfectus est; sed qui ad ipsam perfectionem irreprehensibiliter currit." Augustin. Opera, Vol. VII. p. 307, L.

The expression τὸ τέλειον is also used with reference to the Eucharist,[*] as it is frequently called in the canons of the ancient councils. (Concil. Ancyrani Canones. Can. 4, 5, 6, apud Routh, Rel. Sacr. Vol. III. pp. 405, &c.; Suicer. Thes. p. 1259; Bingham, Orig. Eccles. Lib. I. c. iv. 3.) But the terms τέλειος, τελειόω, τελείωσις, are also used by some of the Fathers, and particularly those of the Alexandrian school, to denote the religious condition of the more advanced Christian, (Suicer. Thes. pp. 1256—9; Routh, Vol. III. p. 227); as may be seen in the writings of Clemens Alexandrinus, in whom the following passage occurs, remarkably illustrating the opinions of bishop Coverdale in this passage: ὁ δὲ ἐν τῷ σώματι καθαρισμὸς τῆς ψυχῆς πρῶτος, οὗτός ἐστιν, ἡ ἀποχὴ τῶν κακῶν· ἥν τινες τελείωσιν ἡγοῦνται· καὶ ἔστιν ἁπλῶς τοῦ κοινοῦ πιστοῦ, Ἰουδαίου τε καὶ Ἕλληνος, ἡ τελείωσις αὕτη· τοῦ δὲ γνωστικοῦ, μετὰ τὴν ἄλλοις νομιζομένην τελείωσιν, ἡ δικαιοσύνη εἰς ἐνέργειαν εὐποιΐας προβαίνει· καὶ ὅτῳ δὴ ἡ ἐπίτασις τῆς δικαιοσύνης εἰς ἀγαθοποιΐαν ἐπιδέδωκεν, τούτῳ ἡ τελείωσις ἐν ἀμεταβόλῳ ἕξει εὐποιΐας καθ' ὁμοίωσιν Θεοῦ διαμένει. Strom. Lib. VI. pp. 464, 5. Ed. 1616.]

[*] Is. Casaubonus Exercit. XVI. 48. adv. Baronium: " τὸ τέλειον, *perfectio* aut *consummatio*, est ipsa Eucharistia, quæ etiam Dionysio dicitur τελείωσις, ut ante observabamus: quia conjunctioni nostræ cum Christo, cujus instrumenta sunt verbum Dei et sacramenta, veluti colophonem imponit participatio corporis et sanguinis Christi in cœna Dominica: nullus enim restat alius modus, quo in terris versantes arctius cum Christo capite nostro conjungamur."

sidering the careful end thereof, as they be inwardly moved by the grace of God, have undertaken to cease and refrain from sin, and from all occasions of sin; and in most diligent wise, as near as they can, with the assistance, grace, and help of God, to be circumspect and wary thereof; albeit they are yet weak, and have not so strong a spirit, as to lay aside and despise all worldly things out of hand. And these are the right true beginners of repentant and *penitent* persons: though they be not new beginners, yet are they unto God the Lord so dear, that all things cannot sufficiently commend and praise it.

This is witnessed unto us by the holy gospel of the unthrifty son; who, when with shameful riot he had wantonly consumed his inheritance, did in time of his extreme hunger convert and turn again to his loving father, and received not only gracious forgiveness of his trespass, but also special tokens of his father's love; as the garment, the kiss, the fat calf, the sweet minstrelsy and melody. This is the first anchor of true repentance. This is the first state concerning the blessed swine-herd, who forsaking the hogs with the cods[1], draff, or swillings, that he sometimes greedily filled his belly withal, and returning to his loving father, is now in his first coming again to his merciful father graciously taken up, received, and rewarded.

Whoso now with this unthrifty son forsaketh his sins, and coming again in true and hearty repentance unto God, his most loving and gracious Father, saith meekly, "O Father, I am not worthy to be called thy son, for I have sinned against heaven and before thee; O make me one of thy hired servants;" to him shall the Father deny nothing. Whoso now with an unfeigned heart and mouth may speak this unto God, and truly and unfeignedly seeketh Jesus, assuredly he findeth him and hath with him a cheerful supper. Look unto whom God in his great mercy giveth such a taste of his grace, let him render thanks and praise unto Almighty God: let him now look for it, that the Father who hath received him, will also nurture him in his own school, and through manifold adversities furnish him, prepare him, and make him more perfect. He hath been fed with the milk; he must learn also to know what hard meat

[1 cods: husks.]

meaneth. Through adversity and troublesome chances he must be tempted and proved, whether he have ought in him of the blessed seed that groweth upwards unto eternal life: which thing shall well appear and be made manifest, if in time of temptation and troubles he be not choked with the thorns, nor trodden down by the high-way-side, nor withered among the stones, but found fruitful in a good and fertile ground.

Other men there be, which are called *reformers*, to whom belongeth somewhat more than there doth unto the other. For like as it appertaineth to the first repentant or penitent persons, that they continually and fervently, with the confession of their sins unto God, with sorrow and lamentation, with prayer, watching, and chastising of the body, do break out away from their old sins, harnessing and arming themselves against others for to come, and earnestly withstanding and forsaking their own evil and naughty customs, if they mind to bring forth fruit, and not to fall away again; even so the reformers in the second order and manner, after the hard rooting out of vice and wickedness, must still exercise themselves in the will of God and in good works, seeking diligently experience thereof in holy scripture, and of those teachers, who by reason of long practice, and by the scriptures, can declare and teach the same way. When these men in such a stedfast purpose to walk and practise themselves in the will of God with his grace and power, do go unto the supper of the Lord, they inwardly with joy and fruit of the godly feast are nourished and refreshed. For whoso desireth to cleave unto virtue and to a godly life, shall nowhere find the same so evidently and plain, as in Christ's passion, whereof he is mindful at the supper with faith and thanksgiving.

The third sort of men are called *perfect*: not that any man here in time may be perfect, as to lack nothing, or to have no sin in him; but therefore are they named perfect, because their exercise is such, that after long accustomate doing of virtuous deeds, after many spiritual fruits brought forth by them in patience, after many temptations, which they with the help of God have overcome, they have so wholly humbled and cast down themselves before God, being reconciled with him, that they are become one spirit with

Christ their head, whom they cleave unto, whose cross and holy passion they follow without fainting, so far as their wit and power may suffer; being dead from the world and the flesh, following only the Lord Jesu Christ, suffering with him, and living with him. These with their minds and hearts step somewhat higher than the others, having their dwelling in heaven, in the sweet contemplation and beholding of God's almightiness, wisdom, and goodness, with fervent devotion. Which men also, by enjoying of the said feast according to their belief and fervent love, receive the more excellent rites, whereby they may expel the temptations that they like not. For the devil keepeth no holy day; he sleepeth not, runneth about as a roaring lion, he ceaseth not; and therefore these men continually get them to their weapons, with the consideration of the passion of Christ. Abraham, the good friend of God, must still drive away the ravenous birds from the sacrifice, till the sun go down, and till a man cheerfully say: "In peace will I lay me down and take my rest," &c.

This probation must be well taken heed unto; for many men not justly considering themselves, neither right discerning this meat from others, receive the food of life unto death. Not that this holy bread was instituted and ordained of Christ, to hurt any man; but because the evil man doth wickedly receive that which is wholesome, and abuseth it through unbelief, therefore justly doth Paul exhort, that there be first had a diligent examination of a man's self, and that then he eat of this bread, and drink of this cup. Thus let every man take good heed to his own state and vocation, that this banquet may set him forward, not unto his hurt, but to eternal life.

Whoso taketh not heed unto this difference, and to himself, as, alas! carnal people do, which are not spiritually instructed; the same faileth oft in many things, and undertaketh to fly high, yea, higher than his knowledge and power may attain. Hereof then it also proceedeth, as we see before our eyes, that so few folks come to stedfast amendment, namely, even hereof, that when men are not exercised in discerning of God's matters from others, a mad heady notion of sensuality provoketh them inordinately to sit highest at the table, whereas yet they are not worthy of the lowest place; and so will they forthwith possess the seat royal, afore they have found the asses, or kept the sheep, as of David and Saul in figure it is read. But thus ought it not to be: for though the grace of the Holy Ghost use not long fetches about, yet cometh no man suddenly to the happiest step. I speak after the common course, as it beseemeth us to talk and do in the church of God, namely, after the ordinance which he hath appointed us.

Behold St Paul, being so perfect in the law, that the world could not accuse him; being also chaste, earnest, fervent, and well exercised in all virtues; whom God, that had separated him from his mother's womb, would call to his service. Though he was taken up into the third heaven, and saw secrets that no man can express, yet doth he not trust so much thereto, as by reason of that great grace to magnify himself, and to take upon him the office of preaching, before he being taught at Gamaliel's feet, and baptized and instructed of Ananias, had perceived in himself and proved that same, which he afterwards out of the perfectness of the Spirit might distribute abroad unto all Christendom. This is peradventure laughed to scorn of the unexpert, proud, worldly-wise: but whoso hath ears circumcised with the fear of God, will think more upon the matter.

He that will sit now at the table of the high King, let him diligently consider what he receiveth in his soul through faith, namely, the body and blood of Jesus Christ, which feedeth and nourisheth him to eternal life, and draweth him to God, altereth him, and maketh him stedfast, which the outward bread taken with the mouth doth point and lead unto: yea, let us ponder, how great love, and what an example Christ there setteth before him, that he also must prepare the like; that is, that he to his power must follow the love, life, and passion of Christ, to the intent that he, being wounded with Christ's love, and fastened with him upon the cross, may abide in him unto the end.

For in the passion of Christ is the instruction of the way which we ought and must follow unto eternal life. There also is information, where and how the same way and the everlasting truth is shewed and found. Thus the penitent findeth the way, the reformer the undoubted unwandering truth, the perfect the very life eternal, which is Christ Jesus, and there is eternal peace. God grant that all they which read this little book, and consider this matter, may so burn in love and fervent devotion, that they continue and live in Christ, and he in them for ever! Amen.

[CHAPTER I.]

THE PASSION OF CHRIST OUT OF THE HOLY EVANGELISTS.

[Matthew xxvi. 1—9. Mark xiv. 1—25. Luke xxii. 1—19. John xiii. 1.]

THE feast of sweet bread, which is also called Easter, drew nigh, namely, after two days. Then said Jesus to his disciples: Know ye, that after two days shall be Easter, and the Son of man shall be betrayed and crucified. At the same time were the chief priests and council gathered together in the palace of the high priest, whose name was Caiphas; and there they counselled, how they might craftily apprehend, take, and kill him. Howbeit they feared the people. Therefore said they together: Not on the holy day, lest there be an uproar among the people. But Satan was entered into Judas called Iscariot, one of the twelve, who went out to the high priests and rulers, intending to deliver him unto them: therefore how he would deliver Jesus unto them, he told them, and said: What will you give me, and I will deliver him unto you? When they heard that, they were glad, and agreed with him, promising him thirty pence. Then promised he them, and sought from thenceforth opportunity, how he might deliver Jesus unto them handsomely and without any uproar.

But afore the feast which is called PASSAH, Jesus, knowing that his hour was come, and that he should depart out of this world unto the Father, while he loved his own that were in the world, he loved them unto the end.

On the first day of sweet bread, when they offer passah, the disciples came to Jesu and said: Where wilt thou that we go and prepare passah for thee? Then sent he two of his disciples, namely, Peter and John, saying: Go and prepare for us, that we may eat passah. They said: Where? Then said he: Go into the city to one: behold, when ye enter in, one shall meet you bearing a pitcher with water; follow him into the house that he entereth into, and say unto the householder, The Master saith unto thee, My time is now here, that I will eat passah with thee. Where is now the place where the multitude shall be kept? Where is the parlour, that I shall eat passah in with my disciples? Then shall he shew you a great parlour that is paved; there make ye ready.

So the disciples went, and found as the Lord had told them; and they made ready the passah. At even came Jesus with the twelve, and when it was time, he sat him down at the table, and the twelve with him.

Now when he sat at the table with his disciples, and they did eat, he said: I have greatly longed and heartily desired to eat this passah with you afore I suffer. For I say unto you, that now from henceforth I will not eat of it, till it be fulfilled in the kingdom of God.

Now as they did eat, Jesus took the bread, gave thanks, and brake it, gave it to his disciples, and said: Take, eat, this is my body, which shall be betrayed and delivered for you; do this in remembrance of me. Likewise also when they had eaten, he took the cup, rendered thanks, and gave unto them, saying: Take and divide among you, and drink ye all thereof. This is my blood of the new testament, which is shed for you, and for many, to the forgiveness of sins. I say unto you, that from henceforth I shall not drink of the fruit of the vine, until the day that I shall drink it new with you in the kingdom of my Father. And they all drank thereof.

NOW FOLLOWETH THE DOCTRINE AND MEDITATION.

HERE should we children of belief diligently ponder and consider, what Christ hath done for our sakes; namely, that he, when he had fulfilled his ministration committed to him of the Father, and now would offer up himself upon the cross for the sins of the world, and with his own death deliver mankind from the captivity of Satan, and from eternal death, declared, how he loved his own until the end, and with what desire he longed to eat the Easter lamb with his disciples, before he suffered. 1 Cor. v. Isai. liii. John i.: giving them thereby to understand, that he was the true paschal Lamb, which, being slain for us, should take away the sins of the world, that the figures of the old testament might be reduced into the truth; that like as the Jews, to whom with a prescribed ordinance it was commanded yearly to eat the Easter lamb, did the same for a memorial of their deliverance out of Egypt; so we believers also might in the new testament have a remembrance and exercise of the gracious redemption, whereas we by his death are delivered from the power of darkness, of the devil, and of sin, and brought to eternal life. John xiii. Luke xxii. Exod. xii.

And to the intent now that the remembrance of such excellent benefits, grace, and merits of the passion of Christ, might ever be fresh and new with his disciples and all believers, our Lord Jesus Christ, when he now would go unto death, and pay the ransom for the sins of all the world, he then did eat the Easter lamb with his disciples, to finish the shadow of the old testament; and that he might be remembered thereby, he instituted the bread and wine for a sacrament and memorial of his holy body and blood.

Seeing then that we are cleansed, delivered, and redeemed with so dear and worthy a treasure, namely, with the precious blood of Jesus Christ, the undefiled Lamb; we ought never to forget such an high benefit, but at all times with thankfulness to remember, that Christ our paschal Lamb was slain and offered up for us upon the cross, that we from henceforth should walk in pureness, singleness, and innocency of life; and that, when we in the supper by true faith do eat his body, and drink his blood, we might through him be so strengthened and fed to eternal life, as to abide and 1 Cor. v.
1 Pet. i.
1 John i.
1 Cor. xi.
1 Cor. x.

1 Pet. ii.

<small>John vi.</small> live in him for ever. For he is the bread of life that came down from heaven, to nourish and strengthen our weak and hungry souls, yea, to make us dead to live again.

But then eat we his flesh, and then drink we his blood, when we through true belief do ponder and consider, what he hath done and suffered for our sakes; then are we partakers of his supper and feast, when we for his sake do live, as he did for his Father's sake. He gave himself whole unto us: so ought we to give ourselves whole unto him, and to our neighbour; to him through belief, to our neighbour <small>John xv.</small> through charitable love. Through faith we abide in him; by working love he abideth in us. The more we love, the more enjoy we of this meat; the more we believe, the more <small>John xiii.</small> we love. In this shall all men know that we are his dis- <small>1 John ii. iii. iv.</small> ciples, if we love one another. God is love; and he that <small>John xv.</small> abideth in love, abideth in God, and God in him. What greater love can there be, than to give his own life for us? The death of Christ ought never to come out of our hearts; that we may do and suffer all things for his sake that died for us.

THE SECOND PART.

[John xiii. 2—17.]

WHEN supper was ended, after that the devil had put in the heart of Judas Iscarioth, Simon's son, to betray him; Jesus knowing that the Father had given all things into his hands, and that he was come from God, and went to God, he rose from supper, and laid aside his upper garments, and took a towel and girt himself. After that poured he water into a bason, and began to wash his disciples' feet, and to wipe them with the towel wherewith he was girt. Then came he to Simon Peter: and Peter said unto him, Lord, dost thou wash my feet? Jesus answered and said unto him, What I do thou knowest not now, but thou shalt know hereafter. Peter said unto him, Thou shalt never wash my feet. Jesus answered him: If I wash thee not, thou hast no part with me. Simon Peter said unto him: Lord, not my feet only, but also my hands and my head. Jesus said unto him: He that is washed needeth not save to wash his feet, but is clean every whit; and ye are clean, but not all: for he knew who should betray him; therefore said he, ye are not all clean. So after he had washed their feet, and received his clothes, and was set down, he said unto them again: Wot you what I have done you? Ye call me Master and Lord; and ye say well, for so I am. If I then your Lord and Master have washed your feet, ye also ought to wash one another's feet: for I have given you an ensample, that ye should do as I have done to you. Verily, verily, I say unto you, The servant is not greater than his master, neither the messenger greater than he that sent him. If ye understand these things, happy are ye if ye do them.

DOCTRINE AND FRUIT.

HERE ought we diligently to consider the unspeakable *Love.* and fervent love of our Lord Jesus Christ, who until the end leaveth nothing undone that may serve for our welfare. Likewise also should we ponder and regard the meek lowli- *Humbleness.* ness of him, in that he the King of heaven doth humble himself, even to wash his disciples' feet, which thing is accounted base and vile amongst men; yea, even unto the man that betrayed him, is not he ashamed, neither refuseth to shew such lowliness and work of love.

By this we learn to declare all works of charitable love unto our neighbour, and not to be ashamed, how high soever we be, meekly to do our neighbour service, though he be poor, base, and small in reputation, yea, albeit he hath already hurt and betrayed us. We ought to learn with Christ our head to do good, not only to our brethren and friends, but also to our adversaries, enemies, evil willers, and such as love us not; even unto them should we shew friendship, serving them, being gentle, mild, and loving unto them. We must pray unto the Lord, that he will grant us grace to fulfil and do that we hear and read of him.

Furthermore, considering that we daily perceive in ourselves spots and blemishes of sin, so that our feet, that is to say, our affections and desires, while we walk in the miry way, are still continually defiled and stained; we ought therefore incessantly to watch and to call unto God, that he with the water of his grace will vouchsafe to make clean our feet, and wash away the mire of earthy and carnal spots, that we in the pureness of faith may abide in Christ our head, and he in us.

OF THE SERMON THAT CHRIST MADE UNTO HIS DISCIPLES AFTER THE SUPPER.

[Matthew xxvi. 31—35. Mark xiv. 18—21. Luke xxii. 31—34. John xiii. 18—38.]

The exhortation and warning of Christ.

THEN said Jesus unto his disciples: This night shall you all be offended because of me. For it is written: I shall smite the shepherd, and the sheep of the flock shall be scattered. But when I am risen again, I will go before you into Galilee. Peter answered and said unto him: And though they all be offended because of thee, yet will I not be so. Then said Jesus to him: Verily I say unto thee, that this night, before the cock crow twice, thou shalt deny me three times. Upon this spake Peter further: Though I should die with thee, yet will I not deny thee: and so said all the disciples likewise. But Jesus said: I speak not of you all, I know whom I have chosen. He that eateth bread with me, shall lift up his heel against me. This I tell you aforehand, ere it come to pass; that when it is done, ye may believe that I am he. Verily, verily, I say unto you, he that receiveth him whom I send, receiveth me; and whoso receiveth me, receiveth him that sent me.

The presumption and rashness of Peter.

The dignity and worthiness of the disciples.

The foreknowledge of Christ.

When Jesus had spoken this, he was troubled in spirit, and protested, and said: Verily, verily, I say unto you, one of you shall betray me, yea, even he that eateth with me. The disciples looked one upon another, and doubting of whom he spake, they were very sorry and dismayed, and began to say one after another: Lord, is it I? Then said Jesus: One of the twelve, even he that dippeth his hand with me in the platter, he shall betray me. The Son of man goeth, as it is written of him: but woe unto him, by whom the Son of man is betrayed! Better it were for him, that he never had been born. Then said Judas that betrayed him: Lord, is it I? Then spake Jesus: Thou hast said. *The presumptuousness of Judas.*

One whom Jesus loved among the disciples lay upon Jesus' lap. To him beckoned Peter, and said: Who is he, that he speaketh of? Now when he leaned on Jesus' breast, he said unto him: Lord, who is it? Jesus answered: He it is, unto whom I shall reach the sop. And when he had dipped in the bread, he gave it unto Judas Simon Iscarioth; and after the sop entered the devil into him. And Jesus said unto him: That thou doest, do it quickly. None of those that sat at the table, perceived why he spake this: some thought, seeing Judas had the purse, that Jesus had commanded him to buy something necessary at the feast, or to give something unto the poor. Now when he had taken it, he went out immediately, and it was night. *Treason cometh of the devil.*

Now when he was gone forth, Jesus said: Now is the Son of man glorified, and God is glorified in him. If God be glorified by him, then shall God glorify him in himself, and shall straightway glorify him. Little children, I am yet a small time with you. Ye shall seek me, and as I said unto the Jews, whither I go, ye cannot come. And now I say unto you: A new commandment I give you, to love one another; as I have loved you, that ye even so love one another. Herein shall all men know and perceive, that ye are my disciples, if ye have love among yourselves. Then said Simon Peter: Lord, whither goest thou? Jesus answered him, and said: Whither I go, thou canst not follow me now, but thou shalt follow me hereafter. Then said Peter unto him: Why may not I now follow thee? I will jeopard my life for thee. Jesus answered, Wilt thou jeopard thy life for me? Verily, verily, I say unto thee: afore the cock crow, thou shalt deny me thrice.

DOCTRINE AND FRUIT.

GOOD virtuous children should hearken most diligently unto the words of their father, and fasten them in their hearts; but specially those words which he speaketh and committeth unto them, now when he mindeth by death to depart from them, and to take his leave of them. For the same words, being the last, pierce very deep into the heart, and are never forgotten. Seeing then that we are God's children, and Christ here nameth us so to be with his disciples; we ought very diligently to ponder and consider all his words and doctrine, but specially such as he uttered unto them when he now would go to his passion. For there shall we find an ardent, earnest, and fervent doctrine, full of most excellent, godly, and inestimable love, proponed[1], and thrust into their hearts, with words sweeter than honey. In this oration bringeth he forth specially that same, which most of all concerneth his disciples. First, the Eternal Wisdom declareth, that he is ignorant of nothing, that unto him there is nothing hid. He knoweth what shall happen unto them through weakness of the flesh and fear of men: albeit our feebleness and imbecility doth always break forth, presume, and brag more than we are ever able to perform, as we have example in Peter. Such heady rashness the Lord rebuketh, admonishing us of our own weakness and fall.

Moreover, we ought to consider in Christ our head and forerunner, how earnestly and lovingly he mentioneth and warneth the traitor, setting his great offence before his eyes, and always touching him, to remove him from his wicked purpose. Yet maketh he mention of him, and of the vice, in such sort, that he never desireth his hurt, but only his conversion and amendment. His desire is, that he were reformed, not that he should be bewrayed, or that any harm should happen unto him by him or others. Such lenity and gentleness ought we also to shew and declare unto our ene-

[1 Proponed: propounded.]

mies, and those that hurt us; if it only concern us, we should not be desirous of vengeance. And though we all ought sore to mourn in the church, that is to say, in the christian congregation, if there be transgressors and naughty people, applying our diligence the best we can, that such be not therein; yet where as their vices be secret, and as yet not opened, we ought in love and patience to bear and suffer them until the harvest, when the Lord shall purge and cleanse his floor. Besides this, we ought not to cease with warning and advertisement, with correction and doctrine, that they may leave off from their obstinate wickedness.

And when the congregation of God through his grace is quit of such evil people, and discharged of such wicked blemishes, God must be thanked, and diligence applied, that no wicked thing breed therein again.

But above all things must we regard that principal and new commandment, which Christ giveth us; namely, upon the love, that he after a new sort hath declared and performed; by the which love he reneweth those that are his, and plentifully endueth them through the Holy Ghost, whom he giveth in their hearts. Love comprehendeth and fulfilleth all laws: therefore Christ leaveth all other commandments, and admonisheth us only of love. *Love.*

Love hath he himself shewed us aforehand; of him must we learn to love. Love is the assured and unfailing evidence of the children of God. Whoso hath not it, though he had all other virtues, yet hath he nothing, neither is it profitable to him that he hath. If he have love, then hath he all things that are necessary for his health and salvation. Therefore ought we to regard nothing so much as love. There is nothing more acceptable, nothing more perfect, nothing better in heaven and earth, than love: for it is of God, and may rest nowhere else but in God. Only love maketh us godly, and shapeth us likest unto God; namely, that love which springeth and groweth out of a pure heart, out of a good conscience, and of an unfeigned faith. Nevertheless we must love one another, not with words only and with tongues, but with the deed, and in the truth, even with our whole hearts, as Christ loved us.

[John xiv. 1—14.]

Jesus said unto his disciples: Let not your hearts be troubled. If ye believe in God, believe in me. In my Father's house are many mansions. If it were not so, I would have told you. I go to prepare a place for you. And if I go to prepare a place for you, I will come again, and receive you even unto myself, that where I am, ye may be also: and whither I go ye know, and the way ye know. Then said Thomas: Lord, we wot not whither thou goest; and how is it possible for us to know the way? Then said Jesus: I am the way, the truth, and the life. No man cometh unto the Father, but by me. If ye had known me, ye had known my Father also. And now ye know him, and have seen him. Philip said unto him; Lord, shew us the Father, and it sufficeth us. Jesus said unto him: Have I been so long time with you, and yet hast thou not known me, Philip? He that hath seen me, hath seen the Father; and how sayest thou then, Shew us the Father? Believest thou not, that I am in the Father, and the Father in me? The words that I speak unto you, I speak not of myself; but the Father that dwelleth in me, is he that doth the works. Believe me, that I am in the Father, and the Father in me. At least believe me for the very works' sake. Verily, verily, I say unto you, he that believeth on me, the works that I do, the same shall he do also; and greater works than these shall he do, because I go unto my Father. And whatsoever ye ask in my name, that will I do, that the Father may be glorified by the Son. If ye shall ask any thing in my name, I will do it.

DOCTRINE AND FRUIT.

When the disciples of Christ heard of his death and departing, what trouble should fall upon them, and what should happen unto them through the weakness of the flesh,

they were very heavy and dismayed; for they had great <small>Adversity.</small>
love unto the Lord, and loath were they to depart from
him, and yet might they not follow him at this time.
Therefore lovingly doth the Lord comfort and strengthen
them, saying: Be not afraid, let not your heart be
troubled. This comfort is spoken unto us all; for while
we live here, we must look for much trouble and adversity, whereof springeth many times heaviness, fear, and
unpatiency in our flesh. Therefore Christ, who corporally <small>Patience</small>
is absent from us, but present among us with his grace,
speaketh unto us inwardly by his Spirit in our hearts, or
outwardly by his word and exhortation, comfortably strengthening and mightily comforting our feebleness; giving us
gladness also in sorrow.

To be without adversity, if it please God otherwise,
is not good for us; to be rash and heady is hurtful.
Therefore bringeth he us in between fear and hope, that
we should turn neither to the right hand nor to the left.
Much adversity suffereth he to come unto us, so that ofttimes fearfulness and sorrow falleth on us: but this keepeth
us in his awe, cutteth our comb, bringeth down our pride, <small>Meekness.</small>
and humbleth us. Out of this we learn, that if any human
infirmity and feebleness fall upon us, as it did upon the
disciples in the Lord's passion, we shall not utterly despair,
nor fall away through fearfulness; but remember, that in
this time it happeneth so of course, that we must suffer
and bear much trouble and adversity, to the intent that the
glory and power of God may be opened in our weakness:
and yet in all our adversity must we be manly and stout,
valiantly fighting for his name's sake. And though of weak- <small>The fear of God.</small>
ness we be fallen in the field, yet will he have compassion
upon us, and graciously forgive our fall. For who would not
be afraid to fall, when the earnest and fervent apostle Peter
fell so sore, and all the other disciples fled from the Lord?
If this chanced to the beloved disciples, no man need to think
the contrary, but the like may happen unto him. He that
standeth, let him stand fast in the fear of God, and look that
he fall not.

Christ unto his own that stand in this conflict and dan- <small>Faith,</small>
gerous battle, giveth the shield or target of faith, which they
cast up, and receive all strokes and shot therein. Believe

ye in me, saith he. Whoso believeth in Christ, believeth in God; for Christ is God. This faith giveth strength, and overcometh all adversity. As if Christ would say: Be not afraid by reason of my bodily absence. Though ye see me no more from henceforth with bodily eyes, yet with my grace and comfort will not I forsake you, but be with you until the end of the world. I will alway remain with you; only look that ye believe in me, continuing and cleaving fast unto me with the belief of the heart; so will I defend, deliver, and save you for ever. Be not afraid for any adversity; put your confidence in me. After your trouble, there is prepared for you an excellent great joy, and an exceeding unspeakable reward. For in my Father's house are many dwellings, which from everlasting have been prepared for all the elect, that believe in me, and follow me under the cross. I will not deceive you, I will shew you no unfaithful touch; I will not disappoint you, into no fool's paradise nor false hope will I bring you. If the mansions were not prepared for you in my Father's house, I would tell it you: but doubt ye not in my promise; fall ye not off from faith and hope; stay your belief and affiance stedfastly upon me; hope undoubtedly for the dwellings to come, which are ordained and prepared of my Father for you. Here is nothing but misery and trouble; here is no abiding, no dwelling, but a pilgrimage. Here ye are among strangers: but in my Father's house are many dwellings, not only for me, but also for you. And forasmuch as now through my death I will furnish and perfectly open and make an entrance into the same dwellings, which were prepared for you of my Father afore the creation of the world; be not you therefore dismayed by reason of my death. My death shall be your life and salvation. Through my death go I before you, and make you a way unto heaven. Look what the Father of his gracious goodness hath ordained for you from everlasting, that will not he give you, but through me; therefore must I die, and with my death open you the entrance unto life.

And albeit that through my death and ascension I shall corporally depart from you; yet will I not fail you, neither forsake you. Like as by my death I open unto you the entrance into the heavenly mansions, so will I send you my holy Spirit, who shall furnish you, and make you meet for such dwellings. That I go from you, it is done for your wealth; therefore be not sorry, that I open the dwellings unto you. I will come to you again, and receive you to myself; that ye may always be with me in my Father's kingdom. For he that serveth me, shall also be eternally with me in my Father's house. Thither will I bring you through my power and grace; fear ye not, and believe in me. Thus ye know whither I go, namely, unto the Father, to work your welfare: ye know also through what way ye must follow me, even through faith and adversity. Abide ye stedfast in faith, and put your trust in me; so will I be your faithful mediator and attorney in the presence of God my Father.

And if we would say, as Thomas did, that we know not the way, the Lord Jesus instructeth us further, and saith, that he is "the way, the truth, and the life." This ought we poor sinners well to fasten in our hearts, that Christ is the only way which bringeth us unto God, and that no man may come unto the Father but by him. We should not therefore erect or choose unto ourselves any other way. Only by Christ must we come unto God: this hath he spoken, that is the truth itself, and cannot lie. In the way is he our guide, and by it he leadeth us unto himself, and so by himself unto God. Through this way we come to life, and though we must die in adversity for his sake, yet in him we find eternal life; for he is the life and resurrection. Whoso believeth on him cannot die, but cometh out of death into life; and though he die, yet shall he live in him everlastingly.

Christ is the only way.

Furthermore, we must take sure hold upon Christ's promise, which in life and death shall strengthen and comfort us; in that he promiseth us, he will give us all that we desire in his name. Wherefore in all our necessity and trouble we ought to have recourse only unto him, or unto God his Father in his name. And then do we pray in his name, when we desire that which may serve to the honour of his Father, that the Father may be honoured through the Son, and in the Son, when we desire such wholesome good things, as the Spirit of Christ moveth us unto.

All this doth stir up in us patience, peace, joy in the Holy Ghost, belief in Christ, who is our God and head; whom by his doctrine and wonderful miracles we have learned to be very good in deed. The holy scripture also, both of Old and New Testament, doth sufficiently declare the same, as Esa. vii. ix. xlii. xlix. lxii. Hier. xxiii. xxxiii. Mich. v. Zach. xiii. Mala. iii.

What doth he else in his whole gospel, but evidently and strongly prove that Jesus is very God? as in the i. ii. iii. iv. v. vi. vii. chapters; yea, in all.

Christ calleth himself the Son of God, and teacheth every where, that we ought to believe on him. Now if he were not very true God, then had he deceived us, then had he taught us wrong, and then were he himself a false teacher; for we must believe in none, save only in God. If Christ now were not God, how should we believe in him? If he were a false teacher, then would not the Father have commanded us to hear him; then had not he spoken from heaven these words, "This is my dearly beloved Son, hear him:" then had not he also confirmed his cause with miracles, raised him up from death, taken him up into heaven, and set him on his right hand: for he hateth all liars, and hath no pleasure in the wicked.

John viii. : "Afore Abraham was, I am." Christ saith, that "the Father hath given him all power in heaven and earth." Matt. xxviii. Which sentence alone were sufficient and strong enough, to prove that Christ is God; for God giveth his glory and honour to none other. Esa. xlii. He saith also, that " what the Father hath, it is his." John xvii. And, John xx., saith Thomas unto Christ: "My Lord and my God." By him were all things created. John i. Col. i. Then must he needs be God; for no creature is the maker or creator of all things. Paul saith: "He is the wisdom of God." 1 Corinth. i. The wisdom of God is eternal. Prov. viii. Eccles. xxiv. Rom. i. ix. In the Epistle to the Hebrews, what doth Paul else, even from the beginning, until he come far within it, but bring in testimonies, that Christ is [1 John iv.] very God? John saith: "Every spirit which confesseth, that Jesus came in the flesh, is of God." Out of the which it followeth, that as concerning his divine nature, he was from everlasting, afore he came in the flesh. Item: Paul to the

Hebrews saith: "God took upon him the seed of Abraham:" [Heb. ii.] then must he needs be eternal God, before the humanity was. As also John saith: "The Word was God, and the Word became man." Item: "No man hath seen God at any [John i.] time. The Son of God which is in the Father's bosom, he hath opened it unto us." John iii. Saith Christ: "No man ascendeth into heaven, save he that came down from heaven." Now canst thou not say, that he came down, as touching his human nature; for that took he first upon him in the Virgin Mary. Luke i. Then must it needs be true, that he came down concerning his Godhead; as he oft saith: "I came [John xvi.] forth from the Father;" and Paul, Phil. ii.: "He took upon him the shape of a servant." Who? God. Also, John xvii., he saith: "Glorify thou me, O Father, with the glory and honour, which I had with thee afore the world was created." And, 1 John v.: "We know that the Son of God is come, and hath given us understanding to know him, who is the true God: and we are in him that is true, even in his Son Jesus Christ. The same is the true God, and the eternal life."

Seeing then that God hath given us his Son to be our righteousness, our sanctification, saviour, redeemer, ransom, life, light, and head, to believe and trust in him, and finally by him to be saved, he must needs then be the true living God; else might not, neither should our heart trust nor cleave unto him. This ought a believing heart fully and well to take hold of, and stedfastly to stand thereupon.

[John xiv. 15—24.]

IF ye love me, keep my commandments; and I will pray the Father, and he shall give you another Comforter, that he may abide with you for ever; even the Spirit of truth, whom the world cannot receive, because the world seeth him not, neither knoweth him; but ye know him, for he dwelleth with you, and shall be in you. I will not leave you comfortless, but will come to you. Yet a little while, and the world seeth me no more, but ye see me; for I live, and ye shall live. That day shall ye know that I am in my Father, and you in me, and I in you. He that hath my commandments and keepeth them, the same is he that loveth me; and he that loveth me, shall be loved of my Father, and I will love him, and will shew mine own self unto him. Judas said unto him, not Judas Iscariot: Lord, what is the cause that thou wilt shew thyself unto us, and not unto the world? Jesus answered and said unto him: If a man love me, he will keep my sayings; and my Father will love him, and we will come unto him, and will dwell with him. He that loveth me not, keepeth not my sayings: and the words which ye hear, are not mine, but the Father's which hath sent me.

DOCTRINE AND FRUIT.

CHRIST promiseth his disciples, that is, such as believe on him, that he will give them whatsoever they make petition for, or desire; yea, if they love him. For faith without love is dead, and hath no strength. Where there is faith in man, there followeth love. Many of us say, We believe in Christ, and we love him, yet we keep not his commandments. *He that loveth worketh.* Such men ought well to note the words that Christ here speaketh: "Whoso loveth me, keepeth my commandments." The disciples thought that they loved Christ right, because they were sorry for his departing; but Christ teacheth us, that love consisteth in the keeping of his commandments. If we will declare our love towards God, it must not be done only with word and tongue, but with keeping of his precepts. *Psal. xxxiv.* "The eyes of the Lord behold the righteous, and his ears consider their prayers." God will not that we, whom he through his grace hath admitted for his own children, and purified through faith, should go idle. Faith, which God giveth us in our heart, standeth not idle: we have for this purpose received it, even to keep his commandments. *God's commandment.* Now is it his commandment, that we deny and mortify ourselves, hate and despise the world, take up our cross upon us, and follow him, stoutly and manfully confessing and acknowledging him before the wicked world, loving one another, as he hath loved us; innocently and godly leading our lives, whereby we may daily receive the more gifts at his hand. For if we keep not his grace that he giveth us, if we do not continually and daily reform ourselves, and with all diligence fashion our lives after his life, it is but right that we lose again what we have received.

And if any man saith, it were unpossible for man to keep God's commandments, (as it is true indeed,) yet unto us that believe in Christ are all things possible, not in ourselves, but in Christ our head. If we abide in him through faith, then hard and unpossible things are light and possible unto us; for in him that strengtheneth us we may do all things. And if we love God, then for his sake that is beloved we may do and suffer all things; for there is nothing but love overcometh it. Our Lord Jesus Christ fulfilleth the commandments and will of his heavenly Father. So far as we now are his members incorporated with him, and abiding in him as our head through faith, our daily exercise, ferventness, and diligence shall be in undertaking to perform and keep his commandments. And if we out of a true belief do apply such diligence to keep his precepts, then may it be perceived that we love God. *All things possible to believers.* *Love overcometh all things.*

And if that, after such diligence in keeping God's commandments, there be aught lacking, (as we shall ever here want something,) we must cry unto our heavenly Father, and pray: "O Father, forgive us our debts and trespasses." And then have we with him a faithful Mediator, even Jesus Christ the righteous, who maketh intercession for us, and taketh our faults upon himself; and what we are not able, that fulfilleth he for us. Thus is it his first and highest commandment, which he earnestly requireth of us, that we believe in him. Where the same faith is right, it brings with it love, which keepeth all the commandments. Now when we begin to break our minds off from earthy worldly things, and to set them upon godly heavenly things, which Christ calleth us unto; then take we in hand to be obedient unto God the Father, after the example and pattern of Christ; for he loved us first. If we now also love him, and practise ourselves in his love, then shall he help us to keep his commandments. *Faith, love, keeping of the commandments.*

And to the intent that we may be able to put our trust

in him, to love him, and to observe his precepts, he promiseth us his holy Spirit, to work all such things in us.

He comforteth also his disciples and all his elect in this world; as if he would say: "Be not ye afraid, neither sorrowful, by reason of my departing. Albeit I now die, and go corporally from you unto the Father, yet will I always have a fatherly love, faithfulness, and care for you; neither will I leave you friendless, as those that are utterly destitute of all help and consolation. I will pray unto the Father, so that he shall send you another to succour and comfort you. While I have been with you myself, I have instructed and taught you in all things that were necessary for your welfare. Unto all such works as are acceptable unto my Father, have I exhorted you; unto all good things have I moved you; from all evil have I defended you; in all trouble and adversity have I comforted you. I have been your teacher, your exhorter, your attorney, your advocate, and mediator; so that ye have lacked nothing, neither hath any man hurt you. Seeing now I have hitherto never failed you, I will also from henceforth not forsake you, but pray unto my Father, who shall send unto you the Holy Ghost.

The office of God's Spirit. The same shall perfectly bring to your remembrance, and be your teacher in all that I have shewed you; he shall exhort and admonish you, aid, succour, and comfort you; so that ye shall not be without consolation. He shall be your tutor and defender; neither shall he be with you only for a time, as I have been, but even in your hearts shall he dwell with you, and never depart from you.

Of this helper, comforter, teacher, and tutor, shall ye also have need; for great trouble and persecution shall the *Comfort and strength in adversity.* world move against you. To overcome the same, is your flesh too feeble: therefore will I send you down from heaven a power, whereby in all adversity ye may be able to stand fast, and to have the victory.

O the unspeakable love of our Lord Jesu Christ, who taketh such diligent care for us, and endueth us with so excellent a gift, namely, his own holy Spirit! With what modesty and soberness, with how pure and honest behaviour ought we to walk, seeing that God hath into our hearts given his holy Spirit, who utterly abhorreth and loatheth all vice and all filthiness of sin? Great diligence ought we therefore to apply, in keeping clean and undefiled our bodies and souls, which God through his holy Spirit hath purified and consecrated to be his own dwelling place and temple, lest we expel the chaste Spirit of God. For in no froward soul abideth he, neither dwelleth he in that body which maketh itself slave and thrall unto sin. The ears of our mind ought we to open, and to hearken whereof this Spirit admonisheth us, and what doctrine he in our Saviour's words doth teach us; and his motion ought we to follow. Afraid ought we not to be: he that is in us is stronger than all our enemies.

This Spirit hath Christ by his prayer and merits obtained of his Father; for he prayed with weeping and tears, and was heard for his worthiness' sake.

He is called also the Spirit of truth, because he proceedeth of the truth, teacheth the truth, and maketh us true: we are else of our own nature altogether liars, inconstant, untrue, and dissembling hypocrites; and whatsoever the world speaketh and doth, it is nothing but vanity and lies. Blessed therefore are they, unto whom God giveth the high gift of his truth.

The world, that is to say, fleshly men and children of the world, receive not this Spirit; for they despise the word of Christ, and laugh it to scorn. Therefore God sheweth not himself unto them, for they love him not; which thing they declare, in that they refuse his word. But whoso receiveth his word, sheweth thereby that he loveth Christ and God: him will God love again, and open himself ever more and more unto him. This is a high reward, which God giveth unto his lovers; that he cometh unto them, maketh his dwelling, and abideth alway with them, working all good things in them and by them. Therefore ought we earnestly to hear his word, to love him, and to keep his commandments. And so even the same his own Spirit, which he gave us at the beginning, shall he still grant unto us more perfectly from time to time. Thus shall that Spirit pour out love in our hearts, and endue them with more perfection. The love of the world, which is not of God the Father, shall this Spirit root out and daily consume; but the love of God it shall continually plant and increase. The more love there is, the more groweth the knowledge of God; yea, the more God's knowledge increaseth, the more fervent and perfect is love. Grant us, O gracious Father, thy holy Spirit, to take possession of our heart; that it may only trust in thee, love thee above all things, keep thy commandments, and cleave still unto thee for evermore. Amen.

[John xiv. 25—31.]

THESE things have I spoken unto you, being yet present with you. But that comfort which is the Holy Ghost, whom my Father will send in my name, he shall teach you all things, and bring all things to your remembrance, whatsoever I have taught you. Peace I leave with you, my peace I give unto you. Let not your heart be troubled, neither fear. Ye have heard that I said unto you, I go, and come unto you. If ye loved me, ye would verily rejoice, because I said, I go unto the Father; for the Father is greater than I. And now have I shewed you before it come, that when it is come to pass, ye might believe. Hereafter will I not talk many words with you; for the ruler of this world cometh, and hath nought in me. But that the world may know, that I love the Father; as the Father gave me commandment, even so do I. Arise, let us go hence.

DOCTRINE AND FRUIT.

THE Lord Jesus continueth his oration in comforting his disciples, and in telling them what the office of the Holy Ghost should be. Whereby we learn, that all reading and hearing, yea, and all doctrine, bringeth utterly no fruit, if the Holy Ghost do not give us understanding, and teach us the word of God. For the disciples were ignorant and forgetful: many things that Christ had told them, they understood not; many things had they forgotten; in many things they doubted. Such like happen also unto us. Therefore ought we at all times to pray unto God, that he will send us his holy Spirit, to admonish and provoke us, to comfort and strengthen us, to instruct and teach us all things that are necessary for us

We must all be taught of God, which is done by the Spirit.

to salvation. He is the right heavenly schoolmaster: when he cometh into us, he expelleth all ignorance away.

But forasmuch as there remaineth much trouble and adversity unto all faithful believers, while they live in this time, Christ doth therefore promise them his peace against the turmoiling, unquietness, and trouble of this world. In the world are many hurley-burlies and adversities; in Christ we find true peace and quietness. And Christ unto those that are his giveth such a peace, as surmounteth all understanding; in the which peace they being coupled and knit, are able valiantly to overcome all enemies and adversity. For inasmuch as they know, and be undoubtedly assured through faith, that their sins are forgiven and taken away by Christ, that the Father of heaven is favourable and gracious unto them, that they be his own children and inheritors, they do little pass what thing outwardly happeneth unto them. All adversity and trouble that outwardly is laid upon them, is through the inward joy and peace which they have in God clean swallowed up, and so forgotten. They settle and stay their hearts upon salvation and eternal peace. *The peace of Christ through the Spirit. Phil. iv.*

The peace of the world seeketh quietness and rest of the body, throweth away the cross, and flieth from it: the peace of Christ rejoiceth in the midst of adversity, and overcometh the cross. For faithful believers look unto Christ, who went before them unto the Father, and after his passion and death took possession of so high honour and glory, and hath carried their nature up so high unto the right hand of the Father, where he now ruleth as a mighty king of heaven and earth. Oh, how great comfort, how sure a hope giveth it unto us, when we see our own nature, our own flesh and bones, incorporated unto Christ, the only-begotten Son and eternal word of God, in so high honour and glory! How can it be otherwise, but we must needs hope, that our weak flesh also shall be taken up? *Worldly peace. Our nature exalted in Christ. Comfort in adversity.*

Look what is past in the head, the same shall assuredly be fulfilled in the members; for without the members cannot the head be. Which thing considered, and through true belief printed in the heart, maketh a man patient and cheerful in all adversity, giveth peace and joy in all trouble. Let the prince of this world, through his ministers and members, stir up all vexation against us, yet hath he no vantage of us, *The devil hath nothing in the faithful.*

<small>We must suffer, that we may be obedient unto the Father.</small> if we be in Christ. Easily might he find somewhat in ourselves, but in Christ nothing; such innocency doth Christ make us partakers of. Tempt us he may, and thrust at us; but to overcome us he is not able, so far as we abide in Christ. In us is death a punishment of sin; in Christ it is obedience and love. For seeing the Father loveth the Son, and of very love gave him unto death for us, the Son would of love obey the Father; and as he also loved us, so would he willingly and obediently suffer death for us, that all the world might see his obedience, and that we might learn of him to obey our heavenly Father, even unto the death, and faithfully follow his precept; and that likewise, whereas it toucheth his glory, we should be afraid neither of adversity nor death, considering how obediently he died for our sakes.

[John xv. 1—8.]

I AM a true vine, and my Father is an husbandman. Every branch that bringeth not fruit in me, he taketh away; and every branch that beareth fruit, he purgeth, that it may bring forth more fruit. Now are ye clean through the words which I have spoken unto you. Abide in me, and I in you. As the branch cannot bear fruit of itself, except it abide in the vine; no more can ye, except ye abide in me. I am the vine, ye are the branches: he that abideth in me and I in him, the same bringeth forth much fruit; for without me can ye do nothing. If a man bide not in me, he is cast forth as a branch, and withered; and men gather them, and cast them into the fire, and they burn. If ye abide in me, and my words also in you, ask what ye will, and it shall be done unto you. Herein is my Father glorified, that ye bear much fruit, and become my disciples.

DOCTRINE AND FRUIT.

UNDER this fair similitude doth Christ teach his Church, that without him we can do nothing, but in him all things.

Now forasmuch as he through his grace hath incorporated us unto himself, we ought with great diligence to apply ourselves, that we may abide in him, and bear fruit. For as long as we are in him, we live, that is, we receive lively virtue and sap of him, namely, his Spirit. For whoso cleaveth unto the Lord, and is incorporated unto him through faith, the same is become one spirit with him. 1 Corinth. vi. For hereby know we that we are in him, and he in us, in that he hath given us of his Spirit. 1 John iv. For why? In the vineyard the branches are of one nature and kind. Thus the only-begotten Son of God took our nature upon him, is become man, and giveth us of his Spirit, and maketh us to be of a godly mind and spiritual nature. Out of the same pith and sap do all manner of godly virtues and good works break forth. Gal. v. Psalm lxxxv. (lxxxvi.) For through his grace are we his operation and work in Christ Jesu, created unto good works, wherein we are bound to walk. And seeing we have received Jesus Christ of God the Father, we ought to walk in him, that in him we may be well rooted and stand fast. *Eph. ii. Col. ii.*

But hereby know we that we are in him, if we walk as he hath walked. For whoso saith, that he abideth in him, then even as he walked, so must we do. 1 John ii. But if we would say, that we were in him, and had fellowship with him, and yet would walk in darkness, (seeing he is the light, wherein is found no darkness at all,) then were we liars, and went not about with the truth. But if we walk in light, as he is light, and we children of light, then have we fellowship and company with him, and the blood of Christ purgeth us from all sin. 1 John i. *What it is to abide in Christ.*

In Christ Jesu may no man be idle and without fruit. 2 Thess. iii. Whoso now is unthankful to the grace of God, and doth not practise himself in good works to God's glory, the same is cut off, and as an unfruitful dry branch, thrown into the fire and burnt. Faith grafteth us into Christ; love declareth that we are planted in, and it knitteth the members with the head. Where the Spirit of Christ followeth from the head into the members, from the stock into the branches, there are fruits of the Spirit; for by the fruit is the tree known. *Punishment of unthankfulness. Gal. v.*

Christ through his word and Spirit hath pacified[1] us, that *How the faithful are clean.*

[1 An error probably for *purified*.]

is, he hath called and separated us from the world and from the filthiness of the flesh unto good works. And into his own service and school of godly nurture hath he admitted us, and written up our names. He hath begun to purge and cleanse us from carnal lusts, and from all uncleanness of the world, accepting us into the number of those that die from the world, and that now from henceforth will live unto him, and bring forth fruit. But that is not enough; we must also obediently wait upon the grace that he hath placed us in, applying our diligence, watching, and praying, that from so high a vocation, from so excellent grace and honour, we fall not away again. 1 Cor. x. It is not enough to have begun, there must be a stedfast continuance. He that forsaketh the head again, hath neither spirit nor virtue; for without him we are able to do nothing. Therefore through faith and love ought we to abide in him, having respect unto him in all things; so shall we bring forth much fruit unto him. Then abide we in him, when we do that he commandeth us, and love that which he promiseth us. Howbeit, these fruits that we bring forth are not ours, but the Father's; to him ought we to bring them forth, unto his honour must they extend. Matt. v. xxviii.

1 Pet. i.
Faith bringeth fruit.
The good works are not open[1].

For when God's light doth appear and shine in our conversation, and many folks thereby are drawn unto God, the Father of heaven is honoured, his name is hallowed, and then are we his disciples. For we have learned of him, how Christ was obedient unto the Father, and sought his glory in all things; and so do we likewise.

Hereunto ought all our prayers to extend, that we may bring and win much unto Christ. Therein is the Father praised, when we bring unto him much fruit; but that might we not, if God had not given us his Son, that we might be his branches, and he our vine.

What we ought to pray.

Where faith is, there is the Holy Ghost, which teacheth to wish and pray for that only, which may serve for God's honour; and that is the cause, why he that prayeth, obtaineth all his desire: for God may not give over his glory. Whoso undertaketh to further that, him doth he assist and help.

[1 Qu. ours.]

[John xv. 9—17.]

As the Father hath loved me, so have I loved you. Continue ye in my love. If ye keep my commandments, ye shall abide in my love, as I have kept my Father's commandments, and abide in his love. These things have I spoken unto you, that my joy might remain in you, and that your joy might be full. This is my commandment, that ye love together, as I have loved you. Greater love than this hath no man, that a man bestow his life for his friends. Ye are my friends, if ye do whatsoever I command you. Henceforth call I you not servants, for the servant knoweth not what his Lord doth. But you have I called friends; for all things that I have heard of my Father, have I opened unto you. Ye have not chosen me, but I have chosen you, and ordained you, that ye go and bring forth fruit, and that your fruit remain: that whatsoever ye ask of the Father in my name, he may give it you. This command I you, that ye love together one another.

DOCTRINE AND FRUIT.

Oh, how excellent great consolation is this to us all, which believe in Jesus Christ, and are undoubtedly assured in ourselves, that Christ loveth us as his own children and disciples, howsoever the world judge us to be forsaken of him! If this love came right into our heart, oh, how earnest and fervent should we be to love him again, to further his honour, to keep his commandments, and in charitable love to serve our neighbours! Then should all good works and keeping of God's commandments flow out of faith; namely, when we believe that God is favourable and loving unto us, yea, that he is our Father, and his Son Jesus Christ our king, head, and brother. This faith worketh through love: for we could not love God, if he had not loved us first. His grace, love, and mercy preventeth us. *Entirely doth Christ love those that are his.* *1 John iv.*

Therefore doth Christ ever still set forth his love before us, as a light torch, to kindle us in love towards him and our neighbours. If we believe this grace, committing us cheerfully unto his love, which he hath declared, and continually doth practise towards us, if we still abide therein; then shall this faith upon the love of God work great things in us and by us, and shall move us with good will gladly and cheerfully to observe his commandments. And if we keep his commandments, every man shall have an assured token, that we be and continue in the love of God; that is, that we keep ourselves unto his love.

<small>Love is an evidence of faith.</small>

Seeing then that he loveth us exceeding much, and we finding the same in our hearts, through faith, do comfort ourselves thereupon, there must needs follow love to our neighbours, joy, peace, softness of mind, gentleness, patience, &c. Gal. v.

<small>What followeth out of the love of God.</small>

Now that Christ doth not slenderly, but most notably love his disciples, and all in them, he proveth it himself divers ways. First, in that he giveth his life for us, and dieth for us upon the cross; for greater love hath no man, than to die for his friend. Thus Christ with his death and blood sealeth his love towards us.

<small>Tokens of God's love.</small>

Secondly, in that he counteth and esteemeth us, not as servants, but as dear friends, brethren, and heirs with him. And the same declareth he in this, that all things which he hath heard of his Father, and sucked out of that fatherly heart, he openeth them unto us, and writeth the same through his holy Spirit in our hearts. All his secret, his godly will he giveth us to understand. For we which be in Christ do know through an undoubted faith, and feel it also in our hearts, that God is our Father through Christ, and that in him he hath admitted and chosen us, that he is reconciled with us through the blood of his dear Son, that he loveth, preserveth, and defendeth us. Therefore do we also patiently and cheerfully bear all adversity in this time for his sake, considering we know, that so is the good pleasure of our dearest Father.

<small>John i.</small>

<small>1 Cor. ii.</small>

<small>Rom. v</small>

Thirdly, Christ declareth his excellent love towards us, in that he did choose us afore the world was created, and loved us when we were yet his enemies, calling us by his word, and appointing us to bring forth fruit unto him.

<small>Eph. i.
Rom. v.
We are chosen to bring forth fruit.</small>

Fourthly, in that we obtain at the Father's hand all that we pray and desire in the name of Jesu.

Are not these sure tokens of an exceeding love of God towards us? After that we once have perceived such love, oh that we always remained therein! Which cometh to pass, when we apply ourselves unto his commandments, and when we in obedience and patience are content to be at his will, as he for our sake was obedient unto his Father, even until the death of the cross. Now that we might know what his commandments be, he concludeth them in a short sum, and saith: "Love ye one another together, as I have loved you." As if he would say: Seeing I have declared my love so worthily, so notably, and with so great faithfulness towards you, that I have not refused to die for you; therefore is it my will, and so is it reason also, that ye likewise shew such love one towards another; for I have given you example afore, that ye should do as I have done, and follow my footsteps. This shall not only be very seemly unto you, but much profit also and great honour shall it bring you. For like as my Father, as ye shall shortly see, shall after my passion bring me unto glory, so shall he also do unto you, so far as ye endure stedfast in adversity, and continue in love one towards another. Like as I with great travail and labour have shewed you the way and will of God my Father, and therefore go now unto death to make you living; so ought ye also to be minded one towards another. Look that ye serve one another in love; lead all men unto God; and the grace of God, which he giveth unto the world through me, publish ye unto all men, though ye must lose your life therefore.

We ought to endure in love.

Phil. ii.

The commandment of God is love.

John xiii. 1 Pet. ii.

[John xv. 18—25.]

If the world hate you, ye know that it hated me, before it hated you. If ye were of the world, the world would love his own. Howbeit, because ye are not of the world, but I have chosen you out of the world, therefore the world hateth you. Remember the word that I said unto you, The servant is not greater than the Lord. If they have persecuted me, so will they persecute you. If they have kept my sayings, they will also keep yours. But all these things will they do unto you for my name's sake, because they know not him that sent me. If I had not come and spoken unto them, they should not have had sin; but now have they nothing to cloak their sin withal. He that hateth me, hateth my Father also. If I had not done works amongst them which none other man did, they had not had sin; but now have they seen, and have hated both me, and also my Father: even that the saying might be fulfilled, which is written in their own law: They have hated me without any cause.

DOCTRINE AND FRUIT.

LIKE as Christ in the aforesaid words hath given unto his disciples, and to us that believe in him, an excellent consolation in his love, which is infinite great towards us; so doth he now comfort us against such trouble and adversity to come, as outwardly happeneth unto us, and against the hate and persecution, wherewith the children of the world recompense us for our love and well doing. Love ought we to have towards all men: such godly love shall move us earnestly to further God's glory, to bring all men to the knowledge and love of God, and to withdraw them from fleshly lusts and worldly vices. When we now of a godly zeal begin thus to rebuke vice, and to reprehend the carnal lusts of the children of the world, then they that are drowned in the shameful vices of the world and the flesh, may not suffer it, but hate, trouble, and vex us, molest, persecute us, and put us unto death, contemning and despising the word which we offer them from God, whereby they might be saved, and going about by all means to root it out.

Exhortation to patience. But all this ought not to drive us back, or discourage us; for in this world must we seek no high honour nor praise, but willingly humble and submit ourselves under the *1 Pet. iii. John xiii.* rebuke and cross with Christ our head. Christ also exhorteth us to follow his footsteps, and to do after his example, and not to forsake the truth and love of our neighbour for their hatred; but constantly to proceed and do our best to *Acts v.* guide all men unto God. And if for such our faithfulness and love there happen reproach and trouble to us, we ought to rejoice, that God doth us so great honour, as to grant us to suffer somewhat for his name's sake. If we lived as do the children of the world, we should not be hated of them, and happily we needed to fear but little danger. But Christ hath taken us from the world, and hath chosen and called us to good works and to innocency of life. Nothing hath he omitted, that might serve to our welfare; faithfully therefore ought we to follow his vocation, and not do as the unthankful Jews, that despise his doctrine and works. He talketh yet daily with us, provoketh and calleth us; therefore ought we to cease from sin, and not to fashion ourselves after the world. Rom. xii. For if we would live to please the world, to serve it, and to hunt after the favour and praise of it, we should not be faithful ministers of Jesus Christ. We ought not to look for worldly honour; but to have respect to the eternal glory, which we shall have with Christ our head, yea, so far as we suffer rebuke and dishonour with him. When he lived in this time, and practised the truth against the Pharisees, he was reviled, put to shame and death. The same happeneth also unto us; for we are not above the Lord. An evil token were it, if the world loved us. Patiently therefore and with joy ought we to bear such rebuke and shame, as happeneth unto us for his name's sake by those that hate the truth. For our honour and reward is great in heaven; but after our trouble shall the same be first opened, as it happened also unto Christ our head first after the cross.

[John xv. 26.—xvi. 7.]

But when the Comforter is come, whom I will send unto you from the Father, even the Spirit of truth, which proceedeth of the Father, he shall testify of me. And ye are witnesses also, because ye have been with me from the beginning. These things have I said unto you, that ye should not be offended. They shall thrust you out of their synagogues, and excommunicate you; yea, the time shall come, that whosoever killeth you will think that he doth service unto God. And such things shall they do unto you, because they know not the Father, neither me. But these things have I told you, that when the hour is come, ye may remember that I told you. These things said I not unto you at the beginning, because I was with you. But now I go my way to him that sent me; and none of you asketh me, Whither goest thou? But because I have said such things unto you, your hearts are full of sorrow. But I tell you the truth: It is expedient for you that I go away. For if I go not away, that Comforter will not come unto you: but if I depart, I will send him unto you.

DOCTRINE AND FRUIT.

FORASMUCH as it is our bounden duty to bear witness unto Christ with our mouth and life, and yet our weak flesh feareth the hatred and resistance of the world; Christ therefore promiseth us here, that he will send us strength from heaven, namely, the Holy Ghost, first in our hearts to bear witness unto Christ, and then to open our mouths, that we may testify the Lord Christ and his truth manfully and without fear. Certain it is, that "all they which will live here godly in Christ Jesu, must suffer persecution." But seeing that to suffer such adversity our flesh is far too slow, cold, and feeble, God giveth us the Spirit of his Son, to move, strengthen, and preserve us in all goodness. This Spirit poureth out love into our hearts, expelleth all fear and terror, as we see in Peter on Whitsunday, and maketh us to overcome all adversity.

Matt. xxvi.
Acts i.
Rom. viii.

2 Tim. iii.

Rom. viii.

Rom. v.
Acts ii.

John xv. We are branches in Christ the true vine, albeit as yet very weak and tender, soon blown away with the wind, or smitten down other ways: but forasmuch as out of Christ we receive yet the sap and virtue of spirit and life, we are in life preserved, that we wither not away. Of this now must we be mindful in all adversity, so that without ceasing we pray unto God for his holy Spirit, who is our instructor, comforter, and teacher. We ought to have respect unto our fore-goer and finisher of our faith; remembering, that we

THE PASSION OF CHRIST

suffer not as thieves and evil doers, but for his sake, yea, 1 Pet. iv. and that of the wicked. This shall make our adversity and cross the more easy and light, when we feel the comfort of the Spirit, and behold how shameful a death Christ suffered for us. Therefore should there no fear make us to shrink from the confession of Christ and his truth. We are not Matt. x. they that speak, but it is the Spirit of the Father which speaketh in us. We may not fear those that kill the body; we may not be ashamed of him: so shall he also knowledge Luke ix. us, and make us honourable in his Father's sight. The John v. honour of this world should not be dearer unto us than the glory of God. And though we die for it, yet ought we not to shrink or stir from the confession of the truth.

This engendereth many times much heaviness and fear in us, that we consider only that which is present, little regarding that which is to come and everlasting; and because we think, that when God thrusteth us into adversity, he is far from us: whereas he then is most of all with us by his grace, comfort, and strength, and trieth us through the cross, standing behind the wall, and looking through the grate upon our Cant. viii. conflict and battle, yea, helping us to fight and to overcome. Therefore must we not always be children, we must not hang 1 Cor. xiv. still at the breast, seeking milk as children do; but grow to a Heb. v. perfect age, learning to know Christ the Lord after the Spirit, as he now governeth, and is a mighty King; under whose banner we must fight valiantly, and endure the cross unto the death; throwing behind us all things in this world, and lifting up our eyes and hearts into heaven, whence our help Psal. cxxi. cometh, and into the which Christ is gone, to prepare for us John xiv. an everlasting dwelling.

[John xvi. 8—14.]

AND when the Spirit is come, he will rebuke the world of sin, and of righteousness, and of judgment: of sin, because they believe not on me; of righteousness, because I go to my Father, and ye shall see me no more; of judgment, because the prince of this world is judged already. I have yet many things to say unto you, but ye cannot bear them now. Howbeit when he is come, which is the Spirit of truth, he will lead you into all truth. For he shall not speak of himself, but whatsoever he shall hear, that shall he speak; and he will shew you things to come. He shall glorify me; for he shall receive of mine, and shall shew unto you. All things that the Father hath are mine: therefore said I, that he shall take of mine, and shew unto you.

DOCTRINE AND FRUIT.

<small>John v.</small>

IN these words doth Christ shew us the office of the Holy Ghost, and what he worketh by his disciples, and by all faithful believers in the world. The whole world is set upon wickedness and iniquity; and when that is rebuked, it hateth and persecuteth those that rebuke it. Whereout it followeth oftentimes, that through imbecility and weakness of the flesh we cease from rebuking of vice and sin.

Now when we find it to be thus, that the infirmity of our flesh, and the terrible threatening of the world, will hinder us or utterly draw us back from the free rebuking of vice; we ought to pray unto God our Father for to give us the Spirit of his Son, that he may pour out love into our hearts, and expel all fear, that with stout stomachs and words we may reprehend the vices of the world, and valiantly resist

<small>1 John iv.
Isai. liii.</small>

them. This Spirit shall teach us the thing, that neither our flesh nor the world is instructed in. All we of nature do err, and every one wandereth his own way, that is, every one followeth his own purpose and intent; and if we believe

<small>John iii.</small>

not in Christ, we perish in our sins. And this is the greatest sin of all, wherein the world is wrapt, afore it receive the

<small>Unbelief is the original of all vices.</small>

truth. Not to believe in Christ is a sin, out of the which all vice and wickedness doth grow. How great this sin is, no man is able to know, only the Spirit of God openeth it: therefore the Spirit teacheth us, how far we go astray. And if we come to Christ from this erroneous way of unbelief, all sins are forgiven us through Christ, and not imputed us to our damnation.

Neither is it enough to know that we have erred, or do yet err; but we must know also, which is the right way, wherein, when error is forsaken, we must walk to attain unto godliness and bliss. This right way doth the Spirit also shew to be even Christ, who is our way, our righteous- ness, and goodness; which way nevertheless the world will not go. To believe in Christ, is the true way to attain unto righteousness and salvation: whoso now departeth not from the erroneous way of unbelief and vice, and will not walk in Christ, the way of all virtue and goodness, which all the world, alas! so abhorreth, the same is convict, that the judgment of eternal pain doth righteously fall upon him, seeing the light is set before him, and he will rather abide and perish in darkness. But is not this a just judgment, that the world should perish in sin, and be punished for ever, considering that God hath graciously sent unto them his own Son, promising everlasting life and salvation in him, who with his blood hath washed away our sins, mightily overcome death, sin, and the prince of this world, delivered us out of his power and heavy yoke, and taken possession of the kingdom and glory with his Father; and yet they will not know, receive, nor honour Christ, as their chief king and Lord, but still serve the prince of this world in vice and sin, and not submit themselves under the easy yoke of Christ, and of his love and virtues? *[margin: John xiv. 1 Cor. i.; John iii.]*

O dear children, let us depart out of the kingdom of darkness into the kingdom of Jesus Christ the Son of God: let us regard his word with diligence; let us hearken what God speaketh in us; and though there be many things that as yet we know not, many that we do not understand and perceive, we will earnestly pray unto God for his Spirit, who is the right schoolmaster and teacher. He shall lead us into all truth, he shall renew us in the spirit of our mind, and teach us to understand, what the good, acceptable, and perfect will of God is. He shall plant and root us in love, that we may comprehend with all saints, what is the length, the breadth, the height, and depth; that we may also know the exceeding love of the knowledge of Christ, that we might be filled in all godly perfectness. Thus the Spirit teacheth us all truth, when he poureth love into our hearts. *[margin: Col. i.; Psal. lxxxv.; Eph. iv.; Rom. xii.; Eph. iii.]*

This schoolmaster teacheth all believers here in time, every one as much as he can comprehend, and kindleth spiritual hearts with greater desire. He that now increaseth in love, that is, whoso loveth that whereof God giveth him knowledge, and desireth to know that which as yet he knoweth not, him doth the Spirit lead into all truth. For the more that love groweth, the more perfect is knowledge. And in this school of the love which the Spirit poureth into our hearts, the faithful believer learneth more, than all books and all men can teach him: but the more a man learneth and can, the more must he acknowledge and confess, that he can nothing towards that which we shall know, when we shall clearly and perfectly see God face to face. Unto us shall it be enough and sufficient, that we in spirit and in the truth know Jesus Christ, which was crucified, and that he shine and be glorified in our mortal body, in our hearts, mouth, and in our whole life.

<small>1 Cor. xiii.
1 Cor. ii.
2 Cor. v.
John iv.
2 Cor. iv.</small>

[John xvi. 16—22.]

AFTER a while ye shall not see me, and again after a while ye shall see me; for I go to the Father. Then said some of his disciples among themselves: What is this that he saith unto us, After a while ye shall not see me, and again after a while ye shall see me; and that I go to my Father? They said therefore, What is this that he saith, After a while? We cannot tell what he saith. Jesus perceived that they would ask him, and said unto them: This is it that ye inquire of between yourselves, that I said, After a while ye shall not see me, and again after a while ye shall see me. Verily, verily, I say unto you, Ye shall weep and lament, but the world shall rejoice: ye shall sorrow, but your sorrow shall be turned into joy. A woman, when she travaileth, hath sorrow, because her hour is come; but when she is delivered of the child, she remembereth no more the anguish, for joy that a man is born into the world. And ye now therefore are in sorrow: but I will see you again, and your heart shall rejoice, and your joy shall no man take from you.

DOCTRINE AND FRUIT.

An excellent comfort doth Christ give here unto his disciples, who by reason of his departing were in great sorrow and heaviness. But like as the disciples of Christ, because of his passion, abode for a little season in great cumbrance, fear, and trouble, and yet received great joy out of the resurrection, when he shewed himself unto them; even so in adversity ought not we to be faint-hearted, but comfort ourselves in this, that the Lord doth not long leave those that are his. Though he hide himself for a time, he shall shortly shew us his gracious countenance again, and refresh us with rich comfort. The adversities of faithful believers are not only short, but also they end with unspeakable joy. After adversity and death followeth everlasting joy and eternal life. We are here with Christ our head in trouble and on the cross, where the world laugheth at us and rejoiceth. For all this ought not we to be unquiet in ourselves. Very shortly will the matter change and turn upside down; so that their laughter and joy shall be altered into weeping and eternal sorrow: but our heaviness shall God shortly end with great fruit and joy, and the same joy shall no man be able to take from us, when we with Christ our head shall everlastingly be glad and rejoice, when all tears shall be wiped away from our eyes, and we discharged of all travail and labour of this time.

[John xvi. 23—33.]

In that day shall ye ask me no question. Verily, verily, I say unto you, Whatsoever ye shall ask the Father in my name, he will give it you. Hitherto have ye asked nothing in my name: Ask, and ye shall receive, that your joy may be full. These things have I spoken unto you in proverbs; but the time will come, when I shall no more speak to you in proverbs, but I shall shew you plainly of my Father. At that day shall ye ask in my name. And I say not unto you, that I will pray unto the Father for you; for the Father himself loveth you, because ye have loved me, and have believed that I am come out from God. I went out from the Father, and came into the world; and I leave the world again, and go to the Father. His disciples said unto him, Lo, now speakest thou plainly, and thou speakest no proverb. Now are we sure that thou knowest all things, and needest not that any man should ask thee any question. Therefore believe we, that thou camest from God. Jesus answered them, Now ye do believe. Behold, the hour draweth nigh, and is already come, that ye shall be scattered every man unto his own, and shall leave me alone; and yet I am not alone, for the Father is with me. These words have I spoken unto you, that in me ye might have peace. In the world shall ye have tribulation; but be of good cheer, I have overcome the world.

DOCTRINE AND FRUIT.

MANY times doth Christ promise us, whatsoever we pray, to obtain the same of the Father of heaven; whereby he may stir up our hearts faithfully to cry unto God, the gracious and loving Father, whose love towards us is exceeding great, neither can he say us nay, that hath given and bestowed upon us his own Son. Yea, not only hath he sent down unto us his dear and only-begotten Son, to take the nature of man upon him, and to die for us; but hath also into our hearts given his holy Spirit, with whom he hath sealed us, and certified us of his love, pouring the knowledge and love of Christ into our hearts. How can we then doubt of his love and faithfulness? How is it possible, that in all our trouble and heaviness we should not unto him only have recourse, seeking help and comfort at his hand? The Son for our sake came forth from the Father, humbled, and made himself of no reputation, took all reproach, shame, and trouble upon himself for our welfare. To the Father was he obedient, until the death of the cross; and after that he through his blood had washed away our sins, and finished the work of our salvation, he arose again from death through the power and might of his Father, overcame death for us, and with his ascension opened heaven, and prepared an entrance unto God, carrying up our nature and flesh unto the honour and glory which he had from everlasting, and giving us therein a hope and sure comfort, that we also shall with him have everlasting joy and glory for ever.

Seeing then that he came out from the Father, we ought to hearken unto him, and not to despise his word. He is the eternal wisdom of God, he is the truth, no false teacher can he be; forasmuch as he cometh from God, and is his only-begotten Son. To contemn so dear an ambassador and messenger of God, must needs have great punishment; and though we are not able in most perfection to understand his doctrine, truth, and love, (for here in this time is our knowledge unperfect;) yet should we consider that the Father loveth us, and faithfully ought we to cry and pray unto him for his Spirit, that shall teach us all truth, so much as is necessary and profitable for us; which knowledge from day to day shall increase, till we shall see him face to face, and have the perfect knowledge of him. Our nature is weak and feeble, the nature divine is high and incomprehensible. We are full of darkness; God is the clear and far-passing light: but when our dark mist is taken away, then in clear brightness shall the godly light open unto us. *Heb. i.* *1 Cor. xiii.*

Some first-fruits and beginnings of God's knowledge have we received already. God hath cast and planted a little seed of knowledge in our hearts, which through his grace and moisture shall daily grow, increase, and prosper. Of such knowledge as we have of God, we may not presume, neither of our weak faith, nor yet ascribe too much unto our own strength. He that standeth, let him look that he fall not. We think many times that we are very strong in faith; but adversity sheweth how feeble we be, and how soon we shrink. Therefore in all trouble and distress of this world we ought to comfort ourselves, and trust only in the grace and strength of Christ. In him shall we find peace and quietness, in him shall we overcome all our enemies: for his overcoming is our victory, his power is our strength. The world is not able to hurt and plague us, more than of our gracious Father is permitted unto them for our wealth.

While we live here, we are in misery, affliction, and distress: but seeing that the head hath overcome, the members ought not to doubt of the victory. Let us with stedfast belief look unto Christ, the fountain of life, our foregoer and finisher of our faith; and let us stoutly step forth after him, let us go the way that he is gone, and hath trodden, and made before. Afflictions shall serve us unto high honour, as they served Christ the Lord unto glory. In Christ we find the peace and rest of our consciences and souls; in him we know and find the goodness and love of God the Father; out of him receive we power, strength, comfort, and eternal life; only let us look, that we turn not the eyes of our heart and faith away from him. Our welfare consisteth in the stedfast belief and love of Jesus Christ the Son of God. Though we may many times stumble, fall, and be proved by sundry temptations and afflictions; yet is the same good and profitable for us, that we may the better learn to know our own weakness, and again, the strength and grace of God. If it were not profitable for us, Christ had not suffered his disciples to fall so grievously. But in all distress he putteth his hand under us, and in adversity he leaveth us not alone, as he also left not his own Son alone. Though all men fly away from us, yet have we God with us.

[John xvii. 1—8.]

John xvii. THESE words spake Jesus, and lift up his eyes to heaven, and said: Father, the hour is come: glorify thy Son, that thy Son also may glorify thee: as thou hast given him power over all flesh, that he should give eternal life to as many as thou hast given him. This is life eternal, that they know thee the only very true God, and whom thou hast sent, Jesus Christ. I have glorified thee on the earth: I have finished the work which thou gavest me to do. And now glorify me thou, Father, with thine own self, with the glory which I had with thee ere the world was. I have declared thy name unto the men which thou gavest me out of the world. Thine they were, and thou gavest them me, and they have kept thy sayings. Now they know that all things, whatsoever thou hast given me, are of thee: for I have given unto them the words which thou gavest me, and they have received them, and know surely, that I came out from thee, and do believe that thou didst send me.

DOCTRINE AND FRUIT.

CHRIST the true, only, and chief priest, who now would offer up himself to the Father upon the cross for our sins, after that he had loved his own unto the end, comforting and strengthening them, turneth now himself in an earnest and fervent prayer unto his heavenly Father, for an ensample *How we should pray.* and doctrine unto his disciples and all faithful believers, that they in all temptations and afflictions should with an earnest and fervent prayer have recourse unto the Father of heaven. That he taught afore in words, the same declareth he now in the deed; shewing not only what, but also how, and after what sort, we ought to pray; not only for ourselves, but also for those that are given and committed unto us of God, and whom we have comforted and exhorted. Our eyes and hands ought we to lift up unto heaven, from whence our help cometh; which doing is a token of a devout, humble, and lowly mind: yea, the eyes, not only of the body, but also of the heart and belief.

But unto this end principally ought all our prayers to be *The sanctifying of God's* directed, that the heavenly Father may be glorified. The *name should we chiefly* devil, the prince of this world, through his adherents, causeth *desire.* the name and truth of Christ, his doctrine and knowledge, to be rooted out and despised. Seeing then that we are God's children, we should in nothing be so earnest, as in saving the honour of our Father, and in furthering his glory. Which thing cometh to pass, when we notify to men upon earth his *What it is to honour the* grace, faithfulness, love, and great mercy, which he by his *Father.* only-begotten and dear Son hath declared and shewed unto mankind; when we lead men unto God from earthly vices and false gods' service, and when we direct all things to his glory. Thus is Christ also honoured and glorified by us, when we through the gospel do publish unto all men his power and goodness, his honour and glory; when we know, that he is our Saviour, our righteousness, and sanctifying; when we know, that the Father hath given all things into his power; that to those whom the Father hath granted to him he may give everlasting life. Which life everlasting consisteth in this, that we know the living God, and his Son Jesus Christ, John xiv. whom he sent into this world. For God the Father cannot be known without Christ Jesus his Son, neither is there any Christ is the way to God. more Gods, but only one, on whom we hope and trust. The way to God is Christ, whom God therefore sent down, that by him the mercy and grace of the Father might be opened and appear unto us. Wherefore if we will have eternal life, that is, the knowledge of God, we must believe in Christ, and know him; and by him as the way and mediator we must know God the Father. Whoso refuseth Christ, cannot have the Father. What should it help thee to think, that thou knowest God, the highest goodness of all, if thou hast not him, by whom thou art delivered from sin and eternal plague?

The knowledge of God, eternal life. Where as God, the original of all goodness, is known, and our mind through Christ his Son assured of his grace; namely, that he is favourable unto us, and that he therefore hath separated us out of the world, to the intent that by his Spirit he might make us like unto his Son, righteous and blessed; there doth there spring in our hearts a comfortable trust unto God, a love, and such joy, as nothing in this world may be compared unto. There also doth arise in us a diligence to keep his commandments, godly and innocently to live. Thus cometh our health originally out of the grace and mercy of our heavenly Father, who, afore the world was created, did choose us in Christ Jesu his Son unto eternal life, and in the book of life wrote up our names. After the The order of our health. same did the Father grant unto us the Son, and gave him power over all men. Now that we are given unto Christ, he openeth unto us the name of his Father, through the outward word, and through his Spirit in the heart. When we believe in him, which to do also cometh of him, then increaseth the knowledge of God in us. Out of that knowledge groweth an assured confidence in God, the highest good; of this assured trust cometh love towards him; and when God granteth us all this, he saveth us, and giveth us eternal life.

This is an high worthiness and honour of Christ, in that the Father giveth him all things into his hand, that he may give everlasting life unto faithful believers. No man can have life, but through Christ. Whoso believeth not in Christ, remaineth in death, and the wrath of God abideth upon him. But then giveth he us eternal life, when we receive his word, and know that he came out from God, and that the Father sent him the Saviour of the world. And when we thus are become faithful believers, then keep we his commandments: for faith studieth and is diligent to please God. This honour and dignity of Christ, his power and kingdom, are first opened unto the world, after his death and cross, in the resurrection and ascension. Of the which honour and glory we also in due time shall, after our measure, be partakers, if we suffer with him. For the high Priest, who hath prayed for us, is heard of the Father, and glorified with eternal honour and glory. Wherefore we may not doubt in the remnant that he prayeth for still on our behalf; he shall be, and is for his worthiness' sake heard, and hath his request. Of this we will consider more.

<small>What it is to keep God's commandments.</small>

[John xvii. 9—23.]

I PRAY for them, and pray not for the world, but for them whom thou hast given me; for they are thine, and all mine are thine, and thine are mine; and I am glorified in them. And now am I no more in the world, but they are in the world, and I come to thee. Holy Father, keep them in thy name, whom thou hast given me, that they may be one, as we are. When I was with them in the world, I kept them in thy name. Those that thou gavest me have I kept, and none of them is lost, but the lost child, that the scripture might be fulfilled. Now come I to thee, and these words speak I in the world, that they might have my joy full in them. I have given them thy word, and the world hath hated them, because they are not of the world, even as I am not of the world. I desire not that thou shouldest take them

<small>John xvii.</small>

out of the world, but that thou keep them from evil. They are not of the world, as I am not of the world. Sanctify them with thy truth: thy saying is truth. As thou sentest me into the world, so have I sent them into the world; and for their sakes I sanctify myself, that they also might be sanctified through the truth. I pray not for them alone, but for those also which shall believe on me through their preaching; that they all may be one, as thou, Father, art in me, and I in thee; and that they may be also one in us, that the world may believe that thou hast sent me. And the glory that thou gavest me, have I given them, that they may be one, as we are one; I in them, and thou in me, that they may be made perfect in one; and that the world may know that thou hast sent me, and hast loved them, as thou hast loved me.

DOCTRINE AND FRUIT.

THIS prayer of our high Priest and mediator Christ Jesus is fervent, earnest, full of the fire of godly love, full of great secrets and spiritual instructions. Herein may we learn to know, what high honour, dignity, and power, Christ by his obedience and patience, hath obtained with his Father, wherein consisteth our peace, joy, and welfare; what care and love Christ beareth towards those that are his, and how he committeth them unto his Father. First, he prayeth for his disciples, whom he did choose to publish his truth; afterward prayeth he for all such as should come to the faith by their preaching until the world's end. And forasmuch as the disciples had a great weighty matter in hand, full of danger and adversity, (for they must needs procure to themselves great hatred of the world,) he first prayeth for them, that the Father will strengthen, comfort, and preserve them through his power, and defend them from all evil.

How the ministers of the word should be prayed for. In this are we taught diligently, chiefly, and specially, to pray for those, unto whom is committed the preaching of the gospel; for a chargeable and great work carry they upon their shoulders, by means whereof, among all others, they have special need of the grace, help, and assistance of God.

But our prayer ought we to frame as Christ hath framed his. First, we must in our prayer to God make special mention of his own grace and mercy; whereby he choosing them to such an office, hath given them unto Christ his Son. Forasmuch then as they are the ministers of him and of his Son, and seeing the Son is so dear, worthy, and beloved unto the Father, our prayer must be, that he for his Son's sake will defend and preserve them, as in him and by him they are worthy.

Secondly, considering that for his sake and his word, which they declare, they are persecuted of the world, it is requisite that God preserve them in his own work. For great need have they of his fatherly protection, while they yet live in the weak feeble flesh, and are mortal men.

Thirdly, their office serveth to many men's health and welfare; their office is necessary and profitable to the whole world, which walketh in blindness and darkness; for they are the light of the world, that through doctrine and living must shine to many men's life; which without the assistance and help of God cannot come to pass. Matt. v.

Thus ought we to pray for the ministers of the word, and to desire, that God through his holy name and power will defend, strengthen, comfort, and preserve them in all adversity; but principally that he will give them grace to be one, coupled together in the band of peace, love, and uniformity; that they may be of one spirit, and of one mind; that in one spirit they may further and plant the honour of God; that like as Christ neither spake nor did anything, but that which was acceptable and well-pleasing unto the Father, they also in their sayings and doings may have respect unto God's glory; and that they, being rooted and fortified in love, be not vanquished nor overcome of the pleasures or threatenings of this world. Ephes. iv. Phil. ii. Ephes. iii.

Secondly, that in all their labour and travail, in all adversity and persecutions, he will put into their hearts his own comfort and spiritual joy. For the world hath manifold mirths, pastimes, and pleasures; much bragging and wilfulness useth it in the riches and fleshly voluptuousness thereof. But the true ministers of Christ, seeing he hath severed them from the world, must and ought to refrain and absent themselves from all worldly joy and voluptuousness; yea, it is John xv.

they that ought to dissuade the world from such wantonness and vanity; by means of whose faithful admonition there falleth much hatred and trouble upon them; neither were it to the furtherance of God's honour and our commodity, to have them utterly taken away out of this world. Therefore doth Christ desire, and so must we with him, that from evil, namely, from the devil the prince of this world, who stirreth the world against them, they may of the Father in the world be defended and kept.

Thirdly, that he will sanctify and cleanse them afore other men, that they may be holy and pure vessels in the house and temple, that is, in the church of God: for they are means and instruments, by whom God ministereth his grace and truth unto men; therefore is it also convenient, that they be pure and holy. This cometh through the truth that God putteth in their mouth and heart by the Holy Ghost, which inwardly purifieth them. But then are they holy, when they teach truth, and live godly. Into the world hath Christ sent them, as the Father sent him into the world. The Father sent Christ into the world, that he should destroy the kingdom of the devil and of the world; that he should declare unto the world the grace and mercy of God towards mankind; that he should bring men from sin and from false idolatrous faith to the true living God, and to a virtuous conversation; that he with the light of truth should shine upon those which sat in darkness; that he should bring the knowledge of God into the world, and exhort men to the amendment of life. Even this hath Christ given in commission to his apostles, and to all ministers of the word to do. This is their office, this is their ministration, unto this have they great need of the grace, power, and assistance of God. Therefore ought we most earnestly to pray for them: for if they fail or fall, it hurteth the whole church; yea, out of the same there groweth slander unto the name of God in the sight of the unbelievers, and an occasion of falling to such as are weak of faith. Therefore Christ also offered himself to the Father for them, and sanctified them, that they might be pure and holy, not in outward appearance, but from the heart, and in the truth; that through their uniformity and love, through the word of truth which they preach, through the holiness of their doctrine and living, all men and the whole world might know and understand, that God hath sent them; yea, that God sent his Son Christ into the world, unto whom they with mouth and life bear record, and who also everywhere shineth out of them with words and deeds.

Not only for them hath Christ prayed, but also for us, as many as hearken and believe the word of truth preached by them. Wherein first we may perceive and see the love, faithfulness, and great care of Christ for us, how earnestly the trusty Shepherd of our souls committeth his poor sheep into his Father's protection, how faithfully our Mediator and Advocate prayeth for us; whereby also he setteth forth a doctrine unto us, how and what we shall pray of our heavenly Father.

First, that he will make us one by his holy Spirit in the truth, in the unity of faith, and in love unseparable, that we may all be of one mind, one body, and one spirit in Christ Jesu our Head, and to keep the unity of the Spirit in the bond of peace; that we all being illuminated by his Spirit, may in word and deed, yea, in our whole life, seek and further the glory of our heavenly Father, that we may all be one among ourselves and with God; whereby all the world may spy, see, and perceive, that we are God's children and Christ's disciples. Phil. ii.
Ephes. ii.

John xiii.

Secondly, that of his fatherly goodness he will defend, save, and preserve us his own poor sheep, which be in the midst among wolves and manifold dangers, and seeing we be yet in the world, do not live after the world; that it will please him to keep us from the evil, namely, from the prince of this world, that though the same our enemy doth tempt and plague us, he never yet have power to prevail against us. Matt. x.

Thirdly, that inasmuch as we, being in sin conceived and born, have hitherto lived in sin, and seeing that albeit we are cleansed already by his word and faith, yet the uncleanness of the flesh and of the world doth daily defile us, it will please him through his truth to purge and sanctify our bodies, our souls, and our whole lives, that we may become an holy temple of his grace, pure, clean, and holy vessels, consecrated and sanctified to God's own use. He hath once purified and hallowed us through the blood of his Son, and unto the Father hath Christ sanctified and offered up himself an holy acceptable sacrifice for our sins; but the devil, the world, and our Psal. l.

1 Cor. vi.
2 Cor. vi.

flesh, is ever busy to lead us away again from God and from true holiness. Therefore must we daily pray unto him, that through his holy Spirit, and through his holy truth, he will continually purge, cleanse, and sanctify us, that we be not dissembling hypocrites, but godly and unfeigned even from our hearts, and that we be not stained in the filthiness of this world, but to refrain from all uncleanness, through the assistance of his grace; that we may also offer up our bodies an holy acceptable sacrifice to God the Lord, as he offered up himself upon the cross for our sakes.

James i.

[John xvii. 24—26.]

John xvii.

FATHER, I will, that they which thou hast given me, be with me where I am, that they may see my glory, which thou hast given me; for thou lovedst me before the making of the world. O righteous Father, the world also hath not known thee, but I have known thee, and these have known that thou hast sent me. And I have declared unto them thy name, and will declare it, that the love wherewith thou hast loved me, may be in them, and I in them.

DOCTRINE AND FRUIT.

AFTER that Christ had committed his unto the Father, that he will care for them, defend, and keep them, while they live in the world; he desireth now that it will please him finally also to save them, and to take them to himself into his kingdom. With the which prayer, he giveth a great consolation to his disciples, and all faithful believers, that we might be the more cheerful to serve him, considering the high reward that is prepared for us; that for his sake we should joyfully and stoutly bear all adversity, seeing he will make us, yea, hath made us already, partakers of his glory and of his kingdom.

Oh the great grace and incomprehensible love of God towards us, who through his mercy and great love, whereas we were children of wrath and damnation, hath made us his own children, elect and beloved; and when we were dead in sin, hath with his Son raised us up from death, Ephes. ii. revived us, and made us sit with him among those of heaven in Christ Jesu; to declare unto the ages to come the riches of his grace in kindness and love to us ward, through Jesus Christ.

Forasmuch now as God hath caused the light of his glory, even Christ, to shine into our hearts, and through the light of faith hath kindled and purified our hearts; it is meet that in this time we live as children of light, to the intent that men may see the brightness of those good works Matt. v. which proceed of faith, to the praise of our heavenly Father. And though we be not as yet bodily with Christ, yet our hearts and minds are always above, there as Christ sitteth Col. iii. at the right hand of God: our conversation and being is in heaven; albeit we are in corporal misery, with heart we desire to die, and to be with Christ. We are sure, if this Phil. i. earthly house were fallen and broken down, that we have 2 Cor. v. one everlasting in heaven. We are dead, but our life is reserved with Christ in God. It is not evident yet what we be: but when Christ our life shall shew himself, then shall we also appear with him in glory; even when we shall rise up, and be taken up in the air, and be with him for ever, and see his honour and glory, which the angels delight 1 Thess. iv. to see and behold.

Oh, how great pleasure and joy is it, to behold the eternal light that never quencheth, in the which no darkness hath place; from the which shall be expelled and cast out all they that would not receive and know the light which God hath sent into the world to illuminate them, but are blinded by the prince of this world, lest the light of the gospel should 2 Cor. iv. shine upon them. No wrong doth the righteous Father unto them, when he plagueth them, and taketh the light from them. A righteous and just judgment is it, seeing the gracious Father so mercifully sent them the light of the truth, and they yet so maliciously and stubbornly have despised and refused it. Yea, reason it is, that they perish in untruth, in lies, and in everlasting blindness; forasmuch as John iii. they would receive darkness rather than the light, lies rather than the truth. And considering that they have forsaken the brightness of the truth and of the Son of God, they must needs be cast into utter darkness, and never enjoy the light.

O gracious Father, grant unto us, which through thy Son have known thy name, that in such knowledge and light of the truth we may increase more and more; that the love wherewith thou lovest thy dear Son may be and remain in us; and that thy only-begotten Son Jesus Christ our head, may in us his members, continue still, work, live, and bring forth fruit acceptable unto thee.

[John xviii. 1, 2.   Matthew xxvi. 36—39.   Mark xiv. 32—36.
Luke xxii. 39—42.]

AND when Jesus had spoken these words, he went out with his disciples, as he was wont, over the brook Cedron, unto mount Olivet, into a village called Gethsemane, where as was a garden, into the which Jesus went with his disciples. Judas now, who betrayed him, knew also the place: for Jesus used oft to come thither with his disciples. Jesus said unto his disciples, Sit ye here till I go yonder and pray. And he took unto him Peter and the two sons of Zebede, and began to be heavy and sorry. And a fear and terror came upon him. Thus said he unto them: My soul is heavy unto the death; tarry ye here and watch with me. And he went from them as far as a stone's cast. Then fell he down upon his face to the ground, and prayed, that if it were possible, that hour might depart from him. And thus he prayed: O Father, unto thee are all things possible; take this cup from me; howbeit not my will, but thy will be done.

DOCTRINE AND FRUIT.

AFTER that Jesus hath established his disciples in faith and love, comforting and strengthening them against adversity and trouble to come in this world, promising also unto them the Spirit, love, defence, and protection of his

Father; he goeth now to meet his traitor and enemies, and beginneth the work of our redemption. Awake up now, O thou faithful and devout soul, and go after thy Redeemer; follow his footsteps; gather up diligently the drops of his blood, and sprinkle them with a true faith in thine heart: take up the bundle of myrrh, and lay it at thy breast, O thou noble bride and spouse of Christ; his passion that he suffereth for thee, write then in thy mind; learn to die from all sin, from thyself, and from the world, that thou mayest be crucified unto the world, and the world unto thee.

Death is ugsome, and very terrible unto the flesh; but joyful and welcome is it unto all such as are instructed in the secret science of God, namely, that death unto faithful believers is an end of all trouble, an entrance into a better and eternal life.

Christ, in that he goeth forth to meet death, declareth that he will suffer, not of compulsion, but willingly; whereby he comforteth us. But whereas he is heavy, and trembleth before his disciples, and confesseth how he feareth death; the same is done for our wealth, to declare unto us the weakness and feebleness that our flesh receiveth at the sight of adversity: for in all things, sin except, it was his good pleasure to become like unto us his brethren; he would take upon a true man, who felt our adversity in his own flesh, and so could have compassion on us. Besides this, he sheweth also to whom our weakness ought to resort for comfort and help in adversity, namely, to our Father in heaven, before whom we must fall down with devout and fervent prayer, and unto him disclose and open our anguish and trouble. *Heb. ii.*

To this prayer, he seeketh and chooseth out a place meet and convenient for the same; for prayer is a lifting up of the mind in God, which among the multitude of men and confusion of worldly matters cannot well be done. Therefore Christ sheweth us, what great diligence we ought to use in prayer, when the enemy falleth in, that the mind may cleave unto God constantly and without shrinking: and what gesture the body ought to shew in prayer, Christ also declareth, in that he falleth down to the earth upon his face, and prayeth with the voice and words. God hath no need of our prayer: but unto us is nothing more profitable and better, than oft and fervently to pray. And the greater the adversity is, the more ardent and earnest should the prayer be; as we see here in Christ our head, whose passion is very great in body and in mind: for the which cause also, as a very true man, he sheweth the same his passion and heaviness to his disciples.

The strongest of all is weak; and the comforter of all hearts hath need of comfort himself: he that expelleth all terror and fear, doth himself fear and tremble. But all this cometh to pass for our learning; that when we be in temptations, we should not doubt in the help of God; and that none of us, being in danger and adversity, and feeling himself loath to suffer, or pensive and slow to tame the motions and wickedness of the flesh, should therefore shrink and be fainthearted; but with a constant faith to resort unto God, complaining to him of his trouble, with hearty prayer that he will bring the hard and painful beginning to a blessed and joyful end; that in all adversity we may consider, as well the excellent and great fruit which proceedeth thereof, as also the gracious good-will of our heavenly Father, to whom we ought wholly and perfectly to give over and offer up ourselves; that neither through the multitude of sins, neither through the greatness of adversity, we despair nor fall away; but with his help and assistance manfully to go through.

[Matt. xxvi. 40, 41. Mark xiv. 37, 38. Luke xxii. 45, 46.]

JESUS came again to his disciples, and found them sleeping. Then said he unto Peter, Simon, sleepest thou? Couldest thou not watch with me one hour? Watch ye, and pray, that ye enter not into temptation: the spirit is willing, but the flesh is weak.

DOCTRINE AND FRUIT.

THE love of Christ towards us is fervent, earnest, and great; but our flesh is so weak, that we not only consider it not, but are also so slow, that we sleep and feel not, for whose sakes Christ hath suffered so great things. Ofttimes is there in us a ready will to take great matters in hand, as

Peter and the other disciples did; but at the last we miss, and have many a sore fall. Therefore Christ, who knoweth us better than we ourselves, willing to expel from us all pride and presumptuousness, teacheth us to be lowly-minded and humble, to be ever watching, and with continual prayer to cleave only unto him, without whom we are able to do nothing, and in whom we may do all things: and even so doth he also in his feebleness, which assaulted him as a very true man, to the intent that we, alway remembering our own weakness, might understand how to tame the rebellious flesh, and in no case to trust it; and that we might be careful and vigilant, lest the subtle enemy in temptations come behind us, fall upon us, and oppress us. It is no time to sleep: the battle is yet a fighting, the enemy is yet alive, and as yet besiegeth he our castle, that Christ hath in keeping. All is full of snares and dangers, which no man is able to escape, save only he, which in fervent belief and prayer doth earnestly watch and stoutly fight, yea, and that continually unto the end.

Neither the present anguish and trouble, nor yet Christ's exhortation, can bring so much to pass in the disciples, as to keep them from sleep; so little it helpeth, where the Spirit giveth not life. Nevertheless Christ's talk and admonition unto his disciples is not utterly unprofitable; for that they now understand not, the same afterwards, when the Spirit cometh, is made plain and evident unto them, and then are they fervent and earnest in godly prayer. Wherefore we should never cease from comforting and exhorting the feeble and weak: for though it help not at this present, the hour shall come, that the Spirit will make it to have life, and to be fruitful in them.

[Matt. xxvi. 42—46. Mark xiv. 39—42. Luke xxii. 43, 44.]

HE went forth the second time, and prayed like as afore: My Father, if this cup may not pass, except I drink it, thy will be done. Then came he again, and found them sleeping, for their eyes were heavy; and they knew not what answer to make him. So he left them again, and went and prayed the third time like as afore, and kneeled down and said: Father, if thou wilt, take away this cup from me; nevertheless not my will, but thine be done. And there appeared unto him an angel from heaven comforting him: and when he was in the agony, distress, and conflict, he prayed the longer, and his sweat was like drops of blood trickling down to the ground. And when he rose up from prayer, and came to his disciples, he found them sleeping for heaviness, and he said unto them: What? sleep ye? Sleep on now, and take your rest. It is enough: up, and pray, that ye enter not into temptation. Behold, the hour approacheth, and the Son of man is betrayed and given into the hands of sinners. Up, let us go: behold, he that betrayeth me is at hand.

DOCTRINE AND FRUIT.

In the perfect example and mirror of our life, Christ Jesus, we find an earnest fervent love, a doctrine how we ought to behave ourselves in adversity. First, we see that Christ of an exceeding great love taketh upon himself all infirmities of mankind, and becometh "like unto his brethren in all things, sin except," being a very true man: he is therefore not ashamed before his disciples to acknowledge his infirmity, sorrow, heaviness, and fear, and to complain thereof unto his Father. A fear, by reason of the death and passion, he receiveth as a very man; for not to feel trouble is not the nature of man, and passion is no passion, if it smart not, if it be not felt. Christ therefore both in his mind and body feeleth the passion; he feeleth the conflict of death, albeit in wrestling withal he overthroweth it. O the exceeding fervent love of our head and foregoer Jesus Christ, who for our health cometh into so great an agony and trouble, that above natural moisture, through the fearful conflicts of the passion and death, he sheddeth his blood and sweateth it! But with hearty desire runneth he to his heavenly Father; to him complaineth he of his weakness and distress; to him giveth he over himself in all obedience and contentation of mind; of him also receiveth he comfort and strength. In the mean season, he forgetteth not his disciples, but cometh to them, exhorteth them to watch and pray, and hath great compassion with their feebleness and sloth.

If we now be the disciples and scholars of Christ Jesu, and have surrendered ourselves up into the school of the heavenly Schoolmaster, we ought diligently to look, what Christ here in himself doth teach and prescribe unto us; that we learning the same of him, and following his footsteps, when temptations of sin, and conflicts of adversity, trouble, and death fall in upon us, may know how to order and frame ourselves therein.

First, that we know ourselves to be poor, full of faults, mortal men, and sinners, having nothing of our own but feebleness. So when the temptation of sin and of the flesh assault us, we must not be ashamed to open such our faults and conflicts unto God our heavenly Father, and to complain unto him of them. God hath not made us to be utterly without temptation, but hath suffered the same to remain in the flesh, that we thereby might be exercised and provoked to seek help at him, and to learn, in how miserable a case we should be, if he withdrew his hand from us. When we now feel Rom. vii. that the spirit is willing and the flesh weak, and that the law Gal. v. of the members withstandeth the law of God in us, that the flesh fighteth and striveth against the Spirit, we must not be ashamed to confess our feebleness before our heavenly Father, (yea, though of weakness we had lain under in the battle already,) desiring his help, that we may rise again, and valiantly to fight it out. Thus must we also do, when the cross and hatred of the world for Christ's sake, or that is contrary to our nature, falleth upon us.

The cup which the Father hath filled in, that we should drink it, the same ought we willingly to drink: and if there grow in our flesh a terror and fear to taste it, we must not be ashamed to complain thereof unto our Father; forasmuch as we see here that Christ, for our sakes being in such heaviness and fear, did not yet, for all that, step aside from his Father's will. The patience therefore of Christians standeth not in this, that they feel no passion, or be not fearful, heavy, or sorry; but in this, that no cross be so great, as to be able to drive them away from Christ. Yea, the more the cross that God the Father hath laid upon them doth make them to smart, and the more it presseth them, (so that they yet bear it,) the more precious and more excellent is their patience; which patience we ought to declare, but not as they that suffer or feel no passion at all.

For here we are instructed and certified of the kindness of our loving Father, that he is not angry, neither taketh it in evil part, when we complain to him of our present trouble, so that we give over our will unto his. All they therefore that be in afflictions, adversity, and temptations, must set this example of the Lord directly before their eyes, and ponder it in their hearts. Not only is the Father not angry, when we complain unto him in our necessity; but in all trouble he sendeth us his own help and comfort, either by his angel, or inwardly by his Spirit, or outwardly by some other mean: he sendeth us strength, giveth us his hand, draweth us, delivereth us, and suffereth us not to be tempted above our power, or else, in the midst of our adversity, he giveth us consolation and strength to overcome it.

O how great comfort bringeth this unto us in our afflictions in life and death, if we ponder, weigh, and consider the exceeding love of God our heavenly Father, who giveth his dear Son into so great trouble, that we might be delivered from eternal adversity and sorrow! If we also remember the love of our Lord Jesus towards us, who for our sakes taketh upon himself so great a fear and passion, how cannot we look for all good things at his hand? What thing is so great, that we his members would not suffer for his sake, if we behold the head in such anguish and trouble? And forasmuch as he suffereth all this for the satisfaction of our sins, we ought to apply great diligence, that we fall not again into sin, for the which Christ suffered this, and from the which Christ with so great a passion hath delivered and cleansed us.

We learn here also to love our neighbours, to care for them, to pity them, if they be impotent and slow, to pray for their infirmity, seeing we are all weak and feeble: and unto such weakness must we so have respect, that we be not arrogant, nor hold much of ourselves, when we see that Peter and others are so full of sleep and sluggishness, that all the admonitions and exhortations of Christ could at that time do little with them. But ever in humbleness of mind, and in the fear of God, ought we to stand; to ascribe all good things unto him; to be careful and watch, lest the devil draw us into his temptations.

O merciful Father, give us grace with fervent hearts to consider the unspeakable love of thee and of thy Son, and never to forget the same; that our faith and trust in thee may be strengthened; that love in us towards thee and our neighbour may be kindled; that above all things we may love thee, the well-spring of all goodness; that we may serve our neighbours in love, care for them, and do them good, according to the love that thy dear Son hath bestowed upon us. O give us patience and stedfastness in adversity, strengthen our weakness, comfort us in trouble and distress, help us to fight; grant unto us, that in true obedience and contentation of mind we may give over our own wills unto thee our Father in all things, according to the example of thy beloved Son; that in adversity we grudge not, but offer up ourselves unto thee without contradiction. Give us strength constantly to subdue the rebellious and stubborn flesh, and to make it obedient unto the Spirit; to cast away all temporal and carnal fear; to resort oft unto prayer; to be earnest and fervent therein; to mortify all our own wills and lusts, and utterly to give them their leave. O give us a willing and cheerful mind, that we may gladly suffer and bear all things for thy sake.

[Matt. xxvi. 47—50. Mark xiv. 43—45. Luke xxii. 47, 48. John xviii. 3—9.]

So when Judas had gotten him a company of soldiers of the high priests, and of the Pharisees' ministers, he came thither with lanterns, links, and weapons, yea, the same Judas Iscarioth, one of the twelve, (as Jesus yet talked with his disciples,) and with him a great heap of people, with swords and staves, sent from the high priests, scribes, and elders of the people. Now had the traitor given them a token, saying, Whomsoever I do kiss, the same is he; take him and bring him warily. So Judas went before them, and came near unto Jesus to kiss him. And when he came, he stept unto him, and said, All hail, Master! and with that kissed him. Jesus said unto him, Friend, whereto art thou come? Judas, betrayest thou the Son of man with a kiss? Jesus, knowing all things that were to come upon himself, went forth, and said unto them, Whom seek ye? They said, Jesus of Nazareth. Then said he unto them, I am he. And Judas that betrayed him stood with them. Now when Jesus said, I am he, they went backward and fell to the ground. Then Jesus asked them again, Whom seek ye? They said, Jesus of Nazareth. Then answered Jesus, and said, I have told you that I am he: if ye seek me, then let these depart: that the saying which he spake might be fulfilled: Of them whom thou gavest me I have lost none.

DOCTRINE AND FRUIT.

CHRIST, the worthy and strong Captain, when he hath wholly given over himself, steppeth forth weaponed, going manfully and stedfastly against the prince of this world and his ministers, yielding and offering himself willingly to suffer for us, as Esay saith, *quia voluit;* for so was it his will. No man had been able to take him, or put him to death, if he had not so willed himself; for he had power to leave his own life. Many times afore did he give place to their fury, and got himself out of the way: but when the hour appointed of the Father was come, he goeth himself willingly, and meeteth death by the way. Here ought we also to learn willingly and stoutly to go into adversity, if it be the will of our Father; if God's honour and our neighbours' welfare so require. For like as the Father suffereth not his Son to die, till the hour of death come, even so standeth our life in his hand. The limits that he hath set unto us, may we neither prevent nor overpass: neither lieth it in the power of our enemies to kill us, when they will themselves. Christ careth for those that are his: the enemies are able to do us no harm at all, no neither in body nor goods, till the Father give them leave. Therefore he saith, "Let these go." The Father, according to his great mercy and gracious will, thrusteth us into adversity with Christ his dear beloved Son, in such wise, so much, and at what time he will himself. Against his will ought we not to strive, but patiently and with obedience submit ourselves wholly unto it.

Oh, what an unspeakable great love is here! The shepherd dieth, to save the life of the poor sheep; the Lord goeth unto death, to the intent that the servant should not die; the Creator spareth not himself, to save his creature. If the Son of God now doth not abhor to suffer death for us, why should we then be ashamed to suffer and die for his sake?

And though he be very God, and sheweth his enemies the brightness of his godly strength, in that he so throweth them to the ground, yet will not he in the same hour use such his divine power to deliver himself: albeit he admonisheth them thereby to cease from their conceived malice; for his godly strength casteth them down, his mercy and grace lifteth them up again. Out of the which great miracle they should have learned not to lay hand on him maliciously; they should have considered, that if it had been his pleasure, he might well have escaped their hands, so that they had not been able to hold him: but the unbelieving rabble are blinded, indurate, and hardened, that neither miracle nor kindness can move them.

O the high majesty of Christ! How shall unbelievers be able to stand before him, when he shall appear in the judgment, whereas before his weakness and humility, when he was now about to be judged himself, they were not able to stand? If his loving voice, wherewith he speaketh so gentle unto them, and saith, "I am he," doth so fear them, and throw them down; what will then the horrible voice of the Judge do, when he shall say, "Depart, ye cursed, into everlasting fire?" O how innocently and godly ought we to live before him, who is among us, and in us, heareth all our words, seeth all our works, searcheth and looketh through all our thoughts, how secret soever they be! Christ at this time withdrew his high power, and in weakness of the flesh, and in wonderful high patience, stept he forth to suffer. By his ensample must we learn, not to take us to our high estate, but with patience and humbleness of mind to meet the enemy.

Like patience and gentleness useth he also towards his

traitor, whom he goeth to meet, not speaking rough words unto him, brawleth not with him, rateth him not, as he was well worthy; but receiveth him with all softness of mind and gentleness, whereas yet he came to deliver and betray him into the hands of the wicked, and unto death. Neither doth the Lord deny him so much as the kiss, the token of friendship, but lovingly also talketh he with him; albeit he also maketh mention of his feigned and dissembling friendship, telling him of it, admonishing him, if he had not been hardened, to cease from his conceived treason. Wherefore we also must learn of Christ, so far as concerneth our own person and estimation, with all mildness, softness of mind, patience, and greatest love, to meet those that hate us and betray us; if peradventure with such love and gentleness of mind we may bring them away from their malice and wickedness.

Matt. v.
Rom. xii.

Here also with great fear and dread ought we to consider of the judgment of God in Judas; that he, being one of the twelve and elect disciples, doth betray and sell the Lord Jesus, his gracious loving master. Whereby we are taught, how that amongst all men there is nothing throughly perfect and whole, seeing that in so holy and small number there is one man so greatly stuffed with wickedness. Therefore he that standeth, let him look that he fall not. Let covetousness blind no man; let the desire of temporal good possess and rule no man's heart: for out of covetousness, the root of all vice, groweth nothing but treason and despair. No righteousness, no fidelity, no truth, no honesty, can be in that heart, where greedy covetousness hath taken root. Judas for very greediness of money giveth over God and all love; and he that afore was a fellow and companion of the holy congregation of God's children, is become a mate, companion, and captain of the wicked and unbelievers; he that was chosen to the preaching of the gospel, is become an enemy, persecutor, and traitor against the truth. O from how high and great honour, to what shame, dishonesty, and vile state falleth Judas; who, having wolvish conditions under sheep's clothing, doth under the token of love practise treason against the truth! From Jesus, the true health, he separateth himself to the children of the devil; he getteth him amongst the blood-thirsty, yea, even he that hitherto in outward appearance had confessed the truth. Thus goeth it, when temptation breaketh in, when the truth cometh into peril and adversity: then the enemies of the truth declare themselves, and hypocrites get them to the adversaries against Christ; then may we learn to know them.

Of these (the more pity!) there be at this day in the church of God many, which, under the pretence and colour of truth, fight against the truth, and that taking the name of Christ in their mouth, betray Christ, yea, with the sword of their venomous tongues kill Christ, and in sheep's clothing are very wolves, false teachers, and most noisome enemies, whom covetousness and vain glory blindeth. And whereas they are not able to root out Christ with the truth, they undertake to do it with weapons and swords, and set the princes and powers of the world to defend their falsehood and tyranny. Yea, many there be of those that, rebuking Judas' act, do even as he did themselves; feigning the truth, when in very deed they persecute the truth.

O our great slothfulness! whereof we are admonished in the disciples that sleep, when wicked Judas in his ungracious work so diligently watcheth, and earnestly runneth about. O that the love and zeal of God might do as much in us, as the ungracious will in the wicked! O that we which are chosen into the service of Christ, were so diligent to minister unto our Father and Lord, as the children of this world are to wait upon Satan their master! For nothing do they omit, that may serve to the persecution of the truth.

O merciful God, grant us poor feeble men patience in adversity; that sudden wrath overcome us not, and that bitterness and desire of vengeance kindle us not to use uncharitable words, and to do hurt, when enemies fall upon us, and brag against us, telling us our faults, whereof we think ourselves unguilty. Grant us ever lovingly to receive all adversity; and that we may know those to be our best friends, which speak unto us, and rebuke us hardest of all. Let no wicked root of envy, malice, and evil will, grow in us; no tediousness, nor sloth. Give us strength to be willing and patient, and with fervent desire to suffer yet more grievous things for thy sake. Pull up the wicked root of covetousness, and the false shine of feigned spirituality out of us. O save us, that Satan bring us not into temptation. Grant us love towards friends and enemies, that we may follow the nature of thee our Father, and the example of thy only-begotten Son, Jesus Christ. Amen.

[Matt. xxvi. 51—56. Mark xiv. 46—53. Luke xxii. 49—53.
John xviii. 10—12.]

THEN came they and laid hands on Jesus, and took him. But when they that were with him saw what would come of it, they said unto him, Master, shall we smite with the sword? Jesus answered and said, Suffer ye thus far forth. Simon Peter had a sword, which he drew out, and smote the servant of the high priest, and cut off his right ear. And the servant's name was called Malchus. Then said Jesus unto Peter, Put thy sword into the sheath. Wilt thou not, that I shall drink the cup which my Father hath given me? All they that draw the sword, shall perish with the sword. Thinkest thou not, that I might pray my Father, to send me now more than twelve legions of angels? but how should the scriptures be fulfilled? It must needs be thus. And when Jesus touched his ear, he healed it. Then began Jesus to speak unto the multitude that were come to him, and to the high priests, and to the chief rulers of the temple, and to the elders, and said: Ye are come forth, as to a murderer, with swords and staves to take me; whereas I yet being daily in the temple, sat and taught, and ye took me not. But this is your hour, and the power of darkness. All this cometh to pass, that the scriptures should be fulfilled. Then the disciples forsook him, and fled all from him. There was a young man that followed after, who had a white linen cloth upon the bare, and him they took. But he left the linen cloth behind him, and ran away naked. The multitude, and the captain, and ministers of the Jews, apprehended Jesus, took him, bound him, and led him first to Annas the chief priest;

for he was father-in-law unto Caiphas, which Caiphas was high priest, and was the same Caiphas, which gave counsel unto the Jews, that better it were one man to die, than the whole people to perish. And all the priests, and scribes, Pharisees, and elders, came together.

DOCTRINE AND FRUIT.

PETER declaring his earnest love which he bare unto the Lord, undertaketh to defend him from malicious violence; but at the same hour it pleased the Lord to declare and shew, not only his own might and power, but also his unspeakable goodness even unto his enemies: therefore is it not his will, that any man on his behalf should have harm; for he was come to bring health, and no hurt; and therefore the uncircumcised zeal of Peter, which was not directed after the will of God, he rejected and reproved, commanding Peter to put up his sword into his sheath; and the servant's ear that was smitten off he set on again, and healed it: for he was ready to be obedient unto his Father's will unto the death, and to drink the cup that his Father had filled for him. Yet doth he shew unto his enemies, that he willingly suffereth, and that if it were not his will, they should not be able to take him. But he affirmed the hour now to be here, that the Father had given him into the power of darkness, and that they shewed such violence unto him, that the scripture might be fulfilled.

The disciples fly from Jesu their Lord, and leave him to tread the winepress alone. In their weakness, fear, and flying, is signified the infirmity of the unperfect members of the Church, which yet, when the Spirit cometh, is strengthened. Let no man build upon his own strength, but pray unto God, that he suffer him not to be led into temptation.

The gracious Lord Jesus is sold unto sinners, that we which were sold under sin, bond, and thrall to the prince of this world, might be redeemed and delivered. He is content to be bound and taken, that we might be quit and free from the snares and captivity of sin.

O Jesu Christ, the mirror of all gentleness of mind, the example of highest obedience and patience, grant us thy servants with true devotion to consider, how thou, innocent and undefiled Lamb, wert bound, taken, and haled away unto death for our sins; how well content thou wast to suffer such things, not opening thy mouth in unpatience, but willingly offering up thyself unto death. O gracious God, how vilely wast thou mishandled for our sakes! O Lord, let this never come out of our hearts: expel through it coldness and sloth out of our minds; stir up ferventness and love towards thee; provoke us unto earnest prayer; make us cheerful and diligent in thy will; bind our stubborn flesh with the cords of thy fear and nurture; yoke us under thy holy work and obedience. Yea, thy bands make quit and free from all sins; thy bands keep us, and draw us in, that we run not at large in curiosity and worldly vanity; they preserve us in thy holy service under continual nurture and blessed perseverance. O grant that it be light and not grievous unto us, to break and yield ourselves; that we do not loath nor abhor to be informed, taught, led, and corrected against our own self-will. Grant that we never become disobedient, unquiet, stubborn, busy, heady, and contentious; that we never be found fighters, neither such as use brawling and scolding. Make thou us quiet, mild, soft-minded, tractable, and meek; ever ready, and not loath to keep thy commandments. Bow down our neck under the yoke of thy obedience; help us, through strait exercises, to tame and overcome our flesh and wicked dispositions, which we are most inclined unto. O Lord Jesus Christ, grant unto us whom thou hast delivered, that fully and perfectly we may yield ourselves unto thee, committing us wholly unto thy Spirit; and to have always before our eyes and hearts, that we are even as sheep appointed to the butchery and shambles; that we defend not ourselves in ire and greediness of vengeance; for thou hast numbered our hairs, and given us thine angels to be our keepers. Wherefore preserve thou our minds from displeasure and desire of revengement; grant us a mild, friendly stomach towards our enemy, that we may love him, speak good unto him, pray for him, recompense him good for evil, that we may be ready to offer the other cheek also. And when we stand in any danger, O grant us, that we do nothing which doth evil become thy children, and that is not agreeable unto thine example.

[Matt. xxvi. 57, 58, 69—75. Mark xiv. 66—72. Luke xxii. 54—62. John xviii. 12—27.]

AND Annas sent him so bound unto Caiphas the high priest. The soldiers took Jesus and led him unto the high priest Caiphas, there as the scribes, the elders, and Pharisees were come together. But Peter followed after afar off into the palace of the high priest, and so did another disciple. The same disciple was known to the high priest, and went in with Jesus into the high priest's palace. But Peter stood without at the door. Then the other disciple, who was known to the high priest, went out, and spake to the damsel that kept the door, and brought Peter in. So Peter went in, and sat with the servants to see the end. They had a fire, and coals kindled in the midst of the palace, and sat about it. Peter also sat amongst them, and warmed him by the fire. The other servants also stood round about the fire, and warmed themselves, for it was cold; and Peter, being with them, stood and warmed himself. Now when the high priest's maid that kept the door, saw Peter, and spied him by the light of the fire, she said, Wast not thou also with Jesus of Nazareth the Galilean? Art not thou likewise one of his disciples? Another said, He also was with him. Then Peter denied before them all, and said, Woman, I know him not; I am not he; neither wot I whereof thou speakest. And when he was gone out into the porch, the cock crew. Then there spied him another damsel, which said unto those that were there, This fellow also was with Jesus of Nazareth. Then denied he again with an oath, and said, I never knew the man. After a little while, as it were about an hour, others that stood there spied him, and said, Verily thou art one of them, for thou art a Galilean; thine own speech bewrayeth thee. Then said one of the priest's servants, a kinsman of his whose ear Peter had smitten off, Did not I see thee with him in the garden? But Peter began to swear, and to curse himself, and to make great protestations, that he never knew the man. Immediately while he yet spake, the cock crew again. And the Lord turned him about, and beheld Peter. Then Peter remembered the word that Jesus had said unto him, Afore the cock crow twice, thou shalt deny me three times. And he went forth, and wept bitterly.

DOCTRINE AND FRUIT.

O THE sudden change! O the great inconstancy of man's weakness! O the unsearchable judgments of God! Not long heretofore would Peter have gone with Christ his master into prison and death: but now he is so afraid of the words of one damsel, that he denieth the Lord. Of the which fall Christ told Peter and the other disciples afore for a warning; but they, believing it not, became presumptuous, and ascribed too much unto themselves: therefore the Lord suffereth them to fall, that they may learn what they have of themselves, and what they have of God; yea, that we all may see what the apostles were afore the receiving of the Holy Ghost, and what they became after the power that was given them from above. Afore they received the Holy Ghost, they were weak, feeble, inconstant, and wavering; but when God had clothed them with power from above, they became fervent, earnest, and stedfast. Grievously doth Peter fall in denying of his Master: which thing yet turneth to the wealth of him and all men; to the intent that thereby we might learn, how hurtful and dangerous it is for a man to trust to himself, to his own strength, and not only unto God, without whom we are able to do nothing that good is. Good godly people do fall many times, and through fear and greatness of the battle they should utterly give over, if they were not fortified and preserved by the power of God.

Therefore the mercy of God, which continually careth for us, hath brought to pass and appointed, that such examples should be noted in the scripture, to teach us and to declare unto us his power and goodness in every thing. Thus the sins and falls of holy and virtuous men are set before us; partly to the intent that if we stand, we should so continue upright, looking well to ourselves that we fall not; and partly that if we be fallen, we should learn to rise up again, to amend our lives, and to bewail our sins. And so have the holy evangelists perfectly and uniformly described the fall and denial of Peter; not that thereby they thought to deface Peter, or to publish and make known his trespass; but that the power of God in him might be known and praised.

As for such sins as holy men commit through weakness and ignorance, God useth them to his glory and our commodity; that with the wounds of his saints he might heal ours, and that the shipwreck of the godly might be unto us a sure port and haven. Peter's fall serveth, first to the knowledge and praise of the power and goodness of God, in that we see how mightily he setteth up Peter again, and strengtheneth him, how graciously he forgiveth him his sins; that we which are fallen should not despair, but hope for assistance and forgiveness of God, who giveth strength and power unto those that are his. Item, it serveth to our commodity and profit, in that we see a good godly man fall and sin, and afterward rise up again and amend; lest we should say, "Alas! I am lost, I have done this, and I have done that:" but forasmuch as we see that Peter by repentance, weeping, and converting again, doth obtain grace, it is meet and convenient, that we acknowledge our offences unto God, desire grace, weep and complain of our sins before God. For both are here set before us, the fall, and the repentance: and this ensample is good and profitable to those that are in the right way of godliness, and also unto sinners. The godly, just, and righteous learn by this to be circumspect, and not to presume: sinners by occasion of this do learn immediately to rise up again from their fall, and not in any wise to despair.

Yea, our own fall learn we to know by Peter's fall: but, alas! our fall is much more grievous and greater than Peter's. Peter sinned through weakness; many a time do we sin wilfully and advisedly: he once, we daily: he was constrained through fear, we many a time through light occasions fall from the way of truth and righteousness: he riseth up again forthwith, we seldom and slowly: he wept bitterly, we scarce do confess and knowledge the sin. Yea, bitterly wept he: which thing all the elect ought to do, if they have sinned.

There should nothing grieve us more, than to have sinned against God, than to have displeased God. This do not wilful sinners, which pass little or nothing upon sin; and when they come into the deepness thereof, care not for it, neither confess nor acknowledge their sin, until afterward with despair, as it is to see in Judas.

But Peter, bewailing the grievous fall and wickedness of his denial, without further falling away into horrible desperation, is preserved through the goodness of God; in the confidence of God's oft proved and accustomed mercy, is he lift up unto blessed repentance, and so healed. Christ's look, the true physician, is unto him as much as a word or speech. Wherein we may learn to know the unspeakable love of God; who even in the midst of sin forgetteth not his own, forsaketh them not, but graciously looketh upon them with the eyes of his mercy, admonisheth them, speaketh unto them through the outward and inward word; with the which gracious countenance he dissuadeth them from sin, and calleth them again to himself, provoking them to sorrow and mourning, lamentation and weeping. He spreadeth out his arms and lap of his mercy, and graciously taketh us up again, and receiveth us with the lost son. Therefore let us knowledge, repent, and bitterly bewail our sins; let us wash them away with tears, and endeavour ourselves with great diligence, that negligently we fall not into them again; let us run to the bottomless well of God's mercy, and pray.

O merciful God, give us the well of blessed tears, that from the bottom of our hearts we may with Peter bewail our sins. O with how great and grievous sins are we laden and entangled! O suffer us not to lie under the heavy burden; let us not sink down in heaviness and desperation. Set thou us up again, and convert us throughly: send grace of thy holy repentance into our heart; wash away all our sins and negligence; grant us the light of new graces and gifts; let not the souls perish, for whom thou didst submit thyself into so many pains and rebukes, and at the last didst suffer the terrible bitter death of the cross. Amen.

[John xviii. 19—23.]

THE high priest asked Jesus of his disciples, and of his doctrine. Jesus answered him: I have openly spoken unto the world; I have always taught in the synagogue, and in the temple, there as all the Jews resort together, and in corners have I taught nothing: Why askest thou me? Ask them that heard me, what I said unto them: behold, they can tell what I said. When he had thus spoken, one of the ministers that stood by smote Jesus upon his cheek, and said, Answerest thou the high priest so? Then Jesus answered him and said: If I have spoken evil, then bear record of the evil; but if I have well spoken, why smitest thou me?

DOCTRINE AND FRUIT.

HERE in the high priest we see an example of those malicious persons, that take in hand to overthrow and condemn the truth, afore they hear it. Great is the arrogancy of man, who dare presume to make himself a judge of God's truth; whereas of more right the truth and word of God should judge our words and works. The understanding of the man and of the flesh perceiveth not the thing that concerneth God; and therefore he refuseth it, and judgeth it unright, and so giveth sentence, afore he know what the matter is. This (the more pity!) do all they that seek their own profit and estimation, and not the honour of God.

Now in such a false and temerarious sentence, how we must behave ourselves towards the unrighteous judges, Christ teacheth us. When the faithful believer is for the truth's sake presented, prosecuted, smitten, hurt, and condemned, he must never hold with the untruth, nor allow it; but disclose their falsehood and contrary doctrine: and as Christ here doth, and Peter teacheth, with softness of mind to give an account of his doctrine, and yet with patience stoutly to bear and suffer what reproach and displeasure soever the wicked do unto him. For albeit that Christ, after the letter outwardly, doth not offer the other cheek unto the stroke, yet inwardly in heart he is after such sort disposed and furnished with love towards his enemies, that he desireth not to hurt them; yea, he is ready to suffer his body to be hanged up upon the cross for them. And yet besides this, he maintaineth and defendeth his doctrine, that it is neither seditious and false, and reporteth himself unto those that heard it. The truth and doctrine he defendeth, not his body: he declareth not his power, but his patience and softness of mind; and yet with valiant stedfastness and truth, not with glosing and flattering the unbelievers.

O God, give thou us patience, when the wicked hurt us. O how unpatient and angry are we, when we think ourselves unjustly slandered, reviled, and hurt! Christ suffereth for us a sore stroke upon the cheek, the innocent for the guilty: we may not abide one rough word for his sake. O Lord, grant us virtue and patience, power and strength, that we may take all adversity with good will, and with quiet silence of a soft mind to overcome it: and if necessity and thine honour require us to speak, that we may do the same with meekness and patience; to the intent that as well the truth and thy glory may be defended, as our patience and stedfast continuance perceived.

[Matt. xxvi. 59—68. Mark xiv. 55—65.]

THE chief priests and the whole council sought false witness against Jesus, that they might put him to death, and they found none. For though there stood many false witnesses, yet did not their testimonies agree. At the last came two false witnesses, and testified against Jesus, and said: We heard him say, This temple made with hands will I break down, and in three days will I set up another again, not builded with hands. And yet their witness agreed not together. Then start up the high priest, and stood there, and demanded of Jesus, and said: Givest thou no answer to this that these testify against thee? But Jesus held his peace, and made no answer. Then the high priest asked him yet once again, and said: I charge thee by the living God, that thou tell me whether thou be Christ, the Son of the blessed God. Jesus said unto him, Thou hast spoken; I am. But yet I say unto you: Ye shall from henceforth see the Son of man sit at the right hand of God, and come in the clouds of heaven. Then the high priest rent his clothes, and said, He hath blasphemed God: what need we further witness? Now have ye heard his blasphemy. How think ye? Then said they all: He is worthy of death. They that had bound him, laughed him to scorn, and mocked him, spit in his face, and blind-folded him, smote him, gave him buffets upon the cheek, and thumps in the neck; and then asked him: Aread[1], who hath smitten thee? and the servants stroke him upon the face, and did him much other villany.

DOCTRINE AND FRUIT.

O HOW unjust people come together against the fountain of righteousness! What false witness and sentence goeth against the truth! And yet all their shifting is, that their malice and hatred may have an appearance of justice. They prevent him with false witness, they press him with perlous[2] and subtle questions, and go about to undermine and supplant the eternal wisdom. The enemies are accusers, witnesses, and judges. And whereas they revile and blaspheme God's Son to the uttermost, they will be seen to be the men that are sorry and displeased, when God is dishonoured. But as much as they seek in the innocent Lamb, yet find they nothing, no not so much as any suspicion of evil; so pure and sincere is all his life, so true and constant are his words.

This example ought all faithful believers to set before their eyes, learning thereby so to direct their life, that the enemies not only find no vice in them, but also no suspicion of evil; that unto the evil speaker there be given no occasion nor cause to slander, and that the name of Christ through them be not blasphemed. But where as the honour of God

1 Thes. v.
Ephes. iv.
1 Tim. iii.

[1 To aread, or areed: to judge, to pronounce. Spenser and Milton.]

[2 Perlous: perilous. Spenser.]

<small>Matt. xv.</small> so requireth, we must openly speak and confess the truth before the ungodly, although they be angry and offended; according as in this place we hear of Christ, who telleth them of his glorious coming in majesty and power, although they take it for a blasphemy. Here ought we also diligently and devoutly to consider, what Christ suffereth for us, what ignominy and reproach he taketh upon himself for our sakes, how vilely he is reputed, and how shamefully in his body and in all the parts thereof he is beaten; and yet in all this, how blessedly he behaveth and sheweth himself; to the intent that it should not grieve us, for his sake to bear vile buffets and all ungentleness: for all this suffereth he for the truth's sake. Even he whom the angels do worship, is blasphemed of unthrifts; he that giveth true answer, is named a blasphemer; the righteous Judge is condemned of the unrighteous, and pronounced to be worthy of death. But the gracious Lord is quietly content to keep silence, and doth suffer: and therefore the more humble he is, and submitteth himself to be misentreated, the more glorious is his victory.

With many wicked evil words is he defaced and scorned, sore beaten and mishandled. That gracious face, which the angels delight to behold, is blindfolded, spitted upon, and buffeted; the head, the face, and neck, beaten with many sore strokes. Christ is become a stranger unto all his friends, forsaken of all his acquaintance and kinsfolks, a mocking and jesting-stock unto all men. Even as if it were a dizzard fool, is he laughed to scorn, that is wisest of all; upon whom the cruel dogs all the night long practise their unsatiable malice and pleasure, with mocking, nipping, pulling, buffeting, spitting, and reviling of him.

In all this doth his swiftness of mind and excellent patience abide still constant and unmoveable: whereby we may justly learn to be ashamed of our presumptuous brags, in our pomp and pride which we use in our soft and costly apparel; whereas Christ for our sakes became most poor and vilely reputed. Very evil beseemeth it us, yea, a shame it is for us, which of Christ are called Christians, and will be his disciples, to seek bodily pleasure and earthly joy and sensuality in all things; whereas the Lord Jesus our head doth bear and suffer all that is contrary thereunto. O how unlike are we to our head and foregoer! How far are we from right and true humility, when for the least wrong and unadvised word we be displeased with our brethren; and whereas we should give thanks for being rebuked to our profit, we are unpatient and miscontent!

O Lord Jesus Christ, grant us so to consider thy holy passion, that it bring fruit in us: make us patient, when hurt and displeasure is done unto us; teach us after thine own living example, not to fear the railing words and persecution of wicked people, neither to be discouraged for any wrongful accusation that happeneth upon us. Teach us to see our own vileness; how justly we are of the people reviled and despised for our sins. Have mercy, O Lord, upon our unperfectness. Thou wast reviled, that thou mightest take from us everlasting shame; beaten thou wast, that from the stripes which we with our sins have deserved thou mightest deliver us; spitted upon and mocked, to bring us from everlasting confusion to everlasting honour. Wherefore strengthen our minds, O Lord, that in lowly shamefacedness we may patiently suffer and bear the hard words and checks that other folks give us for our sins and offences; for many more falser accusations and rebukes hast thou borne with highest patience for us vile sinners.

O let the hard strokes and knocks of thy head be unto us a suaging of all our bodily pains: let that scornful blindfolding of thine eyes be unto us a restraint and keeping in of our sight from all wantonness, vanity, and lightness of eyes: let the vile spitting upon thy holy face expel out of us all carnal lusts; and teach us not to regard the outward appearance, but to hold and keep in honour the virtues of the soul. That carrying about and scornful derision, which happened unto thee undeserved, drive from us all dissolute manners and wanton gestures. Let that refusing of thy worthiness quench in us all desires of temporal honour; let it move us unto things that of the world are contemned and in small estimation. Give us, O Lord, a strong victory in all patience; that from our heart-roots we may acknowledge and confess ourselves to be most worthy of all contempt and slander, of all rebuke, shame, and punishment. Amen.

[Luke xxii. 66—71. xxiii. 1. Matt. xxvii. 1, 2. Mark xv. 1. John xviii. 28.]

EARLY in the morning, at the break of day, went the chief priests and elders of the people to counsel how they might destroy Jesus. And they brought him to their council, and said, If thou be the Christ, tell us. Then said Jesus unto them, If I tell you, ye will not believe me: if I ask you a question, you will give me no answer, neither let me go. But from this time forth shall the Son of man sit at the right hand of the power of God. Then said they all, Art thou then the Son of God? Then said he, Ye say it, I am. They said, What need we any more witness? We have heard it ourselves out of his own mouth. Then arose the whole multitude, as many as were there, and bound Jesus, and led him from Caiphas to Pilate into the judgment-hall. And it was early in the morning. They went not into the judgment-hall, lest they should be defiled, but that they might eat passah. Then went Pilate forth unto them, and they brought Jesus bound, and delivered him unto Pontius Pilate the deputy.

DOCTRINE AND FRUIT.

SATAN sleepeth not, but watcheth and is diligent to drive his household together, to destroy Jesus Christ, to make him sure, and to bring him to his end. For they thought, if they might have Jesus once dead, then had they rooted out the doctrine of the truth. But foolish and vain is their device, for the truth is immortal: the more it is opprest, the more it breaketh forth again: when men undertake for to quench it, then doth the shine and brightness thereof appear more glorious. Shame therefore and rebuke, yea, eternal punishment bring all they upon themselves, that, withstanding the truth, take it prisoner, bind it, and deliver it to the judge. They think they bind the truth: but the truth and word of God cannot be bound; for it maketh all

<small>2 Tim. ii.
John viii.</small>

things free, and such as are tangled and wrapt in the snares of sin, those it delivereth. Whoso goeth about to bind the truth, doth knit and snare himself with unloosable bands, and casteth from him the band of love, wherewith God offereth to draw him unto himself, and to bind him under his yoke. Wherefore let us be obedient unto the truth, and not strive against it; for if we undertake to condemn it, it shall so appear again in high majesty, that through the beautiful, fair, and clear brightness thereof we shall all perish and be blinded.

[Matt. xxvii. 3—10.]

WHEN Judas, which had betrayed him, saw that Jesus was condemned, he repented so, that he took the money, the thirty silver pence, and brought them to the high priests, and to the elders of the people, and said: I have sinned in betraying that innocent blood. They said: What have we to do withal? Look thou to that. So he cast the money from him in the temple, went his way, and hanged himself in a snare. But the high priests took the money, and said: It is not lawful to put it into the treasury; for it is the price of blood. And they took counsel, and bought with the same money a potter's field, to bury strangers in. Wherefore the same field is called *Acheldema*, that is, the field of blood, until this day. Then was fulfilled that which was spoken by Jeremy the prophet, saying: And they took thirty silver plates, the price of him that was valued, whom they bought of the children of Israel, and gave them for the potter's field, as the Lord appointed me.

DOCTRINE AND FRUIT.

LIKE as we have had in Peter an ensample of the grace and mercy of God, so have we in Judas a fearful and terrible ensample of God's righteousness. In Judas are described unto us all unbelieving desperate persons, whom the gracious God of his bottomless mercy calleth to his goodness and service; but they despise it, and follow Satan, who blindeth them, and enticeth them through manifold wickedness, which they consider not; but when they are come into the deepness of vice, they force not of it. The devil also, to whom they surrender themselves to serve, and that hath taken possession of their heart, blindeth them in such sort, that they ponder not the vileness, grievousness, and greatness of their sins, till they have fully finished the abomination: for if they did consider it, they should repent and amend. How many loving admonitions had Judas heard of the Lord, to dissuade him from his purpose! Yet all could not help. At the last openeth he their eyes that they repent, but a godly repentance they receive not. They behold the greatness and grievousness of the sin and offence, but the greatness of God's mercy in Christ they see not; by means whereof they despair in their sins, and are damned.

In the priests that loathe the blood-money, and yet abhor not to shed the innocent blood, is set forth before our eyes an ensample of all hypocrites, which outwardly appear to be good and virtuous, and yet regard not the godliness of the Spirit. A gnat choketh them, and a camel they swallow up.

But unto us poor strangers and pilgrims there is prepared and bought, through the blood of Christ, a field and churchyard, that we, being washed clean from our sins, might find eternal rest to our souls.

Preserve us, O God, from covetousness and despair, from false hypocrisy, treason, and blood-shedding: O lead us not into temptation. And whereas we have sinned, grant us true and fruitful repentance, that we never forget thy goodness and mercy, but immediately cease from sin, and serve thee continually until our end. Amen.

[Matt. xxvii. 11. Luke xxiii. 1—7. John xviii. 29—32.]

JESUS stood before the deputy. Then said the deputy, What accusation bring ye against this man? They answered and said, If he were not an evil doer, we had not delivered him unto thee. Then said Pilate unto them, Take ye him, and judge him after your law. Then said the Jews, It is not lawful for us to put any man to death: that the saying of Jesus might be fulfilled which he spake, signifying what death he should die. Then began they to accuse him, and said, We have found this man perverting the people, and forbidding to give tribute unto the emperor, and naming himself to be Christ a king. Pilate asked him, and said, Art thou king of the Jews? Then answered he and said, Thou hast spoken it. Then said Pilate to the chief priests and to the people: I find no cause nor guiltiness in the man. Then were they more earnest, and said, He hath with his doctrine moved the people to sedition throughout whole Jewry, beginning in Galilee, and from thence hither unto this place. Now when Pilate heard of Galilee, he asked, if he were a Galilean: and when he perceived that he was under Herod's jurisdiction, he sent him unto Herod, who was then at Hierusalem.

DOCTRINE AND FRUIT.

ALL they that hitherto from the beginning of the world have at any time preached the truth, were of the adversaries noted and accused to be seditious and deceivers of the people; which thing was brought upon them, to rid them out of the way. Hereof find we examples enough in the Old and New Testament. Jeremy xxvi. xxxii. xxxviii; 3 Reg. (1 Kings) xviii; Amos vii. In Christ and his apostles we see it evident. Therefore have we no cause to give over the truth; for we are no better than our Master.

And though we be complained upon for the truth's sake, it ought not greatly to grieve us; forasmuch as we see, that the like happened unto Christ, in whose mouth there was never found guile. He is set forth unto us for an example of most perfect patience. We that be spiritual disciples of Christ must go unto him to school, and learn of him meekness, obedience, patience, and lowliness of mind.

Behold, our Head standeth before an heathenish unrighteous judge; wrongfully and sore is he accused, even our Saviour, our King, and Lord; yea, even he that is Judge of us, and of the whole world. Why should we then be grieved, and refuse for God's sake to obey worldly authority, though they oppress us, and do us wrong? He is innocent: as for us, we are in many things guilty. Never should the patience of Jesus slip out of our hearts.

Have mercy upon our impatiency, O merciful Father, and print in our hearts the image of thy Son: grant us grace to follow his footsteps; expel out of us all fear of worldly accusations and false judgments; give us such a gentle spirit, as when we be wrongfully accused, or unjustly punished, is not soon unquieted. O drive thou out of us all fumishness, indignation, and self-will: let thy love increase and grow in us through the contemning of ourselves; and whatsoever is in us, that striveth or resisteth against thy holy will, let the same be clean extinct and die.

[Luke xxiii. 8—12.]

AND when Herod saw Jesus, he was exceeding glad: for he was desirous to see him of a long season, because he had heard many things of him, and he trusted to have seen some miracle done by him. Then he questioned with him many words: but Jesus answered nothing. The high priests and scribes stood forth and accused him straitly. And Herod with his men of war despised him; and when he had mocked him, he arrayed him in white clothing, and sent him again to Pilate. And the same day Pilate and Herod were made friends together; for before they were at variance.

DOCTRINE AND FRUIT.

THE everlasting Wisdom of God is mocked and jested at, as a dizzard fool; the Truth is belied. Us therefore, that of nature are foolish and liars, it should not grieve to be reviled for God's sake. No answer giveth Christ to the ungodly voluptuous king, who, of a curious desire, would fain have seen or heard some new thing of Christ; for at that hour to answer, it could not edify. It was a time wherein it pleased him to suffer, not to do miracles. Thus the innocent Lord Jesus, for us guilty, is drawn and haled from one unrighteous judge to another. All reproach, shame, dishonour, and derision, taketh he upon himself for our sakes; every where is he grievously accused, in every place is there hurt done unto him, and after many questions and examinations they hang him up upon a cross. Thus the high God is brought low, as if he were most vile; the Almighty is defaced, as if he were most weak of all; the wisest of all is laughed to scorn, as if he were a natural fool; the most unguilty is handled as an evil doer.

This spectacle ought we very diligently to behold: for we are laden with grievous burdens of all wickedness, and have for our iniquity deserved so much, that we are worthy of all rebuke, shame, and confusion; yet are we unpatient, when we be despised. Nevertheless all such vile entreating doth Christ suffer for our sakes, to deliver us from eternal shame and confusion, which we justly have deserved.

O Lord, take from us all wantonness and pride. How evil beseemeth it us, thy servants, wilfully and vainly to deck our bodies; whereas thou, Lord, king of heaven, art scornfully despised in a fool's coat! O Lord, set thou before our eyes and hearts the contempt and derision that was done unto thee: teach us to follow thee through the contempt and hatred of ourselves, and to rejoice when we are despised.

Let us never set our hope upon men, upon praise, upon honour, upon power, upon money; but that from the bottom of our hearts we may be able to despise all temporal things, and love thereof, and firmly and stedfastly to follow after thee, O Lord Jesu, our welfare; that as touching all the rebuke and contempt, which thou for us, poor unworthy sinners, hast suffered, we may bear the same in the perpetual remembrance of our heart, and never forget it. Amen.

[Luke xxiii. 13—22. John xviii. 33—40.]

PILATE called together the high priests and chief rulers with the common people, and said unto them: Ye have brought this man unto me, as one that perverteth the people; and, behold, I examined him before you, and find no fault in this man, of those things whereof ye accuse him; no, nor yet Herod. For I sent you to him, and lo, nothing worthy of death is done unto him. So Pilate went again into the judgment-hall, and called Jesus, and said unto him: Art thou the King of the Jews? Then answered Jesus, Speakest thou that of thyself, or have others told it thee of me? Pilate answered, Am I then a Jew? Thy people and thy high priests have delivered thee unto me: what hast thou done? Jesus answered, My kingdom is not of this world: if my kingdom were of this world, assuredly my ministers would fight for me, that I should not be given over unto the Jews. But now is not my kingdom from hence. Then said Pilate, Then art thou a king? Jesus answered, Thou sayest it; I am a king. For this cause was I born; for this cause came I into the world, that I should bear witness unto the truth. Whoso is of the truth, heareth my voice. Then said Pilate unto him, What is truth? When he said this, he went forth again to the Jews, and said unto them, I find no fault in him. But ye have a custom, that I should deliver one unto you loose at Easter. Will ye that I loose unto you the King of the Jews? Whom will ye that I shall let go? Barrabas, or Jesus which is called Christ? For he knew that the priests had of envy and hatred delivered him up. Then cried they all, and said, Not him, but Barrabas. As for Barrabas, he was a murderer; who because of an uproar made in the city, and for manslaughter, was laid in prison. Then spake Pilate further with them, willing to let Jesus loose. But they cried, Crucify him, Crucify him. Then said he unto them the third time, What evil then hath he done? I find no cause in him. Therefore will I punish him, and let him go.

DOCTRINE AND FRUIT.

FORASMUCH as the devil knoweth, that Christ and his ministers apply all diligence with their doctrine, that the kingdom of him, who is the prince of this world, might be destroyed, and that the kingdom of Jesus Christ the Son of God, the chief king of all, might prosper; he bringeth to pass, that Christ and the ministers of the word are noted and suspected of sedition; whereas they seek nothing less than worldly power and dominion. Christ flieth away, when they would make him king: now is he noted and accused, as one that seeketh to be emperor. Nevertheless Christ is a true king, whose kingdom consisteth not in corporal things, but in spirit and in power. Christ despised all honour, riches, power, and pleasures of this world: his ministers therefore must of all the world be contemned. But Christ ruleth through his Spirit and power in their hearts, and they also shall rule with him in the resurrection. He is the truth, and giveth witness unto the truth; and whoso is of the truth heareth his voice, and beareth record also unto the truth.

Here likewise we learn the unstedfastness of the world. They that afore ran still after Christ, and would have made him king, crying joyfully, "Hosanna unto the Lord," cry now, "Crucify him, Crucify him." So little worthy is the praise and commendation of the world to be regarded. They that said afore, "Praised be he that cometh in the name of the Lord," the same cry now, "Away with him, crucify him:" and so they chose a murderer instead of the Saviour. Their request is, that the murderer may live; as for the Saviour and well of life, him they desire to be put to death. If we pondered this well in our hearts, that our Saviour, our Jesus, was esteemed worse and more vile than a murderer, there should be nothing that we would not be glad to suffer for his sake.

Now when the world is in hand with us, and casteth many opprobrious words upon us, we must not be overcome with unpatiency; the false accusation and threatening of wicked people ought not to make us shrink: but if we love

Christ with our hearts, we must remember his patience, when he was falsely accused and reviled for our sakes; and so with stopped ears ought we to let all sharp words pass, yea, to pray for them that speak evil of, or to us.

When our good works and meanings are taken in evil part, our enterprise resisted, our words rejected and refused of every man, we ought patiently to suffer it. For far inferiors are we unto Christ our Lord; over whom goeth so horrible and wicked a cry, "Crucify him, Crucify him."

Hereof should all faithful believers be admonished, yea assured, if they mind to live godly in Christ Jesu, that they must suffer much persecution, and that if they will walk and go forward in the way of God, they must bear many hurtful and noisome things; for no man can please God, that for his sake is not exercised in much adversity. Therefore saith he unto his dear friends: "Blessed are ye when men revile you, and persecute you, and shall falsely speak all manner of evil against you for my sake. Rejoice and be glad: for great is your reward in heaven."

Matt. v.

Wherefore, dear children, let us follow our innocent Lord Jesus; who being refused of wicked men upon earth, but chosen of God the Father, is crowned with eternal glory and godly honour in heaven. No evil saying or curse ought to overcome us, considering that for the same there is so exceeding joy prepared for us of God.

[John xix. 1—12.]

THEN Pilate took Jesus therefore, and scourged him: and the soldiers wound a crown of thorns, and put it on his head. And they did on him a purple garment, and came unto him, and said, Hail, King of the Jews; and they smote him on the face. Pilate went forth again, and said unto them, Behold, I bring him forth to you, that you may know that I find no fault in him. Then came Jesus forth, wearing a crown of thorn, and a robe of purple. And he saith unto them, Behold the man. When the high priests therefore and ministers saw him, they cried, saying, Crucify him, crucify him. Pilate saith unto them: Take ye him, and crucify him; for I find no cause in him. The Jews answered and said unto him: We have a law, and by our law he ought to die, because he made himself the Son of God. When Pilate heard that saying, he was the more afraid; and went again into the judgment-hall, and saith unto Jesus: Whence art thou? But Jesus gave him no answer. Then said Pilate unto him, Speakest thou not unto me? knowest thou not that I have power to crucify thee, and have power to let thee loose? Jesus answered: Thou couldest have no power at all against me, except it were given thee from above. Therefore he that delivereth me unto thee hath the more sin. And from henceforth sought Pilate means to loose him. But the Jews cried, saying: If thou let him go, thou art not the emperor's friend: for whosoever maketh himself king, is against the emperor.

DOCTRINE AND FRUIT.

HERE in Pilate we learn, how hurtful it is, when every one in his office and vocation looketh not diligently about him, but slenderly letteth the thing slip and pass, that he earnestly ought to bring to effect. Pilate was the deputy of a country, and knew that Christ had wrong; whereof he himself also many times beareth him witness with his own mouth. Seeing then that he was a judge, it appertaineth to his office to judge right, and not to suffer the innocent to die. For though Pilate doth, as if he would discharge Christ, yet he mindeth it not earnestly. He goeth about to let Christ loose: nevertheless so far as he displease not the Jews and the emperor, so far as he lose not the favour and friendship of men.

While Pilate now fainteth in the righteousness that he knoweth and is sure of, and holdeth not on stoutly, as he should, to deliver Christ, God suffereth him still to fall, till he come to this point, that he condemneth the innocent to death against his own conscience. Thus goeth it with all those, that for the grace of God lent unto them are unthankful and unfaithful in the little. It is the part of a righteous judge to maintain justice, and to defend the innocent, though it should cost him body, honour, and goods.

The pride also of Pilate, that presumed by reason of his authority, is brought down with the words of the Lord: "There is no power but from above," and therefore should it be godly used; the higher powers are God's ministers. In the which words of Christ the faithful believers that be in adversity are comforted; knowing that no man hath authority nor power over them, except it be given him of God.

Christ is bound, to deliver us from the bands of our sins, and to place us in eternal freedom. He is scourged, to take from us the stripes that we should suffer by reason of our sins; yea, to heal our wounds, is he sore wounded himself. Altogether suffereth he for our sakes; through his stripes are we made whole. "His back," as Esay saith, Isai. l., "offereth he to the smiters, and his cheeks to the nippers," to purge us from all filthiness of sin. He became without beauty, as a leper despised, spitted upon, and mocked, to deliver us from eternal shame and punishment. We had deserved all this, he did nothing worthy thereof; we are the cause of his martyrdom. Oh the great burden of our sins, that the Son of the eternal God must suffer so sore stripes and cruel pains for us, to reconcile us with his Father! Oh the exceeding great love which he declareth unto us, in that he taketh all rebuke upon himself for us! Oh that we considered this with true devotion; so that we might say with Christ and David: "I am ready to be scourged, and my plague is always before me."

O Jesu, kindle us with the fire of thy exceeding love, which thou in so much adversity hast well tried towards us. Grant us the help of thy grace, to the strengthening of our weakness, when the heavy burdens of adversities fall upon us; that through the terrible overcharge of them we be not opprest and thrown down. Give us grace, so to chasten and subdue our body and flesh, that it may be subject unto the Spirit, and obedient unto thy will in all things.

[John xix. 13—16. Matt. xxvii. 12—26. Mark xv. 3—15.
Luke xxiii. 13—25.]

WHEN Pilate heard that saying, he brought forth Jesus, and sat down to give sentence in the place that is called the Pavement, but in the Hebrew tongue Gabatha. It was the preparing of the Easter, about the sixth hour. And he saith unto the Jews, Behold your king! They cried: Away with him, away with him! Crucify him. Pilate saith unto them, Shall I crucify your king? The high priests answered, We have no king but the emperor. And the high priests with the elders of the people accused him in many things, but he gave no answer. Pilate asked him further, and said: Makest thou no answer? Seest thou not, in how many and great things they accuse thee? But Jesus moreover gave no answer, so that the deputy marvelled sore at it. At the feast he had a custom, to let one unto them loose, whom they would desire. Now while the people pressed on, Pilate began to ask them, as he always did, and said: Whom will ye that I let loose unto you? Barrabas, or Jesus who is called Christ?

While Pilate sat in judgment, his wife sent to him, and said: Have thou nothing to do with that just man; for this night in sleep have I suffered much for him. But the high priests and the elders persuaded the people, and enticed them, that they should ask Barrabas, and require Jesus unto death. Then answered Pilate, and said unto them: Whom will ye of these two that I shall let go loose unto you? They said, Barrabas. Then said Pilate unto them: What shall I then do with Jesus, who is called Christ? Then said they all, Let him be crucified. The deputy said: What evil then hath he done? Nevertheless they cried yet more, Let him be crucified.

When Pilate saw that he profited nothing, but that the uproar was greater, he took water and washed his hands before the people, and said: I am unguilty from the blood of this just man; look ye to it. Then answered all the people, and said: His blood be upon us, and upon our children. So Pilate, according to their desire, let Barrabas loose unto them: and Jesus, whom he scourged, gave he over unto them to be crucified.

DOCTRINE AND FRUIT.

PILATE feareth men more than God: therefore doth he against God, and condemneth the innocent, although he thinketh to be unguilty of his blood.

The evangelist maketh mention of the feast of Easter or Passah, to the intent we should consider, that Christ, the true right Paschal Lamb, was put to death and slain for us.

Here we learn what the judgment of the world is: righteousness is refused and condemned; wickedness, ungraciousness, and murder, is delivered and quit. O how lamentably perisheth the righteous, and no man there is that considereth it, or that goeth about to deliver him! The true is given over to the liars; the innocent to the guilty; the godly to the ungracious: the murderer is chosen before Jesus the anointed Son of God: here the wicked is preferred before the just, death before life, night and darkness before the light.

This now in all our troubles, when we are oppressed and falsely condemned, shall comfort and strengthen us, if we set before our eyes the blessed example of Jesus the innocent, who for us was condemned as an evil doer. For we servants are not above our Lord. If the Judge of the quick and dead be wrongfully condemned, how much more convenient is it, that we poor guilty should suffer, when we are judged, whether it be done justly or unjustly!

Christ for our sake was falsely condemned, to take from us the just judgment of eternal damnation, which was gone out upon us for our sins.

Grant unto us, O Lord Jesu, that neither threatening nor slander drive us away from the contemned cross, but that with our whole powers we may gladly follow thee. O give us grace, to fasten our flesh with the temptations thereof, unto the cross; that we, bewailing our former sins, may with-

THE PASSION OF CHRIST

stand and overcome the temptations that are behind. Help us, Lord, in the conflict of the spirit; let thy cross, O Lord, be unto us a medicine against all vice; and grant, that we alway cheerfully take up our cross, and follow thee. Amen.

[Matt. xxvii. 27—34, 38. Mark xv. 16—23, 27, 28. Luke xxiii. 26—33. John xix. 16—18.]

THEN the soldiers led Jesus again into the judgment hall: and when they had mocked him, they stripped him out of the purple robe, and put his own garments upon him, and led him forth to be crucified. And he bare his own cross himself, and went on towards the place of execution. And as they led him, they caught one that was called Simon of Cyren, who came from the field, and was the father of Alexander and Rufus: him they compelled to carry the cross of Jesus, and laid it upon him, that he might bear it after Christ. And there followed him a great company of people, and women, which bewailed and lamented him. But Jesus turned back to them, and said: Ye daughters of Jerusalem, weep not for me, but weep for yourselves and for your children. For behold, the days will come, in the which they shall say: Happy are the barren, and the wombs that never bare, and the paps which never gave suck. Then shall they begin to say to the mountains, Fall on us; and to the hills, Cover us: for if they do this in a green tree, what shall be done in the dry? And unto the place of execution, there were led with him two other, murderers, to be slain. And they came unto the place called Golgatha, that is, a place of dead men's skulls, or the place of execution. And they gave him to drink vinegar mixt with gall; but when he had proved it, he would not drink it. And they crucified him, and with him two murderers, the one on the right hand, the other on the left, and Jesus in the midst: that the scripture might be fulfilled: He was counted among the evil-doers.

DOCTRINE AND FRUIT.

HERE ought we with devout hearts to behold our Saviour Jesus; how meekly he taketh the cross upon him for our sakes, and patiently beareth it, to bring the lost sheep again upon his shoulders. Here we see our King bear his kingdom upon his shoulders, as Esay the prophet saith. He is not only led forth, but it is done with great reproach, even as if he were a ring-leader of murderers and unthrifts. Oh, how was the King of glory blasphemed and misentreated for our sakes! He taketh our sins upon him, and dischargeth us of our burden.

_{Isai. ix.}

In the consideration of this reproach, we should not weep over him, but over ourselves. For if this be done to the innocent Son of God, what are we then worthy of? By this also must we learn patiently to bear our cross in following our foregoer; for he sheweth us an example before, that we should follow his footsteps, even to the death. And if we so consider our cross, it shall be light and easy unto us. We have sworn under the cross, from the which we must not shrink, if we will follow the Lord. The love of Jesu Christ shall make all adversity sweet and acceptable unto us. Our joy and comfort ought to be chiefly "in the cross of our Lord Jesus Christ, by whom the world must be crucified unto us, and we unto the world." He shall cause our slothful flesh to be quick and diligent, and shall kindle our cold heart. He goeth before us in the narrow way, and is a companion of our pilgrimage, a helper in all trouble, a comforter in all adversity, a worker with us in the grievous travail that we suffer for his sake.

_{1 Pet. iii.}

_{Gal. vi.}

O Lord, help us to bear the heavy burdens; that we may be diligent and apt unto all good works. Assist us with thy power and grace; help us according unto thy accustomed mercy; teach us to break and utterly to leave our own will. Make us true cross-bearers and followers of thee: take from us all worldly lust and wilfulness, whatsoever hindereth us in thy love; that in obedience and patience we may alway follow thee, and find rest with thee after adversity. Thou, Lord, wast stript out of thy apparel, and spoiled thereof, that we with virtues might be clothed. The same that was put upon thee to rebuke and shame, is unto us become the highest honour. Thou wast lift up from the earth, that thou mightest draw the hearts of thy faithful believers unto thee from all earthly things, and kindle them in the love of high heavenly things; that thou through thy death mightest reconcile and fully restore all that is in heaven and earth.

O ye righteous and faithful, that delight to serve God, behold with the eyes of your heart, how our God, Lord, King, and Redeemer hangeth on the cross for us: let us consider our lover, who for our sakes hangeth naked and bare in great shame and reproach before the world. He spreadeth out his arms, to call and receive unto himself us poor sinners and lost children, saying: "Come to me, all ye that labour and are laden, and I will refresh you." He sheweth his wounds, out of the which floweth the plentiful river and fountain of his precious dear blood, to the washing away of all our filthiness. He boweth down his head, to speak friendly unto us. Boldly therefore, with great comfort and confidence, ought all sinners to resort unto him, where they shall find help and consolation, defence and protection: there should they lay down the heavy burdens of their sins. Unto us must all the world be a cross, and we unto the world; only let Christ the Lord be our life, and to die with him our greatest advantage. Far be from us all rejoicing, save only in the cross of Jesus Christ: far be from us all confidence in our own works and merits; for all our health consisteth in the cross of Jesus Christ, wherein undoubtedly we may well set all our hope. By him cometh forgiveness of sins; out of him floweth the riches of all deserving; with him is the reward of all righteousness. Through the contempt of ourselves, and of all temporal things, let us barely, nakedly, and simply follow the naked and crucified Lord. Matt. xi.
Zech. xiii.

Teach us, O God, to have delight in contemning ourselves, and all temporal things; and when other folks are in trouble, to be sorry and pray for them. Grant us grace to wish good unto those that hurt and punish us: let us not trust in men; for there be few faithful and constant friends.

Here also should we learn not to be grieved, if we have few lovers and many enemies; for so happened even unto Christ our head. He had many foes; to whom yet he did none evil, but much good, and received great unthank for his labour. Sweet and acceptable should it be unto us, to suffer reproach of the world, and to be despised for his sake; yea, to avoid all voluptuousness and joy of the world, seeing[1] we are fastened unto the cross with Christ. To seek much pastime and pleasure of the world, becometh not him that must suffer adversity. All this learn we in the passion of Christ, and in the cross. Blessed is he that directeth his daily exercise and his whole life thereafter; he shall enjoy the fruit of the tree of life for ever.

<small>Rev. ii.</small>

<small>Psal. lxxxiv.</small> O God, heavenly Father, look upon the face of thine Anointed, who hanged for us upon the cross: be merciful unto us poor sinners, which be laden with great and grievous sins; forgive us for the most worthy merits' sake of thine only-begotten dear Son, who for our sins was beaten and wounded; let him satisfy thee for all our sins.

He is our surety in thy sight, our faithful Advocate and Mediator; him thou gladly hearest, O Father of mercy, and graciously acceptest his intercession for all sinners.

O gracious Lord Jesu, Son of the eternal God, who of very love towards us tookest upon thee our weak flesh, undefiled from all sin, and didst offer up the same flesh unto thy Father upon the altar of thy cross for the safe-guard of the world; have mercy upon us thy servants, for thy everlasting goodness; and for the infinite merits' sake of thy holy passion. For thy deserving excelleth all men's sins, and much greater is the abundance of thy mercy than all our

<small>Psal. cxx.</small> wickedness. Therefore fly we unto thee under the protection of thy holy cross, and with sighing hearts seek we help, grace, and remedy for our wounds. Receive us that are fled unto thee; heal us that be sick; make us just and righteous, that be sinners. Draw thou us up on high, O Lord Jesu, from all worldly things; bind up our flesh with thy fear; wound us with thy sweet love, that nothing else take hold of our heart, save only Jesus Christ.

Out of the wounds of Jesu, and out of the running out of his blood, do we receive hope; there find we medicine for our souls, abundance of grace, and perfect forgiveness. Whatsoever we receive of sinful vices, whatsoever we commit with bodily sensuality, the same is altogether washed and reformed in the fountain of Christ's blood. O the unoutspeakable love, which the Son of God beareth towards his church; that he

[1 Ed. 1593, *saying.*]

washeth and cleanseth it with his own blood, with the blood Eph. v. of the new testament, that it may be holy, pure, and without spot! Not with silver and gold doth God redeem his crea- 1 Pet. i. ture, but with the precious blood of his own Son. O dear children, let us not tread under foot the blood of the holy testament; let us not be unthankful unto our Saviour.

Thy holy blood, O Jesu, make us pure and clean from Heb. x. all sin, and sanctify us throughout; that our spirit, soul, and body may cheerfully wait for thy coming, and live with thee 1 Thess. v. for ever.

[Matthew xxvii. 35—37. Mark xv. 24—26. Luke xxiii. 34—38. John xix. 19—24.]

JESUS said: O Father, forgive them; for they know not what they do. Pilate wrote a superscription of the matter, and fastened it above at the head of the cross. The superscription was written in Greek, Latin, and Hebrew, with these words: Jesus of Nazareth, King of the Jews. This superscription did many of the Jews read; for the place where Jesus was crucified was near unto the city, and the superscription was written in Greek, Latin, and Hebrew. Then said the high priests of the Jews unto Pilate, Write not, King of the Jews, but that he called himself the King of the Jews. Pilate answered: What I have written, I have written. The soldiers, when they had crucified Jesus, they took his garments and made four parts, to every soldier one part, and also his coat. The coat was without seam, wrought upon throughout. Then said they together: Let us not divide it, but cast lots for it, who shall have it; that the scripture might be fulfilled, saying: They have parted my raiment Psal. xxii among them, and for my coat they cast lots. And the soldiers did such things in deed. Then sat they down and kept him. There stood also much people, and beheld.

DOCTRINE AND FRUIT.

THE last words which Jesus spake upon the cross, ought all faithful believers well to write in their hearts, and therein diligently to keep them. First, he spake a loving friendly word, a word full of grace and sweet comfort to all sinners, sufficient and enough to break all hardness of heart, and to provoke fruitful repentance: "Father, forgive them." O how great goodness and lovingkindness is this! how ready is Jesus unto mercy! how well willing is he to forgive his lovers, that sheweth himself so mild and gracious unto his enemies! No angry word, no displeasure poureth he out against those that crucified him; no vengeance nor plague desireth he to fall upon that ungracious people, but speaketh most sweet words, full of ardent love: "O Father, forgive them," &c.

In these words appeareth his exceeding great love with unoutspeakable softness of mind, which through no malice might be overcome. They, like mad and blood-thirsty men, cried: "Away with him; crucify him, crucify him." O the wonderful great lenity of our Lord Jesus Christ! They revile and misentreat him to the uttermost; he prayeth for them, that they, being converted from their wickedness, may acknowledge him the very true Son of God to have appeared in the flesh.

Isai. liii. Here is fulfilled that Esay said: "He hath borne the sins of many, and made intercession for the transgressors," that they should not perish.

Who now being in sin, will despair in the mercy of God, when the great offenders, that crucified and slew the giver of all remission, found so great grace and goodness?

A stedfast hope therefore ought we to conceive and to be sure of, how great soever our sin be. The hope of life standeth yet open, the bowels of mercy are yet ready prepared. Only unto him let us resort; full graciously will he receive us, so far as we give over ourselves unto him. Here likewise, by the example of our foregoer, we must learn to forgive our neighbour, to pray also for our enemies, and for those that do us harm. If we gladly forgive that little, God will forgive us the great. If we so do, we find grace, and are the children of the heavenly Father. As for the recompensing of all despite, and taking of vengeance, we must commit and refer that unto our Father, who judgeth right- 1 Pet. ii. iii. eously.

O Jesu, thou heavenly schoolmaster, teach us this, and grant us grace to do it. Give us also an assured hope of thy mercy and grace, that we fall into no despair through the multitude of our sins; but with faithful minds to consider, that for to heal sin thou camest into this world, and hast shed thy blood. O grant unto us free refuge and sure defence under the shadow of thy wings, and under the invincible token of thy holy cross. Receive us poor sinners, which utterly trust not in any good deed or merit of our own, but only in thy mercy. Amen.

Very spiteful extremity is shewed unto our Saviour, in that he must behold and see, how the vile unthrifts part his clothes amongst them. By this is there set forth unto us a doctrine, how we ought to behave ourselves, if our temporal goods be withdrawn and taken from us. We must be readier to suffer temporal harm, than to be revenged, or with unquiet suit at the law to require our own. He that created the whole world, hath not a corner where to rest his head. He that beautifieth and decketh all things, hangeth bare and naked himself. Whereby we must learn to be patient, if that which is ours be taken from us: we must learn to be content with few things, and to take in good part things of small reputation, and not to grudge, but with quiet minds to be thankful unto God.

O Lord, grant unto us, that we appear not naked and bare before thee; clothe us with the wedding-garment of faith and love; and when we suffer wrong, give us grace to follow thine example in patience, that no sorrow nor heaviness for loss of temporal goods lead us away from thee. Amen.

[Matthew xxvii. 39—44. Mark xv. 29—32. Luke xxiii. 35—43.]

THEY that passed by reviled and blasphemed him, wagging their heads, and saying: Lo, thou that breakest down the temple, and settest it up again in three days, help now thyself: if thou be the Son of God, come down from the cross.

The high priests also mocked him, together with the scribes and elders, and said amongst themselves: He helped others; can he not help himself? If he be Christ, the chosen of God, the king of Israel, let him come down now from the cross, and we will believe him. He setteth his hope and trust in God: let him deliver him, if he will have him; for he hath said: I am the Son of God. The murderers also that were crucified with him, cast the same in his teeth, and reviled him. The people stood there, and waited; and the chief of them mocked him, and said: Hath he helped others, and cannot help himself, and is Christ the chosen of God? The soldiers also mocked him, came, and proffered him vinegar, and said: If thou be king of the Jews, help thyself. One of the murderers that hanged by him reviled him also, and said: If thou be the Christ, help thyself and us. But the other rebuked him, and said: Fearest thou not God, seeing thou art in the same damnation? As for us, we are justly punished, for we receive according to our deeds; but this man hath done nothing amiss. And he said unto Jesus: Lord, remember me, when thou comest into thy kingdom. And Jesus said unto him: Verily, I say unto thee, this day shalt thou be with me in paradise.

DOCTRINE AND FRUIT.

Jesus for our sake took upon himself the most extreme shame, rebuke, and derision, to deliver us from eternal villany[1], and that we should learn gladly to suffer reproach and shame, and to despise the vain glory of the world. He is mocked and contemned of high and low, of spiritual, of temporal, and of every man. For they, being full of gall, bitterness, and poison, pour it out with their false tongues and outward gestures, casting out wicked slanderous words, and sharpening their venomous tongues against the innocent Saviour. They rather should have bewailed their own great sins: but there is no compassion nor mercy in them; their

[1 Villany: slavery.]

hearts are stopped, Satan hath the leading of them. Yet cannot their malice overcome good Jesus; through their wickedness and despite cannot his patience be vanquished. No opprobrious or vile word might cause him to omit the work of our redemption; but he continueth in love, and performeth it with an honourable end. Even as he teacheth us Matt. xxiv. to endure unto the end, so doth he practise it himself, and declareth it unto us in deed and example.

We therefore that will be followers of Jesu Christ, should set before us this excellent example of our foregoer, and learn to contemn the world, and stoutly to abide in our holy vocation and purpose. It is the work of Christ that we have in hand; and before us we have an high perfect example-giver, of whom we ought to learn, even Christ Jesus, who for our sakes was obedient to the Father until the death of the cross. Phil. ii. Wherefore, seeing we are become children of God through grace, we must be obedient to our heavenly Father, looking to his good pleasure, bidding the world farewell, despising the mocks and scorns thereof, looking up ever diligently unto the crucified Lord Jesus, who waiteth for us with outstretched arms, calleth us lovingly unto him, and for a short travail promiseth us eternal reward, and saith : " If thou suffer with 2 Tim. ii. me, thou shalt reign with me; if thou die with me, thou shalt also be crowned with me."

O Lord Jesu Christ, our foregoer and protector, grant us grace stedfastly to continue in our holy vocation, and to abide in thy service; that through no tediousness or sloth we shrink or cease from the ferventness of good works and holy exercises; that we, being alway ready furnished with watching and prayer, may stedfastly stand, and with a constant mind despise all bodily provocations, shewing patience in adversity, not fearing the slanders and despiteful words of the people, neither desiring the praise and honour of this world; that in the only eternal wealth we may set all our trust, and never to go back from the cross for wealth nor woe; but that under the same banner, through true patience, meekness, and obedience, we may finish our life with a blessed end. Amen.

In the offender that received of Christ the promise of grace, there is set before us a comfortable example of the mercy and love of God. For he that afore had been a murderer, and now was become a penitent and repentant person, as soon as he acknowledged the trespass, and was unfeignedly sorry for his offences committed, confessing Christ the fountain of life, there was promised unto him forgiveness of his sins and entrance into joy. Whereby we see, that no true penitent cometh too late, and that no conversion is unfruitful, if it be done unfeignedly from out of the heart. Here should we learn to go into ourselves, to acknowledge and confess our sins, to complain unto God with lamentation, and to desire grace at his hand; affirming also, that we are well worthy of all rebuke and shame, all punishment, pain, and adversity. Nevertheless, in the consideration of God's eternal mercy, we ought not to despair, but to turn us unto the Bishop and chief Shepherd of our souls; and say: "Lord, remember us in thy kingdom, where thou sittest at the right hand of God thy Father:" so shall we undoubtedly hear this cheerful voice: "To day shalt thou be with me in paradise." This word of consolation, this gracious promise, shall strengthen and comfort our troubled heart in the careful and terrible hour; so that we shall be able quietly to die, forasmuch as Jesus so friendly speaketh to us, and receiveth us so graciously.

Great and unsearchable is the mercy of God, that pardoneth so great a sinner and offender, and doth not cast him off: neither will he reject our fervent prayer, which we in true confidence make unto him. He "desireth not the death of a sinner, but willeth that he convert and live." "So loved he the world, that he gave his only-begotten Son, that whosoever believeth on him should not perish, but have everlasting life;" neither came he to call the righteous, but sinners.

Ezek. xviii.

John iii.

Matt. ix.

O Jesu, be mindful of thy promise; think upon us thy servants; and when we shall depart hence, speak unto our soul these loving words: "To day shalt thou be with me in joy." O Lord Jesu Christ, remember us thy servants that trust in thee, when our tongue cannot speak, when the sight of our eyes faileth, and when our ears are stopped. Suffer not the old serpent and wicked enemy, the devil, to find anything in us, though he subtilely tempt us, and craftily lay wait for us. In thee shall we overcome him; for in thee is our strength. Thou takest all our sins upon thyself; so that

THE PASSION OF CHRIST

he shall find nothing in us, but must depart from us with shame. Let them be turned back, and soon confounded; but let our soul alway rejoice in thee, and be joyful of thy salvation, which thou through thy death hast purchased for us.

[John xix. 14, 25—27.]

IT was near hand about the sixth hour. And beside the cross of Jesus stood Mary his mother, and his mother's sister, Mary the wife of Cleophas, and Mary Magdalene. Now when Jesus saw his mother, and the disciple standing whom he loved, he said unto his mother: Woman, behold thy son. Afterward said he to the disciple: Behold thy mother. And from that hour forth the disciple took her for his own.

DOCTRINE AND FRUIT.

IN the passion of Christ, as is mentioned afore, it ought to be considered, that he was most extremely reviled, and suffered most great pain for our sakes. This now appertaineth to the increasing of his pain, that he seeth his mother in all adversity, who might not help him, neither he her. Now doth the sword that Simeon spake of pierce through her heart.

But Jesus, seeing her in sorrow and heaviness, declareth his careful love upon the honour and worthiness of his dearly beloved mother, and giveth her a tutor, such an one as will look unto her. On both the parties may we perceive great love, which we ought to learn of the Lord, and to exercise towards those that be committed unto us. Neither is it written of the evangelist for nought, that she stood; for thereby we see, that though Mary was in very great heaviness and sorrow, yet behaveth she not herself unseemly nor undiscreetly, as carnal men do in adversity many times. She standeth demurely and soberly, being fortified through the strength of the Spirit that stayeth her. Whereby we may learn, when our dear friends die, not to be sorry for 1 Thess. iv them beyond measure and discretion. But chiefly we learn, when adversity cometh, one to have respect to another, to care for our own, faithfully to commit them unto others, that one may brotherly and truly look to another: but specially we ought to be careful for those which are dear unto God.

[Matthew xxvii. 45—49. Mark xv. 33—36. Luke xxiii. 44.]

FROM the sixth hour there was darkness upon all the earth, till about the ninth hour, and the sun was darkened. About the ninth hour, Jesus cried with a loud voice, *Eli, Eli, lama sabacthani?* that is, My God, My God, why hast thou forsaken me? Some standing there, when they heard it, said: He calleth to Helias. Immediately one of them ran, and took a sponge, and filled it with vinegar, and put it upon a reed, and gave him to drink. Other said, Let us see whether Helias will come and deliver him.

DOCTRINE AND FRUIT.

IN all adversity and despite, is all bodily and temporal comfort withdrawn from Christ; that even when he without all consolation doth suffer most grievous extremity, we might perceive his love. The Lord of all creatures, that lacketh nothing, cometh into so great affliction and necessity for our sake, that he complaineth himself to be forsaken of him, who worketh all things in him. This is the voice of the passible mortal flesh, which for us poor sinners crieth upon the cross. His patience is our comfort, his complaint is our help, his sickness is our health, his pain is our satisfaction. The physician came from heaven, that he through great compassion might give over himself into exceeding many torments and rebukes. Therefore with the sick he is sick; with those that suffer he suffereth; with the sorrowful he is sorry; with them that suffer violence he complaineth; for his feeble and weak members he prayeth. And the voice of the flesh and of natural sense is neither rebellious nor desperate. The flesh feeleth great pain undeserved, the innocent holy body suffereth sore punishment: the Godhead nevertheless useth the highest silence; and as for the divine presence, the sensible pain is not minished by it.

But a marvellous stedfastness of patience is here declared, to perform the redemption of mankind. This pain and smart is so great, that even the elements, which have no sense, declare tokens of their compassion. The sun lost his shine, and hid his cheerful light from the wicked rabble, having as it were a displeasure for the death of their Maker. Seeing now that the sun mourneth, and the earth quaketh, much more ought we reasonable men to have compassion, and to consider the death of our Maker.

Behold, O faithful servant of God, how thy foregoer, in all his punishment and sorrowful trouble, endureth still mild and patient, and that there is heard no bitterness out of his mouth. His prayer and complaint sendeth he up unto his heavenly Father, neither nameth he any other, save only God. To him alone he complaineth and openeth his desolation. Even so ought we to do, when adversity, reproach, or any such thing assaulteth us: we must not undiscreetly sorrow, or be angry, but run straightway unto the cross, and at the cross tarry and abide a little while with the Lord. If thou be forsaken, complain of thy trouble unto God the Father; consider, that Jesus also for thy sake was left in great trouble and anguish; learn thou likewise to be soft-minded and patient, without murmuring or cursing; keep thee to the only comfort of God, give over all the joy of this world: so shalt thou not be forsaken of him. All earthly things set apart, turn thou thy mind up into the country of heaven. Take God for thy Father, Jesus for thy brother: thou art of a noble high kindred, namely, a child of the ever-living God.

O merciful Father, we cry unto thee in all trouble, and call upon thee through the crucified Jesus. Suffer us not to sink in great afflictions, give us not over unto our own strength; but the more the enemy presseth upon us, the more be thou our assistance: for in all anguish and trouble thou art the right helper and most faithful friend. If temptation then come upon us by thy fatherly will, grant us grace, O Lord, patiently to bear it, and to lay the burden upon thy mercy; that in all trouble we, being else destitute of all consolation, may put our whole trust only in thee. Amen.

[John xix. 28—30.]

AFTER this, Jesus knowing that all things were now performed, that the scripture might be fulfilled, he saith: I thirst. So there stood a vessel by, full of vinegar. Therefore they filled a sponge with vinegar, and wound it about with hyssop, and put it to his mouth. As soon as Jesus then received of the vinegar, he answered and said: It is finished.

DOCTRINE AND FRUIT.

ADAM satisfied his lust in the forbidden apple; which noisome lust was occasion of our death. But Jesus, for the reformation of this concupiscence, suffereth also upon his tongue, to restore us again from the fall, and to conquer us in this life. His bitter drink is unto us a blessed medicine. Such great unthankfulness of the Jews was prophesied by king David in the Psalms. To him that fed them in the wilderness with bread from heaven, and gave them water to drink out of the hard stony rock, even unto him for a recompence they give vinegar and gall. O the sour and unnatural fruit that the Lord receiveth of his own vineyard, which he had planted and garnished so fair! To us here is prepared a sovereign medicine against gluttony and all voluptuousness of the flesh, through the love whereof God is forgotten and forsaken.

Psal. lxix.

Isai. v.

Now when Christ, who is the fulfiller of the law and all the prophets, had wholly and fully performed the will of his heavenly Father, he saith for a conclusion and end of his life: "It is finished;" as he would say, "Now is finished all that the old law hath written and spoken of me, all that the old testament figured with oblations and sacrifices, with glory and beauty in the God's service. Now are truly fulfilled the holy prophecies of the prophets, and the long wished desires of the holy old fathers. Now is wrought and performed all that belonged and concerned the redemption of mankind. It is all, as it was promised of God, concluded with an honourable blessed end. And look, what is behind shall undoubtedly be fulfilled in due time. I have accomplished the commandment of my Father, who sent me into this world; the work that he gave me to do, have I finished. What could I do more for thee, O my people, that I have not done? Upon the sixth day he finished the work of the creation of the world; and now upon the sixth day and age of the world he performeth the blessed work of man's redemption. Upon the sixth day he created man, and made him of the mould of the earth; upon the sixth day he restored him again, and delivered him with his holy blood. Thus all things are finished: the great work of his mercy and most excellent love is accomplished; the way unto heaven is opened, and the devil's power is broken." _{John xvii.}

In such hope ought we valiantly to travail at this time, in this unconstant world, and not to let fall the work of God that is begun; but by his assistance to bring it unto a blessed end, and stoutly to endure therein. It is well nigh come to the point, that all shall be finished: the evening and end of our life cometh on apace, wherein we may say with glad hearts, as Christ our foregoer did: "It is all finished."

Wherefore, dear brethren, let us ever most diligently and earnestly walk in the way of the truth, and of commendable virtues begun, exercising ourselves in righteousness. We must not think otherwise but to have battle against vice, against the flesh, the world, and Satan. Daily go we on apace towards death, in hope to attain eternal life. O that we might say with Paul: "I have fought a good fight, I have fulfilled my course, I have kept the faith!" We must suffer and have travail yet a little season; the time of our deliverance will shortly be here. _{2 Tim. iv.}

O Lord Jesu, direct thou all our works according to thy good pleasure; illuminate and purify our minds and thoughts. Teach us how we ever, to the praise and honour of thy holy name, may meekly begin, diligently do, and blessedly end all our works and enterprises. O give us grace faithfully to labour in the vineyard of the Lord, that the heat and travail drive us not back, that we faint not; that in the school of heavenly exercise we may stedfastly endure, till we give up the ghost; and that through thy mercy, after many commendable battles and long striving, we may say in the last hour of our life, It is all finished. Vouchsafe thou to be the final occasion of our whole life, and of all our workings: so shall it follow, that thou wilt also be our eternal reward, joy, and salvation. Amen.

[Matt. xxvii. 50. Mark xv. 37. Luke xxiii. 46. John xix. 30.]

AND Jesus crying with a loud voice said: Father, into thy hands I commit my spirit. And when he had thus said, he bowed his head, and gave up the ghost.

DOCTRINE AND FRUIT.

THE life of all living dieth after the flesh: through the painful torment of death doth Jesus depart. But by his death he openeth unto us the way of life, and taketh from us everlasting death. This is a precious, dear, and victorious death, which hath slain our death, and conquered us life again. Let this death evermore continue in our hearts, and let our death be considered in the consideration of his death. This shall bring us comfortable trust and hope, when our death striveth in us; so that we shall neither be afraid, nor despair, if we stedfastly believe that Christ died for us, and that he through his death hath opened unto us everlasting life.

Let us with devout hearts consider the death of him that hath redeemed us, and restored us again. The gracious innocent Lord Jesus dieth miserable and naked, so poor, so destitute, as no man else; and yet unto God is none so dear, although of men he be most vilely entreated. This is even the reward of the world, to despise the children of God, and to recompense evil for good. If the like happen unto us, we must not think it strange; for the servant is not above the lord. The Lord hangeth on the cross, hard pierced, not only with nails, but also with ardent love towards us; sore beaten and hurt in every place, without succour, without help, without comfort, even as a dead man who is forgotten and out of mind. Ponder well, O thou good servant of Christ, who and how great he is, that crying with a loud voice, giveth up the ghost: verily, even the Son of God, as Centurio likewise doth testify.

O dear brethren, let us consider, how great our sins are, for the which the innocent Son of God dieth. Justly ought all the world to be dead unto us in Christ, and we unto the world. And what is our life but a blessed death? He that learneth not to die in this life, is afraid, when the hour of death cometh. Every day go we one day's journey unto death: therefore ought we so to watch, so to speak, and so to work, as if we would die even now out of hand. Before death we must learn to die; lest he suddenly take hold upon us, and make us afraid. Death, unto those that faithfully believe, is through the death of Christ become the gate to life; for their comfort and strong hope is in the words of Jesus, when he saith: " He that believeth on me, though he were dead, yet shall he live." Item: " Whoso heareth my word, and believeth on him that sent me, hath everlasting life." ^{John xi.} ^{John iii.}

In this promise ought we to live and die, casting away all impediments, and such things as hinder us from his love; being with heart and mind separated from the world, and undefiled from the filthiness thereof.

Out of the passion of Christ we must pick out unto ourselves comfortable help and medicine; so that obediently in all patience we offer up ourselves unto our heavenly Father, committing our souls into his hands. In life and in death let the death of Christ be our comfort; and let us set it against all fearful temptations, and between the wrath of God and our sins.

O Lord Jesu Christ, who in the feeble nature of man hast suffered death for us unworthy sinners, grant us grace fervently in our hearts to bear the pain and love of thy most bitter death, and through the subduing and overcoming of all vice and wickedness to use and exercise ourselves daily in following thy footsteps, and dying with thee; and when the end of our life draweth nigh, that we then may depart in thy mercy and grace, and receive the joy of paradise. Assist thou us when we die, and defend us from the old enemy, whom thou through thy death hast overcome. O Father, we commit our spirit into thy hand: thou hast redeemed us, O God of truth. Let these be our last words, when we depart hence. Amen.

[Matthew xxvii. 51—54. Mark xv. 38, 39. Luke xxiii. 47, 48.]

AND behold the vail of the temple rent into two pieces, from above till beneath; and there was an earthquake; the stones cleave asunder; the graves opened; they that had slept rose up, and went out of the graves, and came after his resurrection into the holy city, and appeared unto many. The captain, and they that were with him, which kept Jesus, when they saw the earthquake, and that he gave up the ghost with such a cry, and other things that there happened, they were afraid very sore, and said: Verily, this was God's Son. Centurio likewise praised God, and said: Verily, this was a righteous man. And all the people that were there and saw it, smote upon their breasts and returned.

DOCTRINE AND FRUIT.

THE Jews alway required tokens of Christ; and of such there happened many now in the death of the Lord. For the very earth quaketh at their wickedness and blaspheming of God; the hard stony rocks, with their cracking and cleaving asunder, express a lamentation on their Maker's behalf; the vail in the temple rendeth, for a declaration, that the old covered things in the old testament are laid away, and the hid significations of Christ expressed and opened. For he is the holy true oblation, that taketh away the sins of the world: he is the undefiled Lamb of God; he is the true High Priest, that entereth within the vail into the sanctuary; for the way of holy things is opened through his blood: he is the High Priest, that once entered in, and with one only sacrifice doth perfectly cleanse and sanctify. The graves

Heb. x.

opened for an evidence of his resurrection. Centurio knowledgeth that, which the hard-hearted Jews would not confess.

O good faithful believers, let us not be harder than the stones; let our hearts rend asunder in repentance and sorrow for our sins, that we may enjoy the fruit of the Lord's death.

[Matthew xxvii. 25, 26. Mark xv. 40, 41. Luke xxiii. 49.]

AND afar off stood all his acquaintances; among whom were many women, that came up from Galilee, and followed him, and ministered unto him: among whom was Mary Magdalene, and Mary the Mother of James the Less and Joses, and the mother of Zebedee's children, with many other that were come to Hierusalem.

The Jews then, because it was the sabbath-even, that the bodies should not remain on the cross upon the sabbath-day, (for that was the great sabbath-day,) besought Pilate, that their legs might be broken, and that they might be taken down. Then came the soldiers and brake the legs of the first, and of the other which was crucified with him. But when they came to Jesus, and saw that he was dead already, they brake not his legs; but one of the soldiers with a spear thrust him into the side; and forthwith came there out blood and water. And he that saw it bare record, and his record is true; and he knoweth that he saith true, that ye also might believe. These things were done, that the scripture might be fulfilled: Ye shall not break a bone of him. And Exod. xii. again, another scripture saith: They shall look on him whom Zech. xii. they pierced.

DOCTRINE AND FRUIT.

OUT of the side of him that sleepeth upon the cross, runneth the fountain of wholesome water, with the which our uncleanness is washed away, and the whole world sprinkled, purified, and cleansed therewith. The heart is opened and wounded; love floweth out, the blood gusheth forth, to the washing away of all our sins. This is the true stony rock, which, being smitten upon, giveth water unto our thirsty souls: like as Eve was taken and fashioned out of the rib and side of her husband that slept, so is the holy church, the spouse of Christ, shapen out of the side of her husband. This gate is opened wide to all faithful believers; he that hideth himself in this hole, is sure from all hurt and harm. Of this holy and godly fountain whoso drinketh once, or taketh a draught of the holy love, doth forthwith forget all his adversities and griefs, and shall be whole from all wicked heat of temporal lusts and bodily provocations: fervently shall he be kindled in love, and desire of eternal things; and shall be replenished with the unspeakable goodness of the Holy Ghost; and "in him shall be a fountain and well of living water, flowing into eternal life."

Eph. v.

John vii.

By this creepeth the poor sinner into the loving heart of Jesus Christ, which with exceeding great kindness is pierced through; and there findeth he rest and quietness in the stony rock. Here are opened the conduits and well-pipes of life, the way of our health, wherein we find rest unto our souls, and shadow for heat and travail: this fountain of grace is never dried up. This is the well of the godly river, that floweth out of the midst of paradise, to water the whole earth, to moisture the dry hearts, and to wash away sin.

Out of this plentiful well ought we with great desire to draw and drink; that from henceforth we live not in ourselves, but in him who for our sakes was wounded so deep. Our heart must we give wholly unto him, that hath opened his heart so wide. His heart and ours must be all one. Nothing requireth he of us but the heart. "Son," saith he, "give me thy heart." Our heart must we give to the Lord, not to the world; to eternal wisdom, not to lightness. There do the true herdman's sheep find pasture; there are the water-brooks of life; there may they go in and out. Nothing is there upon earth that so kindleth, draweth, and pierceth the heart of man, as doth Christ's love declared upon the cross. When we thus surrender our heart unto the Lord, when we thus wholly and fully give over our heart into the Lord's hands, that he may keep it and possess it for ever, then have we blessed peace.

O Lord Jesu Christ, draw thou our hearts unto thee; join them together in unseparable love, that they may fervently burn; that we may abide in thee, and thou in us, and that the everlasting covenant between us may stand sure for ever. O wound our hearts with the fiery darts of thy piercing love. Let them pierce through all our slothful members and inward powers, that we being happily wounded, may so become whole and sound. Let us have no lover but thyself alone; let us seek no joy nor comfort, but only in thee.

Thus have we the passion and death of our Lord and Redeemer Jesus Christ. Now, as Paul saith, let us go forth of the tents, unto him that for our sake is despitefully crucified without the city of Hierusalem, and let us help him to bear his rebuke, giving him thanks and praise for his great love. In his death standeth our life: for in his death is our death slain; the sting of death and sin is taken away. Here find we true life and eternal salvation; here sin is forgiven, and pardon granted *a pœna et culpa;* here mercy is denied unto no man; for the virtue and merits of the Lord's holy passion is bottomless. Through his shame cometh eternal honour and glory unto us. His passion is the wholesome plaister for all wounds; his cross the overthrow of all enemies, and victory against all vice. *Heb.* xiii.

From our whole hearts therefore ought we to rejoice in the great and blessed fruits of thy holy passion.

O Lord Jesu, whilst we are in this feeble life, grant us so to live, that we may direct all our works, desires, and intents according to thy godly will and pleasure; that this our temporal course may be found and finished in thy grace; that after the overcoming of all temptations and careful things we may come to the reward of eternal salvation. Teach thou us daily to die, and by the spirit to subdue the flesh; that when the flesh corrupteth, the spirit may be taken to eternal rest. Grant us grace, cheerfully and continually to cleave unto thy holy cross. O give us blessed tears of true repentance, while the door of grace standeth open: grant that we may stedfastly and blessedly finish the thing which commendably is begun.

Let our daily exercise be in the consideration of the passion of Christ; let him be our mirror continually: let us not shrink from the cross, but endure with Christ in life and death; with him on the cross, with him in the grave and death. So shall we continue in rest, peace and quietness; that when Christ our life shall appear, we may rise up with him in glory. God the Father, Son, and Holy Ghost, grant this unto us all! Amen.

[CHAPTER II.]

THE BURIAL OF JESUS CHRIST OUT OF THE HOLY EVANGELISTS.

[Matthew xxvii. 57—60. Mark xv. 42—46. Luke xxiii. 50—54. John xix. 38—42.]

Now when it was late, forasmuch as it was the day of preparation afore the sabbath, there came a rich man of Arimathia, named Joseph, such a principal and famous senator, as was just and righteous. The same had not consented to their counsel and doings; for he also was one of those that waited for the kingdom of God; a disciple of Jesu, but secretly for fear of the Jews. Boldly went he in unto Pilate, and begged the body of Jesu. But Pilate wondered, if he were now dead already. And when he had learned of the captain, that it was, he granted him the body of Jesu, and commanded it to be given him. Joseph had bought a white linen cloth, and took down the body of Jesu, and wrapt it in the fair linen cloth. There came also Nicodemus, who was come to the Lord afore by night, and brought myrrh and aloes, upon an hundred pound, mixt together. So taking the body of Jesu, they wound it with clothes, and prepared it with sweet ointments, according as the manner of the Jews was to bury. And by the place where Jesus was crucified, there was a garden, and in the garden a new sepulchre. There Joseph laid Jesus in his own new sepulchre, which he had caused to be hewn out of a rock, into the which no man had yet been laid. Forasmuch then as it was the Jews' day of preparing, the sepulchre being at hand, they laid Jesus into it; and Joseph weltered a great stone afore the entrance of the sepulchre, and went his way.

NOW FOLLOWETH THE DOCTRINE AND CONTEMPLATION.

In the former little book we have heard of the passion of Christ. Now if our great sin put us in fear, making our conscience unquiet, and press us with the terror of everlasting death and damnation, we ought to remember, that the Lamb of God being slain, and hanged up upon the cross for our sins, hath himself satisfied for them all, and washed them clean away. This holy sacrifice was offered unto God the Father for our welfare, and even the same it is that hath taken away the sin and wickedness of all the world.

Whatsoever is read and spoken concerning the passion of Jesus Christ, it is altogether done for our eternal wealth and comfort. Now it is described of the holy evangelists, with what honour and glory his holy body was buried; and that not of mean persons, but of noble and famous just men, Joseph and Nicodemus, who, while Christ yet lived, favoured him, and were secretly his disciples. But now after his death they step forth somewhat more stoutly and boldly, begging of Pilate the body of Jesu, to bury it. In the which act is declared their worthy and valiant belief and love unto the Lord Jesu. For their bodies, their estimation, and goods, they must needs put in jeopardy, and procure unto themselves the hatred and displeasure of all the world, if they honourably bury him, who in his life-time was taken to be an evil doer, a deceiver, a seditious murderer, and so was condemned unto death. But thus it pleaseth God, in weakness to declare his own strength and glory. Thus the dead wheat-corn bringeth forth fruit in the death of Christ; and thus appeareth the power of his death. For though he verily and truly died as touching the body, yet after the spirit, and in mighty power, he liveth; yea, he himself is the life of all things.

<small>1 Cor. i.
John xii.</small>

This is the power and fruit of his passion, when a mighty and strong spirit doth exercise itself in faithful believing hearts. They that were afore ashamed to go openly unto the Lord, step now forth manfully, all fearfulness set apart, jeoparding their bodies and goods. For besides that they put themselves in peril of losing their life and estimation, they bestow also great cost in linen cloth and in costly sweet ointment. For they bury not Jesus as an evil doer, but as an honourable man and friend of God, according to their custom. Lo, what a thing it is to cleave somewhat unto Christ, how feebly soever it be done; it bringeth alway great fruit in his time. No man therefore ought to be rejected, that cleaveth any thing unto Christ, and earnestly seeketh him. Faith is strengthened in affliction and adversity: the death of Christ giveth power unto the fearful. In death beginneth his honour and glory to appear; there are all things fair and beautiful. Centurio giveth testimony, and maketh an honourable confession, and so do they that were under him.

Necessary it was we should believe and confess, that Jesus verily died upon the cross: therefore do the evangelists describe it so perfectly, how his body was taken down from the cross by Joseph, and was laid in the sepulchre; to the intent that we also might believe and confess, that he hath broken the bands of death, and is from death mightily risen again. For life might not be holden captive in death, neither might death with the rules thereof always bind him that of all things is the life, in whom "we live, move, and have our being."

Here we must learn to know the eternal infallible foresight and providence of God, who for his Anointed appointeth aforehand an honourable sepulchre, and moveth the hearts of his elect to bury the body of Jesu; which else undoubtedly had been vilely cast out, and remained still unburied. Howbeit his burial and rest must needs be honourable, as the prophet saith, Esay xi. For when he by death had finished the course of his life and the work of his Father, this rest appertained to his honour, and the Father heard him, as he prayed afore: "Father, make thy Son honourable, or glorify thy Son." John xvii. This began in the burial: there was the fair white linen cloth, the new sepulchre, the honourable men, and excellent dead-buriers, as witnesses of his death; there were the hundred pounds of precious and costly ointment. All these things were evidences of a glorious, new, and immortal life, which Christ had in his body, as the firstling of his dead, and as we also shall have according to our measure. The sepulchre is new, partly to prevent all wrong suspicion; for if any man had lien in that sepulchre afore, it might easily have been suspected or talked, that Christ was not risen again from the dead, but some other; partly to declare the newness of life in Christ, and in those that are his, as it is said afore.

By this also we see, into what poverty Christ submitted himself: he that in his life-time had neither house nor place where to lay his head, is now covered with strange cloth, and laid in a strange sepulchre. In the which thing, though Christ's body was alway uncorrupt, we are taught fruitfully to consider the corruption of our body. We are earth, and to the earth we must yield and pay earth again. Ashes we be, and into ashes we must return. Why brag we then? Why are we proud and high-minded, seeing that shortly we shall become foul dung and carrion? Why have we such desire to the wicked world, considering it casteth us out so vilely? We should alway remember, that within a small short time we shall be laid down into a foul pit. There is the harborough[1] of all flesh; there lie the rich and poor together in one bed. There is no difference between the noble and base of blood; there neither goods help the rich, nor subtle craft the witty. There the tender is worms' meat, and he that a little while ago went bragging up and down in costly apparel, is now an ugly smell to the nose: there the hardy giant is fain to play stout gallant's part; the praise and commendation of such as are puffed up in foolish pride departeth as the dust before the wind. Thus passeth away all mankind, and all flesh falleth to the place from whence he came, being dissolved by reason of original sin.

Wherefore let us learn in this time so to live, and so to subdue the flesh through the Spirit, that when the flesh corrupteth, our soul may be taken into eternal peace and rest.

Rom. vi. "For all we that be baptized into Christ Jesus, are baptized into his death, being buried with him through baptism into death; that as Christ was raised up from the dead through the glory of his Father, so we likewise might walk in the newness of life. For if we be graffed in him through the similitude of his death, we shall assuredly also be partakers of his resurrection: knowing this, that our old man is crucified with him, that the body of sin might be emptied, and that we should serve sin no more; for he that is dead is made righteous from sin. If we now be dead with Christ,

---

[1 Harborough: harbour. Spenser.]

we believe that we shall also live with him." Look upon the whole sixth chapter to the Romans.

We must die from the world, and from our own flesh, that the world may be crucified and dead unto us, as we unto the world. The old Adam, who in us did live and rule, must be subdued and mortified, that Christ only may live and reign in us. We must bury our bodies with myrrh and aloes, that is, with lamentation and sorrow for our sins, with weeping, with fasting, and with abstinence; which works of repentance are bitter unto the body. But like as those bitter things, aloes and myrrh, do keep the body from corruption; so the cross and adversity sent of God, and borne for his sake, preserveth our flesh from sin.

If we thus die with Christ from the world, and be buried in his death, we shall rise again to a new life, here and in the world to come; and so, as for death, we need not be afraid of it. For the sepulchre is new, and lieth in the garden: which noteth unto us the return to the pleasant garden of paradise, which is opened us through the death of Christ. For he as a guide is entered in before us (John xiv. Heb. ix. x.), that we also after a new sort might escape from death, and rise again to a new life. For in the death of Christ is death killed, overcome, and wholly renewed, and as much as altered into a sleep. For we live unto God; and our bodies, as the scripture testifieth, shall also live again. And this is the cause, that the scripture affirmeth those which are dead in Christ to be asleep. Isai. xxvi. 1 Thess. iv.

Afore-time had death mightily and openly reigned, even over those also that had not sinned like unto Adam, (yet had they put on Adam's image, and were therefore subdued unto the curse:) but when the second Adam, namely, Christ, ap- *1 Cor. xv.* peared, he purchased life again for mankind, through the death of his flesh, destroying the dominion of death, and rising from death again. Then was death renewed and changed, and became like unto a sleep: for it destroyeth us not for ever, but is a gate and entrance into a better and eternal life. Therefore have we a much more perfect hope of the resurrection in Christ, than they of old; which therefore buried the bodies so costly and honourably, because they hoped in the resurrection to come. As for us, we must bestow such cost upon Christ in his members, clothing and feeding the poor, and being ready also to lose all things for his sake.

Grant unto us, O God, that as concerning the world and the old life we may die with thy Son our head, and be truly buried in his death; that with him, and in him, we may rise again to a new life; that we, weak and feeble, may with Joseph and Nicodemus grow in virtue and stedfastness, daily laying somewhat to the heap of godly exercises, being ever still renewed in the spirit; that we in our hearts laying up Christ, who died for our sakes, may so in thankful remembrance bury him, to the intent that our body and soul may still remain pure and unspotted until the coming of our Lord. Amen.

[Matthew xxvii. 61—66. Mark xv. 47. Luke xxiii. 55, 56.]

MARY MAGDALENE and Mary Joses, sitting over against the sepulchre, beheld where Jesus was laid. For certain women there were, which coming with him from Galilee, and following him, beheld the sepulchre, and how his body was laid. Those returned back and prepared sweet odours; but upon the sabbath they rested, because of the commandment.

The next day after the day of preparation the high priests and Pharisees came unto Pilate, and said: Sir, we remember, that this deceiver said, while he was yet alive, that after three days he should rise again. Cause therefore the grave to be kept until the third day, lest his disciples happily come and steal him away, and say unto the people, that he is risen from the dead; and so shall the last error be worse than the first. Pilate said unto them, Ye have watchmen; go, and keep it, as ye know. They went and kept, and provided the sepulchre with watchmen, and sealed the stone.

DOCTRINE AND FRUIT.

HERE we learn to have an earnest, diligent, and fervent love unto Christ, hearing with what zeal and ferventness that devout women cleave unto him, and serve him in life and death. Him whom they loved in life, will they not forsake in death; but cheerfully with constant minds they jeopard their life and goods. What availeth us then, that we cannot shew friendship, love, and service unto Christ, as well as these women? Seeing we have not Christ always bodily with us, who now, being in his kingdom, needeth no corporal ministration and service, we ought to bestow the same upon his poor ones, whom we have always with us. Herein ought we to spare neither goods nor money to serve and please Christ, who unto death did jeopard and give his body and life for us.

But like as in the women there was a devout gesture and good mind toward Christ; so in the Jewish priests and Pharisees there was found a great malice and hatred against Christ. They were not satisfied in persecuting him while he was alive, but undertook also to hinder his resurrection. Yet God by his wisdom useth their wickedness to the glory of Christ; that even the enemies themselves, albeit against their will, must bear record of his burial and resurrection, in that they keep the grave with watchmen, and seal the stone. The truth is immortal: the more it is opprest, the more it breaketh forth. Therefore ought we to beware, that we never go about to hinder the truth; for if we should do so, we should both labour in vain, and procure unto ourselves everlasting hurt.

[CHAPTER III.]

THE RESURRECTION OF JESUS CHRIST OUT OF THE HOLY EVANGELISTS.

[Matthew xxviii. 1—7, 11—15. Mark xvi. 1—7. Luke xxiv. 1—3. John xx. 1.]

<small>Mark xvi.</small> AND when the sabbath was now past, even the sabbath-day at even, Mary Magdalene, Mary James, and Salome, bought sweet spices, that they might come and anoint Jesus. <small>Luke xxiv. Matt. xxviii. John xx.</small> The evening when the sabbath is ended, and the first day dawneth after the sabbath, namely, the first day of the week, while it was yet dark, and the sun brake forth and began to arise, the women came to the sepulchre to see it. But there happened first a great earthquake: for the angel of the Lord came down from heaven, and went and rolled back the stone from the mouth of the sepulchre, and sat upon it. His countenance was like the lightning, and his raiment white as snow; and for fear of him the keepers were astonied, and became as dead men. And behold, some of them that had watched the sepulchre, came into the city, and told the high priests all the things that had happened. Then gathered they themselves with the elders, and took counsel, and gave large money unto the soldiers, saying: Say ye, that his disciples came by night, and stole him away while ye slept. And if this come to the ruler's ears, we will persuade him, and save you harmless. So they took the money, and did as they were taught. And this saying is noised among the Jews unto this day.

Now as the women were in the way going, they said among themselves: Who will roll us the stone away from the <small>Matt. xxviii.</small> door of the sepulchre? (for it was a very great one.) And as they looked, they saw that the stone was rolled away. Then went they into the sepulchre, and found not the body of the Lord Jesu; but saw a young man sitting at the right side, clothed in a long white garment: and they were afraid. But the angel said unto them: Fear not; I know whom ye seek. Ye seek Jesus of Nazareth, that was crucified: He is not here, he is risen, as he said: Behold the place where they laid him. But go ye, and tell his disciples and Peter, that he is risen again from the dead. Behold, he goeth before you into Galilee, as he said unto you. Lo, I have told you.

DOCTRINE AND FRUIT.

The resurrection of Jesus Christ from the dead is very diligently and perfectly described of the four evangelists: for right profitable and necessary is it for the strengthening and stablishing of our belief in Christ. And whereas in the description of this history they speak not all alike, the same happeneth to our wealth, through the ordinance of the Holy Ghost; that we should exercise our faith therein, and apply our diligence, perfectly to learn and comprehend the same resurrection of Christ. For where that is right conceived and believed, there is faith perfect. The evangelists now in describing Christ's resurrection do most of all declare, to what high honour Christ came after death; and that in one order and degree, according as our belief and weakness increaseth and groweth towards perfection.

At the first is faith in us feeble and unperfect; but through the grace of him that hath given it, it daily groweth. Very hard also is it for our natural reason to receive and believe the resurrection of the dead. Therefore do the evangelists right diligently and with many words set forth the same resurrection of Christ, that our belief therein might be assured and stedfast. For whosoever truly and constantly believeth the resurrection of Jesu Christ, is ready and prepared to believe all that concerneth Christ. Neither is there anything that maketh a man more joyful, than when he believeth that at the coming of the Lord he shall rise again, and receive a glorified body after Christ and with Christ. What can be tedious to such a faithful believing man, when he beholdeth so high a reward from God? Diligently therefore ought we to hear, what the holy evangelists write of his resurrection, and to give credence to the witnesses that saw it.

First, we hear again the great zeal and the fervent love and diligence of these devout women, in that they desire to shew honour unto the Lord being dead: but the angel, a messenger of his resurrection, commandeth them to declare this joy unto the disciples, and to get them unto the Lord now being alive. Heavenly is the messenger and proclaimer of the resurrection; for it passeth far all natural reason and all flesh. Therefore are the women also afraid of him, and at the fair brightness of his countenance and apparel. For our feeble flesh is not able to sustain the glorious shine of the heavenly light and godly clearness; but is afraid at it, and feareth. Nevertheless God by his angel doth right soon comfort the women's weakness, taketh from them their fear, speaketh lovingly unto them, maketh them apostles, that is, messengers and proclaimers of the joyful resurrection. So little doth God reject our weakness, that he maketh even women to be the declarers of his resurrection: for he ever delighteth of the last to make the first. Forasmuch then as they were the beginners of death in sin, they are here first, afore the apostles, chosen to be the declarers of that immortal life, which even out of death is come forth unto us in Christ.

As Christ with the earthquake died on the cross, so riseth he with the earthquake; which also was heard in the sending of the Holy Ghost. This signified, that through his death and resurrection, and by the power of the Holy Ghost, when the apostles declare the same in the world, the whole world should be moved and changed; and though the ungracious falsehood of the high priests undertook with their lies to hide and suppress the truth of Christ's resurrection, yet God did direct it another way. Look, wherewith they minded to oppress the truth, even with the same have they helped to set it forth: and thereby was it signified, how the Jewish people should be blinded and refused. And forasmuch as they had no love unto the truth, but rejected it, it was meet that they should be blinded and darkened in lies, and that there should error and blindness enough fall upon them.

The cross is the glorious The angel is not ashamed to call Jesus *the crucified:* for the cross is the token of Christ's victory. Through the cross began his honour and glory; through the cross was death overcome; the cross is the glorious token of all Christians; in the cross is the exaltation of Christ the head, and of all his members. We ought not therefore to be ashamed of the cross of our Lord, which was crucified: for therein standeth our health, life, and resurrection, all our rejoicing and glory. Commission is given, that unto Peter before other disciples they should declare the Lord's resurrection; that from the fear, wherein he stood by reason of the denial, he might be delivered, and so comforted. and victorious token of the faithful.

He sendeth them to Galilee, (thither will he go before them,) that they might be safe from the fear of the Jews, which at that time raged horribly.

Grant us, O God, an earnest zeal and love unto the poor, in whom we may highly honour Jesus thy Son. And whereas we, through the weakness of the flesh, are inclined to be faint-hearted, and not able of ourselves to behold the bright shine and clearness of his glorious resurrection, strengthen and comfort thou us by thy holy angel, that we may constantly believe the resurrection of thy Son; whereby we receiving an holy hope of the life to come, and of the immortal resurrection of our bodies, may be able also to comfort and strengthen others that be weak. O make thou this hard earth of our flesh to quake and move, through the power of thy Spirit, to holy fruitful penance, amendment, and conversion of our life. Preserve us, that we never resist the truth, nor take part with lies. Grant us love unto the truth; keep us from error and blindness. Let our joy be in the cross of Jesu Christ thy Son, and our life in his resurrection; that we with him, and in him, may truly rise again here to a godly, righteous, and sober life, and in the world to come to the blessed life everlasting. Amen.

[Mark xvi. 8. John xx. 2—18.]

AND the women went out quickly, and fled from the sepulchre: for they trembled and were amazed. Neither said they anything to any man; for they were afraid. Mary *Mark xvi.*

John xx Magdalene ran, and came to Simon Peter, and to the other disciple whom Jesus loved, and said unto them, They have taken away the Lord out of the sepulchre, and we wot not where they have laid him. Then went Peter forth, and that other disciple, and came to the sepulchre. They both ran together, and the other disciple outran Peter, and came sooner to the sepulchre. And he stooped down, and saw the linen clothes lying; yet went he not in. Then came Simon Peter following him, and went into the sepulchre, and saw the linen clothes lying, and the napkin that was about his head not lying with the linen clothes, but wrapt together in a place by itself. Then went in also that other disciple, which came first to the sepulchre, and he saw, and believed. For as yet they knew not the scriptures, that he should rise again from death. And the two disciples went away again unto their own home. But Mary stood without at the sepulchre weeping. And as she wept, she bowed herself into the sepulchre, and saw two angels in white sitting, the one at the head, the other at the feet, where they had laid the body of Jesus. And they said unto her, Woman, why weepest thou? She said unto them, For they have taken away my Lord, I wot not where they have laid him. When she had thus said, she turned herself back, and saw Jesus standing, and knew not that it was Jesus. Then said Jesus unto her, Woman, why weepest thou? Whom seekest thou? She, supposing that he had been a gardener, said unto him, Sir, if thou have borne him hence, tell me where thou hast laid him, and I will fetch him. Jesus said unto her, Mary. She turned herself, and said unto him, Raboni, which is to say, Master. Then said Jesus unto her, Touch me not: for I am not yet ascended to my Father. But go to my brethren, and say unto them: I ascend up unto my Father and your Father, unto my God and your God. Mary Magdalene came and told the disciples which had been with the Lord, and now were weeping and mourning, that she had seen the Lord, and that he had spoken such things unto her. But though they heard that he was alive, and that Mary had seen him, yet they believed not.

DOCTRINE AND FRUIT.

The evangelists do most diligently set forth to us the resurrection of Christ, as a thing necessary, profitable, and joyful unto all faithful believers. For in the resurrection we see how Christ is exalted, and what hope we have in him. But this resurrection do the evangelists teach, according as man's understanding may comprehend it. For if Christ had suddenly at once opened himself to his disciples, so that other exhortations and warnings were not gone before, then should they have taken it but for a plain fantasy and vision, as they did when the Lord appeared unto them upon the water. Matt. xiv. Therefore the evangelists describe the matter very distinctly and sundry ways; so that no man can be able to suspect any deceit. First, how the women and men came to the sepulchre, looked, and went in; and how they viewed every thing thoroughly, not once, but oft and many times; the clothes wherein the Lord was wrapped, the headkerchief, every thing folden together in his several place; and how they saw and perceived that the body was not there, that the sepulchre was open, the stone rolled away, and how the angels and heavenly spirits testified that he was risen again. Yet for all this they are weak, and believe it not stedfastly; but be as yet in a doubt. Thus God permitteth them to waver, and to be feeble of belief, and doth not throughly persuade them forthwith, and that altogether for our sakes.

He might well suddenly have certified and assured Thomas and them at the first; but thus is it better both for them and us. For the more a sick man feeleth his own disease and wounds, the more acceptable is the medicine unto him: the weaker that our belief is, the more cause have we to call upon God for the increase of faith; the more weakness we find in ourselves, the farther are we in debt, and the more bound to praise God, when he maketh us strong. And seeing it is his only strength that stayeth us, we ought the less to rejoice in our own. Christ in his life-time had oft Matt. xx. told them afore of his resurrection; but their mind was so dull, that they understood it not, neither perceived they that great mystery. The resurrection of the bodies they could not comprehend, but alway understood it otherwise. There was much written thereof, and that with evident words, in the scripture, as in the sixteenth psalm and in the figure of Jonas; and yet could not they understand it. Which thing nevertheless to believe, Christ had given them occasion sundry ways; as in that he raised up Lazarus, and other which were dead, and made them alive again. In all his preaching and doctrine he declared, that this was unto him in no wise unpossible, by reason of the divine power working in him. For all this the disciples are yet so weak, that they understand it not all.

<small>John xi.</small>

Therefore doth the godly wisdom lead them still by little and little, to make them stronger, declaring unto them certain assured evidences; as that the body was not in the sepulchre, but that the clothes lay there wrapt together; for these were undoubted tokens, that he was risen up again. For if any man had taken him out of the sepulchre, as Magdalene thought, he could not have had so much time and leisure, as to loose up the bands, and to undo the clothes from the body; but had taken and carried away the clothes and body together: for the clothes did cleave hard fast to the body, partly by reason of the blood, and partly through the aloes and myrrh, that the body was dressed withal. But for all this they are weak still, and in doubt, until such time as the Lord himself doth strengthen them. Therefore even Mary also, as fervent as she is, judgeth not the body to be risen again, but to be stolen and privily carried away. Thus God openeth himself unto whom, and when, he will. For though we see sometimes many great and wonderful works, though we read and hear much of the scriptures, yet remaineth our heart still ignorant, neither doth the doctrine take effect, till Christ open it, and till he himself be schoolmaster within.

Whoso would rather have another and higher sense or exposition than this, it may be understood, that Christ appeareth unto those which mourn and weep, and stand in death with Christ in subduing of the flesh, in mortifying of the body, in abiding of the cross. For while they be in adversity under the cross, and buried with Christ, the greatness of the trouble causeth them to think that Christ is not risen again; that is, they have nothing but heaviness and sorrow. Notwithstanding Christ appeareth unto them, comforteth and refresheth them, and maketh them partakers of his resurrection and joy.

Here may we perceive and see a great desire and love unto Christ in the disciples that ran, but especially in Mary Magdalene: for seeing that much was forgiven her, therefore was her love exceeding great[1]. Peter also and John, which were more fervent than others in the love of Christ, and drew nearer than others did, when the Lord was taken, although the one fled, and the other denied him; therefore unto them, as to the principal, was this opened before others. Luke vii.

Mary loved Christ very fervently; for many sins were forgiven her, many devils and vices were driven out of her: therefore unto her did Christ first appear. The cross and trouble was not able to bring Christ out of her heart, it could not quench her love unto Christ; the seed of faith was in her heart, it had taken root, although it were not yet ripe. Very earnestly and with great diligence seeketh she him whom she loveth, declaring her ferventness by her weeping, and her zeal by tarrying still at the sepulchre, when the two apostles were gone away already. The Lord therefore forsaketh her not; but instructeth her, and comforteth her by the angel, appeareth unto her unknown, at last talketh with her, and maketh himself known unto her. The number of seven for many. Mark xvi.

The angels, which are ministers for the wealth of the elect, dissuade her from weeping and mourning, and bring her tidings of great joy. For herein now is no just cause to weep, but rather to rejoice; seeing that Christ hath overcome death for us, delivering and setting us free from the

[1 The language here used by Bishop Coverdale implies his approval of the opinion, which has been held by many persons, that Mary Magdalene is the person of whom mention is made in that chapter, as having anointed the head and feet of our Saviour. That however they were entirely distinct persons, has been maintained by others, whose opinion is entitled to great respect. See the question stated in "A letter to Jonas Hanway, esq., in which some reasons are assigned, why houses for the reception of penitent women, who have been disorderly in their lives, ought not to be called Magdalen houses." Lardner's Works, Vol. v. pp. 459—464. Ed. 1815.]

power thereof, and placing us in eternal life. Like as the angels at the birth of Christ in this mortal life did bring tidings of joy; so do they here also, when Christ is risen again into an immortal life. And hereunto also serveth the brightness of the countenance, and whiteness of the clothes; for all such are tokens of joy.

But some man might marvel, why Christ will not suffer Mary to touch him, seeing he would afterward be touched of the other women, of the disciples, and of Thomas; yea, he provoketh Thomas and the disciples thereto.

It seemeth that Mary, with the ointment which she brought with her, thought to anoint the body of Christ, as she did afore in his life-time, and to reverence him, and to deal with him as with a mortal man; which thing Christ forbad her to do. Hereafter shall we hear, how he offereth unto his disciples his hands, feet, and side, willing them to touch him. But with this inhibition, and that commandment, he hath respect to one only thing; namely, to deliver Mary and the disciples from unbelief, from weak faith and doubting. Unto Mary he will say: " Touch me not of a carnal devotion, as though thou wouldst anoint me. I need it no more. As for such corporal service, it is not necessary to do it unto my body any more. The cause why I became man was not that ye should alway hang upon my corporal flesh, and honour me with bodily service. Thou shalt now shortly understand, that I have like power with the Father. I am in thy heart not yet ascended up unto the Father: that is, thou hast as yet no right knowledge of my Godhead; therefore canst thou not now rightly touch me."

<small>2 Cor. v.</small>

<small>God is a spirit, with spirit will he be worshipped.</small>

Thus learn we also to know and honour Christ now no more after the flesh, and to shew no corporal outward service unto his person. In spirit will he be worshipped, with the faith and love of the inward mind. If any thing bodily be done of us, the same should be done unto the poor, and to the neighbour that hath need thereof. Thus may faith and love well use some outward things, not to do service therewith unto God, but unto ourselves or to our neighbour. As when we take and minister bread and wine about in the supper, distributing and eating it, the same is not done principally to the intent to declare a service unto God; but somewhat to provoke our outward senses and flesh by the exterior signs, that we may the better consider and ponder the grace of God declared unto us in the death of Jesus Christ, and that we may lift up our minds unto Christ, the heavenly food and living bread, which inwardly feedeth us with his flesh, and nourisheth us with his blood.

Thereto also hath Christ our Saviour instituted the figurative tokens and sacraments of his grace, to help our infirmity. For sacraments are gracious evidences of the faith that men have, or should have, to God; in the which they comfortably exercise and practise themselves towards God's promises; wherein also they declare the obedience of their inward faith, and that they faithfully believe the words and promises of Almighty God. For the token without belief is nothing profitable, but rather hurtful. All bodily service that the flesh imagineth, pleaseth not God. He sitteth at the right hand of God: there ought we to touch him with the lifting up of a faithful heart, and with the worship which he through his Spirit worketh and directeth into us: for therefore he died, rose again, and ascended up into heaven, that he might fulfil all things, and reign truly and spiritually in our hearts. Our hearts must we lift up there, as Christ sitteth at the right hand of God, and our conversation ought to be in heaven. Col. iii.
Phil. iii.

Whereas the Lord willed his disciples to touch him, it was done to banish their doubtfulness, and to strengthen their weak faith. Which touching was not required of them as a worship, but that their flesh through the outward handling of his body might be quieted and stilled: and so is it a proof and testimony, that he verily rose with the former body, rather than a worshipping or service. Christ did not therefore take upon him his flesh, that we should alway hang and depend thereon; but that we by his humanity should ascend up to his Godhead. For when we know the high and holy mystery of his passion and resurrection, with the which he hath served our turn, we ought to stir up our minds to know the Godhead, wherein he is like unto the Father.

Therefore unto Mary Magdalene also doth Christ speak of ascending up to the Father; which thing he commandeth to shew the apostles, as if he would say: " Now shortly beginneth mine honour, that I, as concerning the humanity received, shall be taken up to the glory which I have had from everlasting; that is, the flesh which I have taken upon me for your sakes, shall sit at the right hand of my Father."

Oh, how great a grace is this! Oh, how high is the glory that here is promised unto us in Christ! The only-begotten Son of God descended and became man for us, that we, so much as were possible for our nature, should ascend up unto his Godhead. He descended down low, that when we are humbled, he might receive and exalt us to his own promotion. He that of nature is the Lord, took upon him the shape of a servant, that of us which naturally were bond-servants, he might make us God's children.

Forasmuch then as he became man, to make us God's and children of godly grace, he took upon him that which is ours, to give us and to part with us that which is his. Psal. xxii. Therefore calleth he us brethren, and maketh his own Father common unto us; so that he is also our Father and our God: that same which he hath of nature, doth he of grace give unto us. "For his Spirit beareth record unto our spirit, that we are the children of God: for we have not received the spirit of bondage to fear, but the spirit of adoption, in the which we cry, Father, Father."

Rom. viii.

John xv. Christ also calleth those that be his, not servants, but friends and brethren: he will be our God, and we his people; our Father, we his children: and his covenant which he hath made with us shall be everlasting: for it is sealed and confirmed with the blood of his only-begotten Son. Now have we fellowship and company with God the Father, the Son, and the Holy Ghost.

Jer. xxxi.

The glory of the faithful is hid under the cross. But such grace and glory is inwardly seen with the eyes of faith, and felt in the spirit, being hid here in time under the shape of the cross. For Christ doth not straightway by and by declare himself openly unto Mary Magdalene, as he is in his glory; but standeth there as a gardener, and speaketh unto her, by the which voice she knoweth him: he long deferreth the comfort, permitting her a good while to weep and lament, that the joy and consolation afterward may be the greater. But the cause why he so long delayeth his help and comfort from these that be his own, is, that their inward desires may be the more fervent and earnest, and that he may stir up and kindle their faith. Now when the fire is kindled enough, then cometh he with his comfort, as it is evident here in Mary Magdalene, and in the woman of Cananee. Matthew xv.

Moreover he sendeth Mary Magdalene from him, to bring the apostles tidings of this glorious exaltation; whereas she doubtless had rather have been longer with him, and to have had the comfortable fruition of the sight of him. Howbeit he directeth her forth, to declare that felicity, and pointeth her to the work of charitable love, to the service of her neighbour. For here in time we cannot as yet come to the beholding and sight of God face to face; it shall first begin after this time. Now while we live here, we must serve our neighbour in charitable love, and do him good.

O God, strengthen thou our weak faith in the resurrection of thy beloved Son; that by it our consciences being examined may well answer: illuminate our minds, and expel out of us all darkness, through the light and brightness of the glorious resurrection: O strengthen our weakness through the power of thy Spirit. Raise us from the death of sin, in the same Rom. i. Spirit and power wherein thou hast raised up thy Son from the dead. Comfort and strengthen us in adversity, and make us constant therein; that we may press through the same in stedfast hope to the joyful and blessed resurrection. Kindle in us the fire of thy godly love, that with earnest and fervent desire we may seek and find thee through Christ. Withdraw our hearts from all earthly love of creatures, and from filthiness, up to heaven-ward, where Christ sitteth at thy right hand, that we may lead a godly and heavenly life upon earth. Set up the spiritual kingdom of Christ Jesu in our hearts, that in us thy name may be sanctified, and thy will performed; that we may become thy virtuous children, and never displease thee, our gracious Father; that we, continuing still in thy merciful covenant, do never fall away from the company and fellowship of thee and thy Son. And 1 John i. whereas thou hast given us such knowledge, grace, and understanding, grant that we may make the same known unto many, being alway ready through charitable love to serve our brethren. Amen.

It followeth now further in the history, how the women that were first with Mary Magdalene at the sepulchre, and being afraid, fled away (no man saying ought unto them), returned now more stoutly and boldly to the sepulchre, to see what would come of that wonderful terrible matter.

[Luke xxiv. 4—11. Matthew xxviii. 9, 10.]

WHEN the women came to the sepulchre, and found not the body of Jesu, they were sore troubled in their minds. And behold, two men stood by them in shining garments. And as the women were afraid, and bowed down their faces to the earth, they said unto them: Why seek ye the living among the dead? He is not here, he is risen. Remember how he spake unto you, when he was yet in Galilee, saying, That the Son of man must be delivered into the hands of sinful men, and be crucified, and the third day rise again. And they remembered the words of Jesu; and returned from the sepulchre, and told all these things unto those eleven, and Matt. xxviii. to all the remnant. And as they went to tell his disciples, behold, Jesus met them, saying, All hail. And they came and held him by the feet, and worshipped him. Then said Jesus unto them, Be not afraid. Go tell my brethren, that they go into Galilee, and there shall they see me.

But when the women, namely, Mary Magdalene, and Joanna, and Mary Jacob, and other that were with them, told these things unto the apostles, their words seemed unto them feigned things, neither believed they them.

DOCTRINE AND FRUIT.

LOVE is not idle, but diligent and zealous: which thing may well be perceived in these women, that ran again to the sepulchre, although they had found it empty afore. Gladly would they have found the body, and done reverence to their Lord whom they loved. This fervent zeal of the women confoundeth our coldness and unmercifulness towards the poor.

Ofttimes do they seek him that is absent, and that with great diligence; we receive him not, when in the poor he cometh unto us. No travail, labour, nor cost grieveth them: as for us, we pity our substance, when we should distribute to the poor, which are Christ's. O that we could rightly consider, how precious a treasure we gather unto ourselves in heaven, when we give of our goods into the hands of the poor, lending the same unto Christ! Then should not we garnish and build timber and stone, but the living temples of God, keeping them from wind and rain, and from decay; namely, that they suffer no extreme poverty, nor be destitute of help. Such a treasure had Tabitha laid up in store: for when she died, it was not stones and stocks that commended her benefits, but the bodies of the widows; they lamented her death, and declared how merciful she had been. *Acts ix.*

Christ openeth and sheweth himself unto those that earnestly seek him, and those he suffereth to touch him; to the intent that, forasmuch as they must declare his resurrection to the apostles, their weak faith must be strengthened, to know and to be assured, that he was verily risen again. For not only the angel, but Christ also himself commandeth them so to do. He comforteth them, and taketh from them the fearfulness and sorrow. Thus we ought not to doubt he shall in all adversity and trouble meet us, he shall cheerfully appear unto us, and with his joyful presence and resurrection shall he comfort and preserve us.

But we lack an earnest and strong faith; our hearts are slow and cold; diligent we be in seeking of temporal things, but godly things we either despise or neglect. Love hath no rest, she ceaseth not to run and seek, till she find him whom she loveth; and when she findeth him, she holdeth him fast, that she loose him not again: glad is she also to make others partakers of the treasure that she hath found.

O God, kindle our cold hearts with the fire of faith and love, that we may earnestly seek thee; and that when we have found thee, we may fervently receive and keep thee, and with a right spirit worship thee. Expel all hardness and ungentleness out of our hearts; make us loving and merciful unto the poor ones. Take from us the terror of all doubtfulness, unbelief, and fear of the world; and comfort us in all adversity. Grant us the faith of thy resurrection; that we, despising all transitory things, may set all our comfort and hope in the blessed resurrection to come. Amen.

Here also we learn, how exceeding weak and ignorant our flesh is to receive and believe the truth, if the Spirit of God give not light and strength. For afore the hearts of the apostles were illuminated and instructed by the Holy Ghost, they esteemed the truth of Christ's resurrection, opened unto them by the women, to be a foolish and feigned thing. Nevertheless Christ forsaketh not those whom he hath once embraced; but still openeth himself unto them more and more, to expel out of them all dubitation and unbelief.

[Luke xxiv. 13—24.]

AND behold, two of them went that same day to a town called Emaus, which was from Hierusalem about a threescore furlongs; and they talked together of all these things that had happened. And it chanced, that while they communed together and reasoned, Jesus himself drew near, and went with them: but their eyes were holden, that they should not know him. And he said unto them, What manner of communications are these, that ye have one to another, as ye walk, and are sad? And the one of them, whose name was Cleophas, answered and said unto him: Art thou only a stranger in Jerusalem, and hast not known the things which have chanced there in these days? He said unto them, What things? And they said unto him: Of Jesus of Nazareth, which was a prophet, mighty in deed and word before God and all the people; and how the high priests and our rulers delivered him to be condemned unto death, and have crucified him. But we trusted, that it had been he which should have redeemed Israel. And as touching all these things, to-day is even the third day that they were done. Yea, and certain women also of our company made us astonied, which came early to the sepulchre, and found not his body, and came, saying, That they had seen a vision of angels, which said that he was alive. And certain of them that were with us went to the sepulchre, and found it even so as the women had said; but him they saw not.

DOCTRINE AND FRUIT.

The longer the more, is set forth unto us the unoutspeakable love and trusty faithfulness of Jesus Christ our Lord, who forsaketh not those that any thing love to talk of him. For look, whom he admitteth into his school, those he teacheth still continually, how weak so ever they be, until he bring them to perfect understanding, and expel all doubtfulness out of their hearts. Forasmuch now as these his disciples speak of him in the way, he getteth him to them, albeit he holdeth their eyes that they know him not; that by the means thereof they themselves with their own words might knowledge and confess their doubtful wavering and weakness of faith; that they might open their disease unto him, and he to give a convenient medicine for their unbelief; that through the long delay, friendly talk, and opening of the scriptures, their hearts and desires might more and more be kindled and set on fire; that their doubtfulness might be taken away, and their weak faith strengthened. For though they held Jesus for a great and principal prophet, and for an innocent good man, yet speak they uncertainly of the matter, and their heart wavereth; yet were not they assured that he had overcome death, and by his own death purchased life for all the world; that he was risen again into an immortal life, and made us undoubtedly partakers of the comfortable and joyful resurrection and eternal life in himself.

Now forasmuch as they gladly talk and willingly hold of him, how feebly and unperfectly soever it be, yet the gracious and loving Lord approacheth near unto them, and instructeth them. It shall never be unfruitful, it shall never pass without profit, but assuredly do good, where Christ is gladly and with a good heart spoken of. Where two or three be assembled in his name, there is he in the midst among them, and informeth them. That he doth to the disciples in the way by mouth, the same declareth he alway unto us inwardly by his Spirit in our hearts, and outwardly with the scripture and word, and with the teachings of good godly men. He that well and faithfully useth the little talent, shall not be denied a greater, if he earnestly desire it.

Wheresoever he is earnestly and fervently thought upon and talked of, there is he present, and instructeth and teacheth the ignorant. For he is not ashamed to resort unto those that lack knowledge and be in error, and to talk with them.

This lowly and gentle condition ought we to learn of our Head, that we shame not to repair unto such as are not yet right instructed, that we may inform them, and commune with them. We should despise no man that with a single heart seeketh God; though as yet we perceive much wavering and weak faith in him. For if the eternal Wisdom was not ashamed to humble himself, and to instruct the ignorant, much more ought we to do it; seeing we are neither sufficiently instructed in the scripture, nor yet diligent and careful to do that which we know.

[Luke xxiv. 25—35.]

Luke xxiv. THEN said Jesus unto them: O ye fools, and slow of heart to believe all that the prophets have spoken! Ought not Christ to have suffered these things, and so to enter into his glory? And he began at Moses and all the prophets, and interpreted unto them in all scriptures which were written of him. And they drew nigh to the town that they went unto; and he made as though he would have gone further. And they constrained him, saying, Abide with us; for it draweth toward night, and the day is far passed. And he went in to tarry with them. And it came to pass, as he sat at meat with them, he took bread and blessed it, and brake, and gave to them: and their eyes were opened, and they knew him; and he vanished out of their sight. And they said between themselves: Did not our hearts burn within us, while he talked with us by the way, and opened to us the scriptures? And they rose up the same hour, and returned again to Hierusalem; and found the eleven gathered together, and them that were with them saying: The Lord is risen indeed, and hath appeared unto Simon. And they told what things were done in the way, and how they knew him in breaking of bread.

DOCTRINE AND FRUIT.

CHRIST saith (John v.), " Search the scriptures, for they testify of me;" also, "If ye believed Moses, ye should believe me, for he hath written of me." Christ therefore, willing to strengthen the weak, and to teach the unlearned, expoundeth unto them the scriptures, beginning at Moses, and so throughout all the prophets. For whatsoever is written in the scripture concerning the mercy, goodness, and wisdom of God, the washing away of sin, and satisfying for the same, it belongeth properly to Christ. For so worthily and evidently have they described the passion and glory of Christ, that one would think them not to write of a matter which were to come, but done already; as it is plain in the Psalms and Prophets. Psalm xxii. Isaiah liii. 1 Pet. i. &c.

Thus out of the scripture we learn, partly, the testimonies of the passion and resurrection of Christ; partly, by what way Christ came to so high honour and glory of his Father; that we first believing, that Christ died for our sins, and rose again for our righteousness, might by his resurrection be sure of a good conscience, and consolation of the life to come.

Secondly, that we in patience and obedience might learn to be obedient to our heavenly Father, to take up our cross, and to follow our Lord Jesus Christ: if we will have joy with him, we must also suffer and travail with him. Our Head goeth to eternal joy through adversity and trouble; and will we enter into it through the pleasure of the world and lust of the flesh? It passeth the bounds of all humanity, and comeliness, and honesty, for the servant to be sluggish and slothful, when the master taketh upon him such travail and pain. This is the narrow gate that we must enter in at: for through many tribulations, vexations, and miseries, must we come into the everlasting kingdom of heaven; and "all they that will live godly in Christ Jesu must suffer persecution" in this world. He that will possess an inheritance, must bear and suffer all the charges belonging to the same.

The eternal inheritance is appointed us of our heavenly Father through Christ; but with this addition, that we receive the possession of it in such sort as the Son hath done, namely, with and through the cross and trouble. Blessed are they, whom God the Father maketh partakers of the passion of his only-begotten Son: for whoso is a companion with him in suffering, shall have his eternal fellowship in heaven, and enjoy with him everlasting bliss and rest. He that understandeth not this, is a "fool, and slow of heart to believe" the scriptures. Let that man beseech God to open the scriptures unto him, and to make him understand it. Where that cometh to pass, ignorance vanisheth away, and the heart is fervent, and receiveth understanding: for the Lord is the right and perfect schoolmaster, that toucheth the heart, and pierceth it through with the arrows of his words and ardent love.

In breaking of the bread, they know the Lord: for afore in his life-time, when he now would go to his passion and death, he took bread, rendered thanks, brake it, and gave it them, admonishing them, that as oft as they did the same, they should do it in remembrance of him. Whereby they now thinking on the same words, and being admonished of the act, remember that it is he. Thus the breaking of the bread before our eyes in the supper is an admonishing token, that Christ's body was broken, and died for us on the cross; and the drink an admonishing token, that his blood was shed for the washing away of our sins. And so when we break the bread, and drink the drink, we ought thereby to know the Lord; thanking him for his death, which is our life, being mindful of him, and following his great love, wherein he died for our sins.

[Luke xxiv. 36—43. John xx. 19, 20.]

As they thus spake, (it was very late the same day, which was the first day in the week; and where the disciples assembled together, the doors were shut for fear of the Jews,)

Jesus came, while they sat at the table, and stood in the midst among them, and said unto them: Peace be with you. But the disciples were afraid, thinking that they had seen a spirit. Then said Jesus unto them, Why are ye troubled? and why do thoughts arise in your head? And he said yet again unto them, Peace be with you. And with that shewed he them his hands, feet, and side, and said: Behold my hands and feet, that it is even I myself; handle me and see, for a spirit hath not flesh and bones, as ye see me have. The disciples were glad, when they had seen the Lord. And while as yet they believed not for joy, and wondered, he said unto them: Have ye any thing to eat? So they offered him a piece of broiled fish, and an honey-comb. The same he took, and did eat before them; casting in their teeth their unbelief and hardness of heart, because they believed not them which had seen that he was risen again from the dead.

DOCTRINE AND FRUIT.

In that the evangelists describe the true resurrection of Christ, they declare withal, unto whom such a high mystery was opened and shewed. For when we hear how the disciples were minded and behaved themselves, we learn thereby, what becometh us, that we also may believe that Christ is truly risen again; yea, not only to acknowledge the same with the mouth, but also to prove and feel it in the taste of the spirit. So have we heard afore, what the desire and ardent love, which God stirred up in Mary Magdalene, did bring to pass, and what good came of the ferventness and diligence of Peter. This we see now here: for God hath a pleasure to stir up our desire, when he will open himself unto us. And therefore all the same day, from morning early until night, were the disciples still more and more endued with new joy, that the desire to see Christ might be kindled more and more in them. And as they were assembled in love and uniformity, (for those two things please God well,) Christ cometh and appeareth unto them. He openeth himself unto those that, longing after him, are coupled in love and uniformity, and being assembled, do hold themselves together. For where love is, there is God; where discord is and division, there is the devil.

O dear brethren, let us regard charitable love; let us care for our brethren, that the brotherhood be not broken, and that love be not spotted; for else farewell faith. No man needeth to boast himself of faith, that hath not charitable love, but stirreth up and seeketh division.

Moreover, we see here that the disciples of Christ stood in great danger of their bodies and life: for when the Jews had no more power to rage against Christ, they raged against his disciples. Look, what men are partakers of the cross and passion of Christ, they verily shall understand the high mystery of his resurrection. For undoubtedly, God with his own consolation shall visit and comfort those that suffer any danger and harm for his name's sake. Forasmuch then as the good disciples of Christ must still be in conflict and battle with the Jews, the Lord speaketh unto them with this comfortable word, "Peace be with you:" as if he should say, "Be of good cheer; your matter shall stand in good case; in me ye shall have peace, and be safe, and quiet, how hard soever it go outwardly: fear not, be not afraid; howsoever the Jews do rage, ye shall do right well." This salutation was common among the Jews; therefore doth Christ also use it. Such a charge gave he likewise unto his disciples, when he sent them to preach, that entering into an house they should say, "Peace be to this house."

<small>Luke x.</small>

And though the disciples were somewhat amazed and afraid at the first blush, yet was their gladness great, when they were throughly instructed that it was the Lord. Now was fulfilled that which Christ had said, and promised unto them afore, John xvi. "Ye shall mourn, and the world shall rejoice: but I will see you again. Your sorrow shall be turned into gladness, your heart shall rejoice, and your joy shall no man take from you." For the joy of a faithful believing heart is constant, and endureth. If the resurrection of Jesus Christ were rightly and truly believed, and the same joy comprehended as it ought to be, all sorrow must needs vanish, all hurt and adversity must needs be little regarded. For what can be grievous unto a man, when by faith and hope he is assured, that he in a glorified and

THE RESURRECTION OF CHRIST

immortal body shall arise again with Christ his head, and have everlasting joy with him?

And this is the cause that Christ appeareth so often unto his disciples, instructing them so much and so perfectly of his resurrection; even to make them stedfast in this faith, and to assure them of this joy. Therefore sheweth he them his body, and giveth it them to handle. The palpable body certifieth them, that it is a true body; the immortal body sheweth that it is glorified, and of highest honour; the prints of the wounds declare, that it is even the self-same body that it was afore. He sheweth them the tokens of victory, as a mighty overcomer of death; and so doth he the wounds that he had gotten for them in the battle; and likewise the side that was opened, declaring his great love. His wounds sheweth he to them, to heal the wounds of their unbelief. As if he would say: "Look upon me, and fight manfully; without a battle shall no man be crowned. But unto him that overcometh in the conflict will I grant to eat of the bread of heaven, and will crown him for ever." 2 Tim. ii. Apoc. ii.

Whereas he eateth before them, it is done for the probation of the true human nature, and not for the great necessity of the body. To them was it very needful, not unto Christ. Even so we, knowing how to further our neighbour's faith, must and ought many times to do somewhat, and to leave somewhat undone, that for ourselves we need not.

O God, grant us true love and uniformity, take from us all schism and division; gather us together through thy holy Spirit; remove all discord and variance out of thy holy church. Give us patience in adversity; send thy godly comfort and joy unto all such as be in distress and trouble for thy name's sake; strengthen the weak, lift up the feeble, establish the doubtful, and in the battle help those which be thine own; that they lie not under, but that in thee they may overcome all danger and harm. Amen.

[John xx. 24—29.]

THOMAS, one of the twelve, which was called Didymus, was not with them when Jesus came. The other disciples therefore said unto him, We have seen the Lord. But he said unto them: Except I see in his hands the print of the nails, and put my finger into the print of the nails, and thrust my hand into his side, I will not believe. And after eight days again his disciples were within, and Thomas with them. Then came Jesus, when the doors were shut, and stood in the midst, and said, Peace be unto you. And after that said he to Thomas, Bring hither thy finger, and see my hands, and reach hither thy hand, and thrust it into my side; and be not faithless, but believing. Thomas answered and said unto him: My Lord, and my God! Jesus saith unto him: Thomas, because thou hast seen me, thou hast believed: blessed are they that have not seen, and have believed.

DOCTRINE AND FRUIT.

THAT which was spoken afore is here evident and plain, namely, that Christ openeth himself unto those, which are desirous of him, and long after him, associating themselves together one with another in true love, and being partakers of the passion and cross. Forasmuch then as Thomas is less fervent, and therefore absent from the rest, he saw not Christ with the other disciples; but when he obtained a desire to see Christ, and was associate and joined to the other, he became also partaker of the joy that they had.

And here we learn the nature and condition of true belief, (which is an illumination of the grace of God, yea, a very godly property,) that he maketh others partakers of his holy and glorious joys, and that through love, which seeketh not her own profit, neither is disdainful; to the intent that the glory of God may be preferred among all men. Therefore the disciples of the Lord make Thomas their companion partaker of such gladness, as they had received of Christ's resurrection opened unto them; for he was

very faithless, and too stiff in his own opinion. Which
unbelief God suffered to happen unto him, and to continue
somewhat the longer, that his slackness and lack of faith
might serve to our commodity; that through his unbelief
we might be provoked unto faith, forasmuch as we hear
that he, so perfectly proving, seeing, and feeling the thing,
came so to an undoubted faith; that we also might believe,
that the body of Christ, which was hanged upon the cross
for our sins, was of the Father raised again unto life. For Acts ii.
if we believe in our heart, and confess with our mouth, that Rom. x.
God hath raised him up from the dead, we shall be saved.
Yea, believe we must, that Christ, according to his words John ii.
afore, hath through his godly power erected up again from
death the temple of his body. Therefore through the doubting of Thomas we learn the mystery of the resurrection of
our own bodies. For Christ hath sufficiently proved, and
Thomas hath confessed, that the body of Christ, which was
hanged upon the cross, is verily risen again from death.
Wherein our faith is confirmed to believe, that our bodies
also shall truly and lively rise again to eternal life.

When Thomas is with the other disciples, Christ sheweth
himself unto him. For they that in the unity of faith and
of undivided love do not associate and accompany themselves
with other faithful believers in the church, shall not be partakers of heavenly joys. Truth it is, that to believe with
the heart justifieth; but the confession that is made with the
mouth belongeth unto health, and serveth unto love and
unity of the Church and congregation of God; without the
which there can be no hope of health. He that saith he
believeth, and doth not join himself unto other Christians, his
faith is vain and of none effect. And therefore did Christ
for his church institute the sacraments, that is to say, exterior signs of his grace; that his people might be associate
together in the unity of faith. The church of God is it
that preserveth us poor ones, as did the ark of Noe aforetime in the flood, and bringeth us through this raging sea
unto the haven of eternal salvation. Not that the grace and
health is therefore to be ascribed to the elements and outward things; but that it may appear, how effectuous faith
is, and what it worketh through charitable love in the
church. Christ maketh mention of the words which Thomas

had spoken afore to the disciples in his absence; namely, "Except I see in his hands the print," &c. Therefore saith Christ, "Thomas, bring thy finger hither, and see," &c. Whereby it is evidently proved, that Christ is God: and even so doth Thomas understand and confess.

The wounds are shewed of Christ, specially to this intent, that his passion might be printed and sealed in men's minds. For a very deep and high mystery it is, that Christ's side is opened, out of the which floweth blood and water; whereby the spiritual and faithful believing minds may well perceive Christ's good loving will towards mankind. Now when we look upon his hands, touching his side inwardly with our desire of inward faith, and considering why and with what love Christ suffered for us, it shall be no hard thing unto us to believe his resurrection. If Christ were dead but even as another pure man or prophet, we could have no hope of the resurrection. Whoso believeth it, cometh soon to this knowledge, that immortal life is given unto us. Now where there is hope of an immortal life, there is the Lord served with great diligence. For if God hath not spared his own Son, but given him for us all, what good thing may we not look for at his hand? If we be only true believers with Thomas, then shall God faithfully perform that he hath promised us. Christ desireth no more of us weak feeble ones, than that we be not faithless, but stedfast believers.

Rom. viii.

Thomas is immediately obedient unto the voice of Christ, and becometh forthwith a new man. The Pharisees could by no doctrine, by no miracles, be brought to give credence unto Christ, and to believe in him, although they saw Lazarus raised again from the dead; malice and hatred did so hinder them: but Thomas acknowledgeth him freely to be his Lord and God. He seeth and handleth man; he confesseth God, whom he saw not. He acknowledged, that he whom he saw was his God and Lord. Through the same faith was his unbelief and sin forgiven him.

O merciful God, grant us love, that we seek not our own commodity nor honour, but the profit of our neighbours and thy glory in all things. Expel out of us all disdain, greediness, ungentleness, headiness, and flattering of ourselves. Preserve us from discord and division; bind us together in uniform love; that we may be one body, and of one mind.

Stablish also our faith; that our minds may be always comforted in the resurrection of thy Son, and immortal life purchased by him. Amen..

[John xx. 30, 31.]

AND many other signs truly did Jesus in the presence of his disciples, which are not written in this book. These are written, that ye might believe that Jesus is Christ, the Son of God; and that ye so believing might have life through his name.

DOCTRINE AND FRUIT.

LIKE as Christ, while he yet lived, did miracles before his death, to declare his godly power; even so after his rising again from death, he worketh many tokens in the presence of his disciples, to prove his resurrection in the flesh. Some of the same are described of the evangelists, not of any curiosity, or for vain-glory, but to confirm our faith therewith. To write all, John thought it not needful; for who could have written all? or who could have fastened and borne them all in mind? Whoso will not believe these few that are written, shall never believe a greater multitude. A faithful believer is well satisfied with these. For these that be written of him are therefore written, "that we should believe that Jesus is Christ, the Son of God, and that we through his faith might have eternal life." Seeing then that all things which are written do extend and serve to this end, that we might believe in him, and be saved by him, what lack we then? or what can we desire more? So that hereby we learn, with great diligence to read, to consider, and to apply into our own life, whatsoever the evangelists have written of Christ; as they have written nothing but that which is altogether excellent, dear, holy, and godly, and such things as do lively describe, set forth, and print Christ unto us; that our faith, hope, love, patience, meekness, and all good things might grow with blessed fruit; that we in our life might become thankful for such an excellent grace, and in no wise to contemn or despise it.

A scornful thing is it, and the evidence of a great unbelief, whereas some think by these words to prove, that forasmuch as all things are not written in the book, it is lawful for certain men to add the rest, and to devise and ordain what they will. For in these things that are written doth John comprehend the whole sum of faith; which consisteth in this, that Jesus is the Son of the living God, who for our salvation came down from heaven, died, rose again, and purchased for us eternal life. Jesus the Son of Mary is the anointed King and High Priest, the Saviour of the world promised of God, and spoken of afore by the prophets. And even he it is, who being of the heavenly Father anointed king everlasting, was to come after David, and to reign for ever. This king is the Redeemer and Saviour of mankind, and the very true Son of God. If we believe in Christ, we believe in the true God; one only God we honour, one only God we worship. Seeing now that we honour and worship Christ, we worship God; for only God is to be worshipped. Forasmuch now as we worship the Son no less than the Father, it is certain that Christ is of one nature with the Father; yea, this ought we to believe, and that he came down into this world to die for us, to wash and wipe away our sins, and to kill sin in our mortal flesh, when he maketh us partakers of his passion, and mightily worketh in us by his Spirit, in mortifying our carnal desires. We must also believe, that he by his godly power arose again from death to a new, glorious, and immortal life. For if we thought that he died, and believed not that he were risen to life again, we should have no life in him. For us he died, for our sakes he rose again, for our welfare reigneth he for ever. A new godly and blessed life worketh he in us with his resurrection, and after this life have we in him life everlasting.

[John xxi. 1—14.]

AFTERWARD did Jesus shew himself again at the sea of Tiberias. And on this wise shewed he himself. There were together Simon Peter and Thomas, which is called Didymus, and Nathanael of Cana in Galilee, and the sons of Zebedee, and two other of his disciples. Simon Peter saith unto them, I will go a fishing. They say unto him, We also will go with thee. They went their way, and entered into a ship immediately; and that night caught they nothing. But when the morning was now come, Jesus stood on the shore; but the disciples knew not that it was Jesus. Jesus saith unto them: Children, have ye any meat? They answered him, No. And he saith unto them: Cast out the net on the right side of the ship, and ye shall find. They cast out therefore, and anon they were not able to draw it for the multitude of fishes. Then said the disciple whom Jesus loved to Peter: It is the Lord. When Simon Peter heard that it was the Lord, he girt his coat unto him, (for he was naked,) and sprang into the sea. The other disciples came by ship; for they were not far from land, but as it were two hundred cubits; and they drew the net with fishes. As soon then as they were come to land, they saw hot coals, and fish laid thereon, and bread. Jesus saith unto them, Bring of the fish that ye now have caught. Simon Peter went up, and drew the net to the land full of great fishes, an hundred and three and fifty. And for all there were so many, yet was not the net broken. Jesus saith unto them, Come and dine. And none of the disciples durst ask him, What art thou? for they knew that it was the Lord. Jesus then came and took bread, and gave them, and fish likewise. This is now the third time that Jesus appeared to his disciples, after that he was risen again from death.

DOCTRINE AND FRUIT.

WE read in the holy evangelists, that at the first Christ called his disciples, namely Peter and the others, from fishing; which they also left, and came to Christ, who told them that he would make them fishers of men. Now, when he will send them out to that office, and depart from them, he appeareth again unto them at their fishing. And, like as he did afore at their vocation, he doth before them a great miracle; in the which he admonisheth them of their office, and chargeth them diligently to care for his sheep committed unto them. But first he proveth his resurrection, to stablish and confirm their weak faith thereby; commanding them afterward, to bring other folks also thereto.

This history in itself is evident enough: therefore ought we first to consider it after the letter; for the letter also teacheth for itself. Christ, like as he appeared unto those that were sorrowful and mourned, so doth he appear unto those that labour and travail. Christ gave his disciples authority out of the gospel, that they preach, to take a competent honest living, as food and necessaries of the body; and yet did he not restrain them, that they should not or might not labour, when occasion serveth. Therefore Paul also used not that liberty at certain times, but laboured with his own hands, and won his meat. So did the disciples of Christ exercise themselves in their labour. For when they were come into Galilee from the feast of Easter, which they had kept at Hierusalem, afore the Holy Ghost was given unto them, they would not go idle, and thereby become a burthen unto other men, (for he that goeth idle liveth upon other folks, eating that theirs is, and overchargeth them,) but undertake to get their own living with their handy-work, which they had used afore. Whereby we must learn to apply ourselves unto labour, and not to be idle; for idleness is the mother of many and great vices. Every man ought to have an honest travail, to be exercised either with the body or with the mind. Whoso laboureth not, must not eat. Man was created to labour, as the bird to fly. Therefore ought every father to bring up his children in honest exercise from their youth up, that the devil get no place in their hearts; which yet cometh to pass, if he find them idle. The first commandment given to our forefather Adam after the fall was this: "In the sweat of thy face shalt thou eat thy bread."

Now when we in true faith and confidence unto God do take in hand the work that he hath committed unto our charge, we ought not to doubt God shall prosper it, and give us his rich and gracious blessing in it; as it is written, Prov. iii.: "In all thy ways remember the Lord, and he shall direct and order thy doing." Eccles. v. ix.

Here is also to be considered, how Christ uttereth his godly power before his disciples, in the great miracle that he did in their sight, to confirm our faith in him. For out of the appearing of Christ groweth faith. Psalm lxxxv. And [Psal. lxxxvi.] his true resurrection will he print in them, in that he appeareth unto them, and eateth with them.

Here we see the ardent desire of Peter, which leapeth into the sea, as soon as he heareth that it is the Lord: he that afore had denied him, maketh now speedy haste again unto him. Though we of man's feebleness and fear, do fall into sin, yet always when we hear God in his word, we ought forthwith to turn again unto him; and so shall he with the Luke xv. lost son graciously receive and embrace us again.

In that Peter covereth himself being naked, we learn nurture and shamefacedness, to walk and dwell with all honesty in the sight of men, specially in the presence of our superiors and governors.

In the corporal works and deeds of Christ, there is nothing in vain, nothing without effect. Besides the outward appearance of the work, there is described somewhat more excellent, whereunto a faithful believer ought to direct the eyes of his mind. As when he maketh the blind to see, it is an outward act, and a declaration of his godly power, and an alteration there is outwardly in the eyes of the blind, in that his sight is restored unto him again: nevertheless over and besides the outward work there is given us to understand, that Christ is the true light of the whole world, which driveth away the blindness of our heart, and illuminateth the eyes of our mind, according to the scriptures. Esay xlii. xlix. John i. ix. xii., &c.

Christ, taking bread and wine, giveth the same to his disciples to eat and drink. This, as no man can deny, was an outward act, and they commanded outwardly to do it, albeit in the remembrance of him. Besides and above the outward eating and drinking, the faithful believer must lift up his heart, and look with the eyes of faith unto that which is spiritual; namely, how that Christ is the true living bread, which feedeth our souls to eternal life; how his body was broken for us upon the cross; how we through his death are made living, and washed away from our sins by his blood. In this is set forth unto us the highest love of all, namely, that Christ gave himself unto the death for us: whereby we are admonished of his grace, yea, not only in this described unto us, but also the Holy Ghost doth mightily and fruitfully work the same in the hearts of the true believers, which in faith at the supper receive the true body and blood of Christ; whereby their hearts are kindled in love towards God and their neighbour, so that they dwell in Christ, and he in them, &c.

So here likewise the outward fishing representeth a fishing spiritual. Like as in fishing it lieth not in the fisher's power or wit to take many or few, but it is the power and blessing of God; and as the labour of the disciples is in vain afore Christ commandeth them, but when they have his commandment, and cast out the net upon the same, they draw up a multitude of fishes: even so cometh it to pass at this present day, that we bring forth no fruit, so long as the Holy Ghost worketh not with us inwardly; but when Christ biddeth cast out the net, that is, when he giveth his Spirit, we are able to draw up many men, and to win them unto Christ. For all the night long had they taken nothing, till Christ came unto them: even so can we do nothing, if Christ be not with us by his Spirit. On Whit-sunday, when the Spirit came upon his disciples, they brought much fruit, and drew many men unto Christ.

_{Acts ii.}

Hereby declareth Christ unto them in this taking of fish, how it should go in their office, and how the time was now at hand, that they should shortly draw many men out of the sea of this world unto him, and that they should prosper and have good success therein. The world is this wild raging sea; the shore is the quietness of eternal life that we have in Christ, unto whom we make haste with Peter and the other disciples; neither do we bring men unto ourselves, but unto Christ, and to the haven of everlasting life. Faith is not idle, but is always occupied in the Lord's business, causing us to contemn all perils, and to speed us apace unto Christ with the clothing of virtues, especially with faith, the wedding-garment; that we appearing not naked, may make haste unto the land of the living, where Christ is, the conqueror of death;

for the faithful believers are not far from the land, when their conversation is in heaven. Without Christ we must begin nothing, without faith may no man please God. In Heb. xi. the night of sin our labour is vain and unprofitable; yea, "whatsoever is not of faith is sin." Upon the right hand must Rom. xiv. the net be cast out; that is, in the office of preaching must respect be had to the only glory of God, and edifying of the 1 Cor. xiv. church, and not to our own profit or preferment.

Christ hungereth after our health: this is the meat which he desireth, that we do the will of his heavenly Father, that John iv. vi. we put our trust in him and love one another, that we lead a just and innocent life, that we keep ourselves from the filthiness of the world, and bring much people unto God. Such meat is brought unto Christ by the apostles, when they through their teaching do catch men, and bring them unto God. Therefore doth he ask them, whether they have anything to eat. They said, Nay: for afore the receiving of the Spirit they could do nothing; but when he came, they brought many profitable things to pass. The harvest was so great, that they must needs have many workmen.

So when God helpeth the faithful ministers of the word, that they in the ministry of preaching have prosperous success, so that they draw up many men through the net of the gospel, and find much fruit; then the disciples whom Christ loveth, and which love him again, do know that it is the Lord, and that the same cometh not of their own virtue, but of the power of God. And hereof then groweth there in them a great desire to come unto Christ, and to be with him. The office therefore of apostles and of all ministers of the word is this, that when they do what Christ commandeth them, they turn them to Christ again, and ascribe the honour unto him. And if aught would let or hinder them to come unto Christ, they ought to refuse all the same, and to haste unto him with the loss of their life. John knoweth Christ afore Peter; but Peter cometh to the Lord before him: whereby we may note the diversity of ministrations and gifts in the church. Though Peter be more fervent, yet is he not ashamed to learn of John.

The fishers come with the fish unto Christ, the shepherds with the sheep to one manner of salvation. For they are not careful only for themselves, how they may be saved; but also for those whom they have caught, to bring the same with them unto the shore of eternal rest. It is our salvation, when we become Christ's meat, yea, when Christ is our food and sustenance. For they that in the sea of this world do faithfully labour to draw the fish unto the haven, shall obtain great fruit, and enjoy an eternal banquet at Christ's table in his kingdom. For Christ prepared them a dinner, wherein he set forth unto the ministers of the word, what they ought to do, namely, to feed the people committed unto them. A great honour is it, to bring much people unto Christ. Great commendation and unspeakable joy shall those teachers have, that faithfully travail in scriptures and word of God.

By the multitude and great number of the fishes that the apostles drew into the net, is figured the multitude of the heathen, who through the preaching in the whole world should be brought into the unity of the faith. And although many schisms and erroneous divisions arise, yet of those that are ordained unto life there shall no man fall out of the net. God "knoweth those that be his;" and they shall alway hearken unto the voice of their Shepherd. Thus shall there ever be one only church, which cannot by us be throughly purged: evermore will hypocrites do all their diligence to continue therein, though the makers of division shall not be without great travail and labour. As for such vices as be manifest, great, and offensive, they that be in authority are bound to suppress them, according unto the ordinance of Christ. Matt. v. xiii. xviii.

First, they that be faithful believers, and ordained unto life, do cleave unto Christ their head, and then to the members, that is to say, all faithful Christians. For they that are faithful believers, be knit together in perpetual unity. And although some at this present day be in contention, yet so far as they are of the number of the elect, they will agree together again one with another, afore they depart hence; that they may die in the unity of God's congregation and church, without the which there is no health.

After the great labour that the ministers of the word have in the raging sea, Christ rewardeth his with a very costly and glorious feast in his kingdom: there will he be the bread of life, that feedeth and satisfieth them for ever.

O merciful God, grant unto us all, that we may faithfully

cleave unto thee, and follow thy commandment. Tame thou our body and members in honest labour, that we loiter not in vices. O draw our hearts alway upward; that, all temporal things set apart, we may haste only unto thee. O gracious Father, give us such faithful fishers, as being true and careful in their office, may with the net of thy holy word draw us out of the raging sea; that we with them, and they with us, may enjoy the everlasting banquet. Amen.

[John xxi. 15—17.]

So when they had dined, Jesus saith to Simon Peter, Simon Joanna, lovest thou me more than these? He saith unto him, Yea, Lord; thou knowest that I love thee. He saith unto him, Feed my lambs. He saith unto him again the second time, Simon Joanna, lovest thou me? He saith unto him, Yea, Lord; thou knowest that I love thee. He saith unto him, Feed my sheep. He saith unto him the third time, Simon Joanna, lovest thou me? Peter was sorry, because he said unto him the third time, Lovest thou me? And he said unto him, Lord, thou knowest all things; thou knowest that I love thee. Jesus saith unto him, Feed my sheep.

DOCTRINE AND FRUIT.

FORASMUCH as Peter had taken a special grievous fall, Christ lifteth him up with a special comfort; but so, that he setteth forth unto all shepherds of his sheep, what their office is. Peter had many sins forgiven him; therefore was it Luke vii. meet that he should love the Lord the more. And seeing he had thrice denied, he maketh now a three-fold confession; so that now the tongue doth no less service unto love, than it served fear afore. Christ sheweth him, that he is received again unto grace; so that he may safely put his trust in him, seeing he committeth unto him his own sheep. As if Christ would say: "As for thy denial, I will no more remember it. And for an evidence hereof, I put thee in trust to keep my sheep. In no wise do I refuse thee; but a shepherd of my sheep will I make thee." Neither doth he cast him in the teeth with his denial, but saith: "If thou love me, then take upon thee the care of the brethren. The love that thou hast willed to declare unto me in all things, and wherein I delight, the same declare thou now unto my sheep, whom I so dearly have bought. Thy life that thou wouldest have offered for me, give now for my sheep[1]." Now, to the intent that Peter should not say he were expelled from the apostleship through his denial, the Lord therefore giveth him a new commission to keep his sheep. As for Peter, he was no more so rash and foolish-hardy; but answereth more advisedly than afore, and taketh the Lord to witness. For he remembereth, how it had happened unto him already: therefore standeth he not arrogantly in his own conceit, neither speaketh he against the Lord; so witty and circumspect is he become through the fall.

Arrogant had he been, and high-minded; and therefore through the denial he fell very sore. But his weeping, through faith and sure confidence, purifieth him again; and in love he becometh more fervent, pondering that much is forgiven him; so that where sin was great, grace is more abundant and plentiful. Rom. v.

In Peter is the office of the other apostles, and of all preachers of the word, described: for here may we see, who are meet to be called to guide the people, and what care and diligence they ought to take for them.

John vi.
But here principally we must note this, that Christ, minding to stablish his special excellent doctrine, did ever first work a notable token and miracle. As when he fed the five thousand men with few loaves, he taught immediately upon the same, how we must be sustained with the bread of heaven; even so here, when the disciples had taken a great

[[1] The author appears to have had the following passage of Chrysostom in view: Καὶ τί δήποτε τοὺς ἄλλους παραδραμὼν τούτῳ περὶ τούτων διαλέγεται; ἔκκριτος ἦν τῶν ἀποστόλων .... ἅμα δὲ καὶ δεικνὺς αὐτῷ, ὅτι χρὴ θαρρεῖν λοιπόν, ὡς τῆς ἀρνήσεως ἐξεληλαμένης, ἐγχειρίζεται τὴν προστασίαν τῶν ἀδελφῶν, καὶ τὴν μὲν ἄρνησιν οὐ προφέρει, οὐδὲ ὀνειδίζει τὸ γεγονός· λέγει δὲ, ὅτι, εἰ φιλεῖς με, προΐστασο τῶν ἀδελφῶν, καὶ τὴν θερμὴν ἀγάπην, ἣν διὰ πάντων ἐπεδείκνυσο, καὶ ἐφ᾽ ᾗ ἠγαλλιάσω, νῦν δεῖξον, καὶ τὴν ψυχὴν, ἣν ἔλεγες θήσειν ὑπὲρ ἐμοῦ, ταύτην ὑπὲρ τῶν προβάτων ἐπιδὸς τῶν ἐμῶν. Chrysostom. in Evang. Joann. cap. xxi. Homil. lxxxvi. p. 566. Vol. II. in Nov. Test. Ed. Paris. 1636.]

heap of fishes at Christ's commandment, and were afterward fed of him, he told them immediately upon the same, what their office is, and that they should look even so to nourish and feed those that are committed unto them. This was spoken unto Peter, and in him to all others.

Christ, who searcheth and knoweth all hearts, doth not ask this question as one ignorant, or as one that first would prove and learn; but to teach faith, and to declare it unto others. Such a question demandeth he, Matt. xvi.: "Whom say the people that the Son of man is?"—shewing thereby, what confession and faith he requireth of those that are his. Even so here the schoolmaster of the whole world, minding to put them in trust, will declare unto them with this question, how they ought to be, and the same will he print sure into them with this threefold interrogation. Here also will the Lord teach, how necessary it is, that he who is to be made a shepherd and teacher of christian people be first well known, proved, and tried, and that in many things aforehand he be found faithful. It is not requisite to take children unto such an office, but such godly and apt men as have been tried and tempted; namely, such men as have proved, suffered, and felt somewhat by experience, whereby they have learned humility and nurture.

The first thing that Christ in his examination requireth of those which must guide the people, is a great, fervent, and a notable love to God. Without this love shall soul-shepherds do no good. This love to God shall bring with it love towards the sheep committed unto them. Forasmuch then as at this day the love of Christ is so greatly quenched, therefore are many curates and soul-shepherds so faint and cold to preach and teach Christ. They burn not in the love of God against vice, they print not virtue and godliness fervently into the people; for there is no love of God's name in them. Seeing then that they have no heavenly zeal unto the glory of God, and to the amplifying of his name, it is no marvel, that their preaching is so cold and unfruitful. Therefore saith our Saviour Christ unto Peter, *Agapas me* (ἀγαπᾷς με)? *Lovest thou me?* For *agapao* (ἀγαπάω) among the Greeks signifieth *fervently, earnestly, and right heartily to love;* yea, to love with a great good will; and this word he useth in the two first questions. In the third question he saith, *Phileis me*, (φιλεῖς με)? *Lovest thou me?* *Phileo* (φιλέω) signifieth so to love, that one be loving to another, and shew him friendship. Therefore doth Peter take the Lord himself to witness. As for the high excellent love, he dare not brag of it, but saith, *Philo se* (φιλῶ σε): which is as much to say, as: "I have hitherto done all that becometh a friend to do. If any derogation or hindrance be done to thy honour and name, I am heartily sorry; as a friend is justly grieved, if his friend be vilely entreated."

Thus the Lord with the three questions layeth hard unto Peter; for a notable love is it that he requireth of those to whom he committeth his sheep in his absence. Peter had a good conscience, and knew no falsehood or deceit by himself; but bare a fervent and notable love unto Christ. Yet by reason of his former fall, and this oft questioning, he was partly out of quiet, fearing lest peradventure there lay yet hid in him some secret thing, that displeased the Lord, or were against him, or that happily he should not stand in such favour with Christ. Therefore said he: "Lord, thou knowest all things, thou knowest the hearts of all men, and wottest that I bear thee a good heart and friendly mind:" which words proceed of a meek fervent heart. Christ knoweth better how we love him, than we ourselves. Thus a shepherd ought to have an ardent love unto Christ, and yet not to stand high in his own conceit, or to brag of himself, although he love, and be garnished with virtues more than other men.

Wherein may it be perceived, that a soul-shepherd loveth Christ, and is his friend? Verily, in loving his sheep, which Christ hath committed to him. Therefore saith Christ alway upon the same: "Feed my sheep." But Christ useth here two distinct words. First, he saith, *Vosce* (βόσκε), that is, feed them, pasture them, fodder them. Secondly, he saith, *Poimene* (ποίμαινε), that is, be thou unto them a herdman, take thou care for them, as it beseemeth a shepherd; be thou a shepherd unto my sheep, keep them from the wolf, and from all such hurt. First, he requireth of him a fervent love; then committeth he his sheep unto him, a treasure great and dear, redeemed and bought with the precious blood of Christ. As if he would say: "If thou love me, declare the same in care and love toward my sheep, whom I commit to thy charge."

The sheep are Christ's, not the shepherd's. As for such shepherds as keep them so, that they make them hang upon themselves, those love themselves, not Christ. They that seek their own glory, profit, and lucre among them, are not faithful shepherds. Against such doth cry the threefold voice of Christ: "Feed and keep my sheep:" "mine," saith he, "not thine. Feed them, oppress them not, slay them not. Feed them, not thyself; seek my glory, not thine own." For some there be which, as Paul with weeping tears com- Phil. iii. plaineth, seek themselves, not the glory of Jesus Christ. Of these spake Paul also afore, 2 Tim. iii. "Men shall be lovers of themselves, covetous," &c. Where the wicked root of self-love is in a curate, there follow all the vices which he in the same place maketh mention of. Whoso now will be a lover of Christ, and a faithful shepherd of his sheep, let him not love himself. This vice, self-love, must Philautia: be abhorred of those that are to be made overseers of the (φιλαυτία.) people. For so fervent and great love ought a soul-shepherd have to Christ and his sheep, that he be ready to die and jeopard his life for the glory of Christ and profit of the people; and that through such fervent love all natural and carnal fear may be driven out of him.

Behold, how worthy and high an office the ministers of the word are put in; how great love, what care, what diligence, what earnestness, what labour and travail they must have, to whom so precious a treasure, and so dearly beloved of Christ, is committed. He maketh not of Peter and his Luke xxii. apostles princes, kings, emperors, but committeth and giveth them a ministration, yea, the most honourable ministry: he commandeth them to become faithful shepherds, willing them to love the people, and to pasture them with the fodder of God's word. He committeth to their charge the sheep, whom as he himself, the true Shepherd, hath with his own death delivered from the pit of hell, so have they a desire to hear their Shepherd's voice. He speaketh not to them John x. of the milk or wool, (which the thankful sheep yet give unto their shepherds,) that they should not have respect to their own lucre; but only with what faithfulness they ought to feed the sheep.

"Feed them," saith he, "kill them not, murder them not; be a shepherd, not a wolf; build, break not down. Peter, if thou love me and art my friend, then put I thee in trust with my best beloved treasure, even mine own sheep, whom I so dearly have purchased. If thou wilt shew me now a friendly part, then take the charge of them, and watch them faithfully. I shall now corporally depart from you; therefore canst thou from henceforth serve me no more in the flesh; but do thou service to my sheep, which hear my voice. If thou faithfully keep them, and take diligent care for them, then shalt thou declare, that thou art my friend, and lovest me; and herein shalt thou do me chiefest service of all."

O gracious Father, grant us to have a fervent love unto thee and thine; but specially provide us with such good faithful soul-shepherds, as earnestly loving thy sheep, and caring unfeignedly for them, may both truly feed them, and valiantly withstand the wolves and all false doctrine. Give grace to those rulers, and unto all such, as by virtue of thy commission do call, choose, and appoint ministers of the word; lest they, being blinded by affection, favour, disfavour, love, hatred, bribes, and such like, prefer unworthy and unmeet men; but to pick out such as be apt, virtuous, godly, and well expert, and that seek thy glory and edifying of thy people. O grant unto all high governors and magistrates, that whereas the goods of monasteries have heretofore served the wicked lusts of unprofitable priests and vain religious, they may, after their decease, be converted by the said rulers into good and godly uses; as provision for the poor, for widows and fatherless children, for bringing up of youth in the scriptures of God, and in honest necessary sciences, that they may be fruitful and comfortable to the whole christian congregation. If this might come to pass, then should there be no lack of wise councillors and active men, profitable to be in common authority; and also amongst christian people there should be found men meet to be made overseers in the ministry of God's word, with which men the people should be well and worthily provided for.

Good virtuous teachers bring forth a virtuous and godly people. And doubtless, the meaning of those that gave such goods to monasteries and churches was at the first that they thought thereby to serve God, and to do good unto the poor. If such goods then, as heretofore have been evil bestowed, be now profitably and blessedly turned to the honour of God and commodity of the whole church, then is the last will and meaning of the founders fulfilled. They also that must pay such rents, tithes, and goods, will be the readier so to do, if they see that the same is well and profitably bestowed. Then shall not they untruly, but faithfully perform and pay all things, when they consider that they do service unto God himself.

Grant us all, O God, to hearken and be obedient unto the voice of true shepherds; and give us hearts to have in great honour, and worthily esteem of such faithful shepherds, as upon earth are thy ministers and stewards, by whom and in whom thou speakest to us and with us: that we, shewing unto them all reverence and honour which they be worthy of for thy sake, may give them honest livings, and consider, how that Christ thy Son our Lord teacheth the same, Matt. x. and Paul thy servant, 1 Cor. ix. Reason it is, seeing they sow spiritual things unto us, that they of us reap things corporal. O Lord, remove away the contempt of thy word and ministers; for the same never escaped without great punishment and harm.

[John xxi. 18, 19.]

JESUS said unto Peter: Verily, verily, I say unto thee, when thou wast young, thou girdedst thyself, and wentest whither thou wouldest: but when thou art old, thou shalt stretch out thine hand, and another shall gird thee, and lead thee thither as thou wouldest not. This he said, signifying with what death he should glorify God. And when he had spoken this, he said, Follow me.

DOCTRINE AND FRUIT.

IT is not sufficient to have begun, except the soul-shepherd continue in his office and faithfulness. For to take the cure and charge of the sheep bringeth great danger, loss, travail, and labour with it. Many a time must a faithful shepherd jeopard his life for his sheep. Such peril doth Christ promise unto Peter, namely, that he must die, and with what death. Aforetime, when he was young, he sought that which pertained to the flesh; he might not away with the cross: but now after the receiving of the Holy Ghost, he is stout, and dieth for Christ's sake, and for his sheep. Behold, such an end had Peter, that of love he dieth for him, with whom to die he rashly promised afore[1]. But necessary it was, that Christ should first die for Peter's health, and that Peter afterwards should suffer death for his name's sake.

The presumption and headiness of man would have set the cart before the horse; but the everlasting truth hath appointed this order. Peter thought he would have jeoparded his life for Christ, and have redeemed the Redeemer: but Christ came to give his life for his sheep, of whom Peter was one. Now after that Christ died for those that be his, there is strength given in the hearts of such shepherds and sheep as be faithful, to suffer death for Christ's sake. Death is not now so to be feared of us, that we would therefore go back from the truth; for by death do not we lose life, yea, Christ hath made death to be the way unto life; and by his resurrection he hath set forth unto us an example of another life, which is immortal. Peter was first afraid, and feared death; and would have dissuaded Christ that he should not die. But now that the precious treasure of Christ's blood is shed, he followeth his Redeemer, yea, even unto the death of the cross goeth he after him; therefore is he now no more a Satan, but a Peter.

Matt. xvi.

Petrus of the rock.

But from whence cometh such strength into a feeble man? Even from God, who dwelleth in the hearts of the faithful: for else is the nature and flesh of man impotent and weak, being afraid of death; which fear, natural heat being abated, is the greater in them that are old. And though we all wish to be with Christ, and be desirous of eternal life, yet would we fain have it without any grief of death, if it might be. Thus came the conflict of death even upon Christ, whereby he declared himself very man; but the will of God

[[1] Eusebius, Hist. Eccles. Lib. II. cap. xxv. p. 83. Ed. Reading, 1720; also Caii Fragm. apud Routh. Rel. Sacr. Vol. I. pp. 168. 179—80.]

had the mastery above man's in the wrestling. Peter also went not with his will to death; but with his will he both suffered it, and overcame it. Christ likewise, to comfort us, was heavy: who nevertheless came upon earth, that he would die; neither was it necessity that moved him to die, but his own good-will and love: for he had power to give his soul, John x. and take it again.

Now though the fear of death be great in nature, yet is it overcome through the strength and greatness of the love 2 Cor. v. which we bear unto him who is our life, even Jesus Christ. And albeit he was the life itself, yet pleased it him to suffer death for us. Seeing then that he alone died for us, we ought not to be ashamed; neither should it grieve us to die also for him, specially considering that the publishing of so excellent grace is committed unto us. When the shepherd dieth for the sheep, it is no great matter if the sheep die for the shepherd's sake. Forasmuch now as the faithful shepherd with his love directeth and encourageth many of the sheep to die for his name's sake; how much more meet is it, that the shepherds be the first which jeopard their lives, striving for the truth, and even unto blood to resist sin, when Christ hath put them in trust to feed his sheep? This is now the occasion, why our Saviour Christ telleth Peter of his death aforehand, and strengtheneth and encourageth him thereunto: for though the will be constant in the saints, yet Rom. vii. is the flesh feeble and weak. No man dieth without pain Matt. xxvi. and grief: which thing is appointed unto us by the wisdom of God, to the intent no man should kill himself. For seeing the devil doth now and then persuade some to murder themselves, how should it go, if the soul were not so loth to depart from the body? With these words therefore thought not Christ to make Peter afraid, or to discourage him, but to furnish him and make him ripe. For Peter had a good desire to suffer somewhat for Christ's sake: nevertheless, being yet young, he could not follow. But when he was old, he followed him: therefore will Christ perform his desire. As if Christ would say: " Peter, thou hast hitherto been weak and fearful; but I will strengthen thee: so that henceforth thou shalt deny me no more, but manfully die for me. Thou hast been tender, in that thou wast afraid at one woman's voice: but now shalt thou stretch forth thy hand to the cross to be bound." For by the stretching out of the hands, he understandeth and signifieth with what death he should die, namely, upon the cross. Which death aforetime was most shameful: but after that Christ was hanged upon the cross, it is now an honourable and glorious death, with the which the faithful do glorify God; and therefore saith the evangelist, that the Lord would thereby signify, " with what death Peter should glorify God."

For in God's quarrel and for Christ's sake to die is the highest honour, whereof no man ought to be ashamed. This ought all soul-shepherds to ponder and consider, that they, faithfully and constantly following Christ the Lord, go not from that they have taken in hand, but proceed and bring their course to an honourable end, keeping fidelity and trust with their Lord, and being fully appointed in themselves to die for the sheep of Christ. Therefore should they consider aforehand, what things they must suffer for the truth; lest they destroy that, which they have of long time builded and taught.

O gracious Father, strengthen thou us in thy work and in thy truth; that in the thing which thou hast begun in us, we may stedfastly continue to the end. Expel out of us the fear of death, and stablish us through thy holy Spirit, that we manfully may despise and jeopard this life for the life eternal. Grant, O God, to the shepherds of thy sheep a fervent love to the truth and thy glory. Strengthen them with thy Spirit, that they valiantly standing by the flock, may even with their death confirm thy people in the truth.

marginal note: 2 Tim. iv.

[John xxi. 20—25.]

PETER turned about, and saw the disciple whom Jesus loved following; which also leaned on his breast at supper, and said, Lord, who is he that betrayeth thee? When Peter therefore saw him, he said to Jesus: Lord, what shall he here do? Jesus saith unto him: If I will have him to tarry till I come, what is that to thee? Follow thou me. Then went this saying abroad among the brethren, that that disciple should not die. Yet Jesus said not to him, he shall not die; but, If I will that he tarry till I come, what is that to thee? The same disciple is he, which testifieth of these things, and wrote these things, and we know that his testimony is true. There are also many other things that Jesus did, which if they should be written every one, I suppose the world could not contain the books that should be written.

DOCTRINE AND FRUIT.

The former words which Christ spake unto Peter, "Follow me," were spoken unto him in this meaning; that he should follow the footsteps and passion of Christ, namely, with word and deed to go the way that Christ had gone. But inasmuch as Peter is a figure of the church, Christ spake those words not only unto him, but unto all faithful believers. For the church of Christ, while she dwelleth here temporally in many troubles and afflictions, she followeth Christ her spouse and head, who also delivereth her from all adversity. She loveth Christ, and in the behalf of his truth she striveth until the death; for seeing Christ died for all, it is meet that they which are his do follow his footsteps. To follow Christ is nothing else than stoutly to suffer and overcome despite and poverty in the world for his sake. And God truly, even in his wrath, which we with our sins deserve, cannot forget his mercy. Over and besides the manifold comfort and help which he otherwise declareth unto us, he hath given us his own Son to be our Mediator; by whom, if we put our trust in him, we should be saved and delivered from eternal death; that we living from henceforth still in faith, hope, and charitable love, as pilgrims in this world, and being in all troubles and adversities preserved by the corporal and spiritual comfort of God, might walk innocently before his sight in him who is become our way unto God. It is no vile thing to suffer and to be put to death for Christ and his truth's sake; yea, a man cannot die a more honourable death, than when for the truth innocently he suffereth with a good conscience and with an upright mind. No man ought indeed to put himself in danger arrogantly, wilfully, or for vainglory.

Whereas Peter asketh a question concerning the disciple whom the Lord loved, what he should do, it is a niceness and unprofitable curiosity, that serveth nothing to edification; and therefore it pleaseth not the Lord. Whatsoever edifieth not, that ought not we to desire of Christ. Let every man look to himself, waiting upon his own business and office, and not to be curious in another man's matter. Whatsoever is not committed unto his charge, and belong not unto him, let him not meddle withal. Peter loved Christ: so did he John[1] also: therefore asked he what should become of him, and whether he should remain still, or die; for he was very loth and unwilling to depart from him. And so he passed more upon John, than upon the precept and commission of Jesus Christ. Such curious back-looking doth the Lord rebuke.

We many and sundry times do regard and esteem more the thing that we love, than that which God commandeth and biddeth us. But such love is very hurtful, and especially in those that should be soul-shepherds. Christ's will is, that they have respect to his work and commandment, and with a fervent love to perform the same, not meddling with other business not needful.

To inquire curiously of other men's matters bringeth not alway profit, but much rather unquietness. Therefore Christ, removing Peter from such curious questions, draweth his mind unto a better thing, namely, to follow him. As for that which he desireth to know, Christ telleth him, that it is no point of his charge; as if Christ would say: "What hast thou to do with other folks' business? Thou hast heard what I have commanded thee; look that thou faithfully do the same. What inquirest thou after other men's matters?"

Thus looking diligently and faithfully to our own charge, and expelling the affection of the flesh, we should neither desire curiously to ask any thing beyond the will of God, neither to look upon any other men; but uprightly to follow the Lord.

Here also we learn, that in the commission and final departure of the faithful there be manifold differences. Some rest in the Lord blessedly, without any special heavy affliction; but some it pleaseth God to bring through sore travail and exceeding trouble, laying the greater burden upon him;

[1] Ed. 1593, them.

according as it was told Peter aforehand, that he should be crucified, but not John.

They now that are admitted to feed Christ his sheep, prepare themselves, and be always ready, without any curiosity to follow the will of God.

Whereas John, in the conclusion of his book, refuteth the erroneous opinion of some, it is an evidence of his meekness and sincerity. It was not so spoken of the Lord, saith he, that the same disciple should not die: whereby John confessed, that he himself also was mortal. His writing will he have credited; for he hath written nothing save only the truth, whereof he may well testify that which he hath seen; yet saith, he hath not written all, but only that whereby we may obtain eternal life; as we have heard sufficiently afore.

[Matthew xxviii. 16, 17. Luke xxiv. 44—49.]

THE eleven disciples went away into Galilee, into a mountain where as Jesus had appointed them. And when they saw him, they worshipped him; but some doubted. And Jesus said: These are the words which I spake unto you, while I was yet with you, that all must needs be fulfilled, which were written of me in the law of Moses, and in the prophets, and in the psalms. Then opened he their wits, that they might understand the scriptures, and said unto them: Thus it is written, and thus it behoved Christ to suffer, and to rise again from death the third day; and that repentance and remission of sin should be preached in his name among all nations, and must begin at Jerusalem. And ye are witnesses of these things. And behold, I will send the promise of my Father upon you. But tarry ye in the city of Hierusalem, till ye be endued with power from on high.

^a Matt. xxviii.

DOCTRINE AND FRUIT.

THE Lord, minding to make his disciples assured of his resurrection, instructeth them first well in his passion, which he declareth out of the scripture, and printeth it in their hearts. He teacheth them, that it was necessary that Christ should suffer and die, yea, even thus to die, namely, upon a cross, upon a tree. On the tree was the transgression committed, upon the tree behoved it the restitution to be made; upon the tree was death fetched, upon the tree was life given; upon the tree must satisfaction be made for the lusts of the flesh, which on the tree were first conceived. And would God that we rightly knew the passion and cross of our Lord Jesus Christ! Then should the glory of the resurrection be well known and loved of us.

O Jesu, grant us grace right to consider, what, wherefore, and with what love and ferventness, thou hast suffered for us. Then shall our heart feel and profitably enjoy the sweet fruit of thy resurrection; then shall our life become new and of another sort, if we take upon us true penance, being sorry for our sins, converting us unto thee, amending and changing our conversation, which with the gracious forgiveness of our sins is declared and promised unto us in the gospel, according to thy commandment.

<small>Isai. ii.
Psal. cx.

John iii.</small>

O what a joyful message is this, that such great grace should out of Sion be shewed unto us, which come of the heathen! From this grace is no man shut out: it is common unto every man, unless the unthankful exclude himself; as do they that love darkness more than the light, and they that disdainfully inclose thy grace, and hedge in thy church, which thou, by the preaching of repentance and forgiveness of sins, hast commanded to be gathered unto thyself in the whole world, not only at Hierusalem, but also in Samaria and Galilee, even unto the end of the world. O God, suffer us not to be subject unto vain-glory and headiness; remove all contention and strife out of thy holy church. Preserve us from schisms and all dissensions; knit us together in uniform love, which is an undoubted token of thy children.

It behoved Jesus Christ to suffer, not for himself, but for our sakes, to become the sacrifice for our sins; that he, so satisfying the justice of God, might make amends for our trespass, and deliver us from death. It behoved him also to rise again, that he by his power might raise us up from the death of sin to a new life, and by his own resurrection to make us assured of ours, and of immortal life.

[Matt. xxviii. 18—20. Mark xvi. 15—18. John xx. 21—23.]

JESUS came to his disciples, and said unto them: To me <small>Matt. xxviii.</small> is given all power in heaven and in earth. As my Father <small>John xx.</small> hath sent me, so send I you. And when he had thus spoken, he breathed upon them, and said, Receive ye the Holy Ghost. Whose sins ye forgive, they are forgiven; and whose sins ye retain, they are retained. Go therefore, and teach all people, <small>Matt. xxviii.</small> baptizing them in the name of the Father, and of the Son, and of the Holy Ghost, teaching them to observe all things whatsoever I have commanded you. And, behold, I am with you every day until the end of the world. Go ye therefore into the whole world, and preach the gospel unto all creatures. Whoso believeth and is baptized, shall be saved; but <small>Mark xvi.</small> he that will not believe shall be condemned. The tokens which shall follow those that believe are these: In my name they shall cast out devils; they shall speak with new tongues; they shall take away serpents; and if they drink any venomous thing, it shall not hurt them; they shall lay hands upon the sick, and they shall be whole.

DOCTRINE AND FRUIT.

WHEN Jesus with many evidences had certified his disciples of his resurrection, he sheweth them now, to what excellent glory and how high power his heavenly Father had brought him, whereby their hearts might be established; and how that all things are justly subdued unto him, who through the cross hath overcome, gotten a glorious victory, and suppressed the prince of this world. And though some now declare themselves contrary to his kingdom, and are not obedient unto his power, but persecute and kill him in his members, saying, "We will not have him to reign over us," resisting and gathering themselves together against God and his anointed King; how mighty soever they be, yet shall he bruise them with an iron rod, and as an earthen vessel all-to break them; yea, they must become his footstool, and he shall reign for ever.

<small>Luke xix.</small>

<small>Psal. ii.</small>

<small>Psal. cx.</small>

As if he would say: "In most perfect humility, in highest patience, and being in greatest contumely, I have hitherto served you and all mankind; but now is the time come, that my Father will glorify me, and bring me to high honour, which I had afore the world was made, that in my name all knees should bow; for I am set above all power and dominion, having all things in my hand. From henceforth shall I be worshipped and honoured of the angels in heaven, and of all men upon earth. And forasmuch as I have received a whole power over all flesh, I send you, not only unto the Jews as afore, but unto all nations in the whole world; for in myself have I sanctified the whole nature of man. Look therefore, that ye declare this joyful and gracious message unto all men, and plant them in with baptism unto the Father, to the Son, and to the Holy Ghost. And those whom ye baptize, see that ye teach to observe and keep all that ye have received of me. Ye must also be stout, and not faint-hearted. Many afflictions, much evil-will, great persecution, shall happen unto you: but consider how mighty a Lord ye have, unto whom is given all power in heaven and earth; he is able enough to defend and save you from all enemies. And albeit that I go now from you, as touching corporal habitation, yet will I be still remaining with you with my power, grace, working, and protection, until the end of the world. Wherefore go your way, set your whole delight in me, keep yourselves unto me alone; so can ye not miscarry."

<small>John xvii.
Phil. ii.</small>

<small>Matt. x.</small>

O how excellent and great consolation is this unto all faithful and believing hearts! O how mighty a strength is it in all adversity and dangers of this world, to hear and consider, that all power in heaven and earth is given unto Christ our Lord and King, under whose protection and wings we are safe and well preserved! And who cannot understand, that this promise reacheth not only unto the twelve disciples, unto whom it was then made, but unto all faithful believers, which through their doctrine are come unto Christ? For those twelve did not continue in this life until the end of the world; and yet he saith: "I will be with you until the end of the world." Wherefore we may well perceive, that Christ, until the end of the world, will be with all the faithful believers; that is to say, with his holy church, to instruct, teach, strengthen, comfort, defend, and deliver it against all malicious violence of this world. In his hand they are safe and well kept; and no man is able to pluck them out of his hand. Although the world rage, and the devil, the prince of the world, set all his power, great as it is, against the church of Christ; yet are not the gates of hell able to do anything against it; for it is founded and strongly builded upon Christ the rock; and he that is with it unto the end of the world is mightier than all enemies. John xvii.

John x.

Matt. xvi.

Now, forasmuch as the disciples of Christ should bring the heavenly doctrine throughout the whole world, man being yet of himself unable to comprehend the doings of God; he therefore first expounded and declareth the scriptures unto them, as Luke mentioneth; and seeing they were simple unlearned men, he opened to them their understanding. But to the intent they might not think, What should we poor simple bodies do against so many learned and wise men? who will arm us against those that are so mighty? therefore he breatheth upon them, and saith, "Receive the Holy Ghost," whom he there giveth them, and therewith strengtheneth them inwardly; but with much more power and might upon Whit-Sunday. Whereupon he commandeth them to wait at Hierusalem, where he will send them the promise of the Father; clothing the weak with heavenly strength, as with a garment, and arming them as with a shield. Joel ii.

What good thing then can he lack, or what evil thing can hurt him, which is his messenger, that hath all power in heaven and in earth, and with whom such a king is ever abiding?

But when Christ would send out his disciples, he saith unto them: "As my Father hath sent me, so send I you." Whereunto did the Father send his Son into the world?

Even that he should open the glory of the Father unto the world; that he should declare the will of the heavenly Father; that he should offer health unto the world. This to do, Christ also sent forth his disciples. He sent them not to seek after vain-glory, after power and riches, after bodily pleasure and worldly pomp; but to do as he himself did. Christ sought the lost sheep, brought men unto the knowledge and love of the true living God, taught them to lead a virtuous and honest life. He was a physician, went to the sick, helped them, and healed them; he was not come to do his own will, but the will of his Father; he was not come to condemn the world, but to save it.

<small>Luke xv.</small>

<small>Matt. ix.</small>

<small>John vi.</small>
<small>John iii.</small>

In all this ought the ministers of the word to follow Christ, and to do as he did. Unto this new, heavenly, and godly life and work, Christ giveth them the Holy Ghost. For like as he himself was risen into a new life; even so through his holy Spirit will he grant and give a new life unto those that are his. Therefore breatheth he upon them, to declare, that it is he, who at the beginning made man, and now by his death had quickened him, and renewed him; and that even he is the fountain and giver of the Spirit. Thus unto his disciples he gave the firstlings of the promised Spirit, and with it a taste of more and greater perfection, as an earnest-penny.

All this declareth, what belongeth to true apostles and ministers of the word, which are sent of Christ, (for no man sendeth himself;) what their office is; and that they which seek the pleasures of the body, honour, praise, and riches, are not followers of Christ and successors of the apostles. Wherefore ought we most diligently to pray unto God, that he will give us faithful ministers of the word, which, looking truly to the work of Christ, may lead us unto God.

But forasmuch as without the Holy Ghost nothing can be fruitfully done, we must nevertheless pray for his holy Spirit, who may in us stir up holy thoughts and devout desires, directing and moving our will, and so giving power and strength to accomplish the works of God, and stedfastly therein to continue; and that the same Holy Spirit may illuminate and kindle our minds, and provoke them unto all good and godly works. Considering then, that the keys which were promised unto Peter, and in him to the whole church (Matthew xvi.), are here given of Christ, we shall also entreat somewhat thereof.

These keys are nothing else than the gospel. Christ now deduceth his oration from the common custom of men. Like as things corporal are shut and opened with the key; so be the consciences of men shut or bound with the gospel. Thus are these the keys which Christ giveth unto the apostles, unburdening of consciences and souls. And that cometh to pass, when the Holy Ghost illuminateth the mind, that it understandeth the mysteries of Christ, and committeth itself thereunto. To be discharged or unbound is, when the mind that hath despaired of health or salvation, is lift up to an assured and undoubted hope. To bind is to leave the obstinate and unbelieving mind unto itself. Jesus therefore sendeth forth his disciples, to publish this health unto the whole world, and to exclude and separate no man from this grace. Of the keys.

But first he giveth them the Holy Ghost, as John saith; that is, he openeth their minds, that they may understand the scriptures, as Luke saith; for what is it else to open the understanding, but to give the Holy Ghost? Meet is it also and convenient, that they which by the gospel should bear Christ throughout the whole world, should receive the Holy Ghost. For if they should preach Christ, it was necessary they had Christ's Spirit, seeing that they and Christ had one manner of thing in hand. As Christ was sent of God, so were they sent of Christ. Without fruit verily should the ministers of the word preach the gospel, if they were not endued, illuminated, and inspired with the Holy Ghost.

"Preach," saith he, "the gospel;" that is the key, wherewith the gate of heaven is opened. Whoso believeth the gospel, when he heareth it preached, and understandeth it, feeleth comfort in his conscience, that he is delivered from sin.

Now doth the gospel set before us, not only the grace of God by Christ, through the which grace our sins are forgiven us; but also it teacheth and requireth a new life. Neither doth any man begin a new life, unless he first be ashamed of the former old and wicked life. Therefore saith Luke, that Christ "opened the minds and understanding of the disciples, that they might perceive the scriptures," namely, that he Luke xxiv.

might thus and thus suffer, and rise again; and that in his name, that is, in his commandment and power, conversion of life and forgiveness of sins should be preached and declared among all people.

Therefore when the poor sinner through the preaching of the Holy Ghost heareth his wicked and sinful life, (for the holy gospel rebuketh the world of sin,) he beginneth to know himself a sinner, and to be displeased, repentant, and sorry for his sins; he considereth also, that he is well worthy of eternal punishment and damnation: by means whereof, through the multitude and greatness of his sins, he utterly despaireth in his own power and righteousness, and eternal salvation. But therewithal he heareth also, that Christ, by reason of his sins, came down from heaven, and died for him upon the cross, washed away all his sins with his blood, hath reconciled him with God, made him God's child, and an eternal inheritor of his kingdom; and this he stedfastly believeth. I pray you, doth not such a man's heart leap for joy, when he heareth, that through Christ he is discharged of all the sins that so sore pressed him?

The keys, therefore, are the pure word of God; which teacheth men to know themselves, and to put their trust in God through Christ. With that word, with those keys, do the ministers of the word open. For they that so are taught and instructed by the word of God, that they put all their confidence in God through Christ, those verily are loosed and discharged of their sins. But he that either will not hear, or when he heareth, will not receive and believe this grace declared to the world through Christ, and offered unto him by the ministers of the word, him do the ministers bind, that is, they leave him still in his error; according as Christ commandeth his disciples, (Matt. x.) that from such as will not receive and hear their word they shall depart, and shake off the dust from their shoes upon them. Thus did Paul bind, Acts xiii. xviii.

To bind then with the word, is nothing else but, when the word of the grace of God is preached, and not received, to leave such impenitent people, and to have no fellowship, neither aught to do with the despisers of the truth and grace. For in the day of judgment it shall be easier unto Sodom and Gomorrha, than unto such.

Now, although the word that the Apostles preach is not their own, but God's, and no man may cleanse, unbind, and discharge from sin, but only God; yet Christ of his grace, and according to the property of the scripture, ascribeth such unto the apostles. For the gracious Father, of his abundant love and kindness, and by reason of the covenant that he hath made with us, doth oft ascribe unto us many things which can properly belong unto none, save only to himself. Neither is this any marvel, seeing he hath given us his only-begotten and most dear Son to be our own; for "how cannot he give us all things with him?"

Notwithstanding, we ought not by reason hereof to be high-minded and proud, and to ascribe unto ourselves that which only is God's; but much rather be thankful for his grace, and diligent in our vocation, faithfully to employ and bestow the high treasure and gifts of God, and not to abuse them. This thing therefore extendeth not so far, as that every one man, properly to speak, doth of his own power and authority forgive sins. But forasmuch as the apostles and ministers of the word do publish and declare remission of sins, they bring the keys, and forgive sins ministerially and as ministers. Nevertheless, if herewithal the Spirit of God do not work in the hearer to believe the word when it is preached, then is not the sin forgiven. All the power therefore and working is God's.

Thus the apostles may damn no man, but undoubtedly they may by the word declare damnation to the unbelievers. Where an assured promise of grace is declared, there sins are forgiven. Now when the apostles shew unto sinners remission of sin, they do it out of the Holy Ghost, and are not deceived; for they preach that our sins are pardoned us through Christ, who hath made satisfaction for them. If this faith upon Christ be lively in us, so that we abhor sin, and be desirous of heavenly things, then are our sins forgiven us through the Holy Ghost; for "no man can say that Jesus is the Lord, but by the Holy Ghost." *The Holy Ghost that worketh in the apostles forgiveth the sins.* *Note this condition well.*

The key, therefore, extendeth to this end, that the minister declare remission of sins through Christ. Whoso now believeth the gospel preached, "shall be saved; he that believeth not shall be condemned." And seeing that the faith is an inward thing in the soul inspired of God, the minister cannot know who in the sight of God believeth, or believeth not; for God only knoweth the heart. Howbeit, by the outward confession, which is done with the mouth, and by receiving of the preaching, and by the fruits, the minister may judge. For whoso receiveth the word, openly confessing Christ, and doth not outwardly defile himself with vile deeds, to such the minister openeth with the key, and dischargeth them; that is, he taketh them into the church of Christ, numbereth them among the people of God, and receiveth them into the kingdom of heaven. As for those that will not hear the word preached, or that, when they hear it, do refuse it, not confessing Christ, or uttering their unbelief with foul, gross, and open vices, those the minister bindeth; that is, he shutteth them out of the church, and banisheth them out of the realm of heaven. To him that is in the church is forgiveness of sins promised: whoso despiseth charitable love, hath not faith; upon such one remaineth sin still, and the wrath of God.

Now, what the apostles and ministers of the word do, that do they not in their own name, not in their own power; but as they which are sent of God, and that declare his word, the holy gospel, out of the power of God, even out of the Holy Ghost, who being given unto them, doth work and speak by them. What these bind is bound before God and in heaven; for out of God is it that they judge: and what they unbind is unbound before God; for God will ratify and allow what they do, that being sent of him, keep themselves in exercise, and meddle with in his word and commission. As for him that is not sent of God, and declareth not his word and gospel, but of his own proper power will bind one man, and unbind another, set this man in heaven, and that man in hell; is it any marvel, if such one do many times miss, and be called a wolf, and not a shepherd, seeing his proceedings cometh not of God?

Here also we learn, with what desire and thankfulness we ought to receive the ministers of God, that bring us his holy word, and comfort of our conscience; how we ought to esteem them that have the Holy Ghost, who speaketh unto us by them. For if we despise them, we despise God himself. St Paul, therefore, exhorteth us to be obedient unto them, and to have them in worthy estimation, that shew us

Luke x.
Heb. xiii.

the word of God. Worthy they be of double honour; partly, 1 Tim. v. for that through them God speaketh, whose ministers and 2 Cor. v. ambassadors they be, (for the highest king of all sendeth them out unto us with his commission;) partly, for that they be charged with so dangerous and heavy office and travail. For though, as concerning themselves, they live justly, well, and blameless, yet if they regard not the life of their sheep, but neglect them, they must look for great and sore punishment: not only for themselves must they give account, but for all the souls that are committed unto them, if one of them perish through their negligence. We should not therefore have respect to the infirmity or baseness of the ministry, but unto him that sent him, and whose commission he executeth. When a prince or king sendeth out a mean servant with a commission and charge, who will despise him without the wrath and indignation of the prince? How can we then contemn the ministers of the high eternal King without plague and punishment?

This be spoken, not that unworthy and unmeet men should be placed in so high an office, or that we should delight in their evil; but to the intent that malicious judgment may be avoided, and that there be no villany done to the anointed of the Lord. More respect and regard should we have to the word of God, that they bring unto us, than to their living and faults; more to the giver, than to the minister. It is not they that work, but God worketh through his own power; he cannot fail us in his promise. The minister lendeth his hand and mouth, but the Holy Ghost worketh in the hearts of the believers; neither can the wickedness of the priest diminish or hinder that operation. If we ourselves have pure, clean, and faithful believing minds, it is not the uncleanness of the minister can either defile or hurt us.

This is now the story of the resurrection of Christ; wherein we see, how the goodness of the Lord wonderfully striveth with the weak faith of those that are his. For when the angels could not persuade them that he was risen again, he himself appeareth unto them alive, and proveth by many evident testimonies, that he is of a truth risen again and revived, talketh with them, eateth with them, offereth himself unto them, that they may see him and handle him; sendeth the women and certain disciples for witnesses, and leaveth nothing unattempted that may persuade them. For in the faith and belief of the resurrection of Jesus Christ lieth all our welfare. We must therefore beseech Almighty God to establish in us this faith, and by his Spirit mightily to work, that we from sin may truly rise again to a new and godly life, and afterward with our bodies to enter into an immortal and everlasting life. Hereunto help us God the Father, the Son, and the Holy Ghost! Amen.

> Here endeth the Sermons upon the Resurrection
> of Jesus Christ, according to the true copy
> of the Author; and now followeth the
> Sermons of the Ascension.

[CHAPTER IV.]

THE ASCENSION OF JESUS CHRIST, OUT OF THE HOLY EVANGELISTS.

[Luke xxiv. 49—53. Acts i. 4—14. Mark xvi. 19.]

JESUS led his disciples out unto Bethany. And when he had brought them together, he spake unto them of the kingdom of God, and commanded them that they should not depart from Hierusalem; but to wait for the promise of the Father. For John, saith he, baptized with water; but ye shall be baptized with the Holy Ghost after these few days. When they therefore were come together, they asked of him, saying: Lord, wilt thou at this time restore again the kingdom to Israel? And he said unto them: It is not for you to know the times and the seasons, which the Father hath put in his own power; but ye shall receive power, after that the Holy Ghost is come upon you; and ye shall be witnesses unto me, not only in Hierusalem, but also in all Jury, and in Samaria, and even unto the world's end. Now when Jesus had spoken these words unto them, he lifted up his hands, and blessed them, and was taken up, and a cloud received him out of their sight: so that he departed from them, and was carried up in heaven, and sitteth on the right hand of God. And whilst they looked stedfastly up towards heaven, as he went, behold, two men stood by them in white apparel, which also said: Ye men of Galilee, why stand ye gazing up into heaven? The same Jesus, which is taken up from you into heaven, shall so come even as you have seen him go into heaven. So when they had worshipped him, they returned with great joy into Hierusalem from mount Olivet;

which is from Hierusalem a sabbath-day's journey. And when they were come in, they went up into a parlour, where abode Peter and James, John and Andrew, Philip and Thomas, Bartholomew and Matthew, James the Son of Alpheus and Simon Zelotes, and Judas the brother of James. These all continued still with one accord in the temple, lauding and praising God, and making their prayers, with the women, and Mary the mother of Jesu, and with his brethren.

DOCTRINE AND FRUIT.

<small>John xiii.</small> CHRIST, who loved his disciples, declareth unto them his love, even unto the end; yea, he never ceaseth to love them. <small>Matt. xxviii.</small> For though he leave them, as concerning his bodily presence; yet with his love, grace, and power, he is ever still with them. Forasmuch now as after sufficient proof of his resurrection he will depart from them, and go to his Father that had sent him; he taketh them forth with him unto the place, from whence he mindeth to depart from them. And manifestly, before their eyes, he ascendeth into heaven into the glory of his Father; that they might be witnesses, as well of his glorious ascension, as of all other things which they had heard and seen before. O how fervent words spake he then unto them! How deeply entered he into their hearts! How earnestly printed he those his last words into them! The eternal wisdom speaketh nothing vainly, nothing slenderly, nothing without profit. Although the disciples, as men yet somewhat carnal, do ask questions concerning the restitution of a bodily and temporal kingdom, yet maketh he no answer unto their demand, but directeth them unto that which is for their profit, and belongeth to their office; drawing their hearts from the earthly kingdom, from the which they ought to be mortified, unto the kingdom of heaven, even unto the kingdom of God; in the which he himself is king, and into the which they now were received as citizens, that they should declare the same throughout the whole world, and offer it unto all men.

This is the gospel of the kingdom of God, which for a

testimony unto all nations must be preached in the whole world, to witness the grace of God unto the elect; but to the damned and unbelievers, a testimony of their damnation; in that they are convinced of their own infidelity, and shall have no excuse, if they contemn and despise the grace offered unto them. By this ought we also to learn to see such things which are most profitable and wholesome unto us; and which bring us the nearest way to put our trust in God, and to love our neighbours; for that part of the play is ours. As for unprofitable and contentious questions, if we meddle not with them, then the less division, and the more love and edifying in the church of God shall follow. Many times are we too much careful for such things as we desire ourselves; as, what end this thing or that will come unto, when God will set up our prosperity, and what shall be done hereafter, when and how God will punish those that are against us. And this temptation, carnal zeal, and curiosity, chanceth oft even in the hearts of the faithful; as we see here in the disciples of Christ. Sometimes there be froward and wicked minds, which, pretending to be Christians, seek out of the gospel nothing but honour, lucre, and profit: but such be both false and feigned. Notwithstanding, all these set apart, we ought to commit and refer all things unto our merciful Creator and gracious Father, who can right well order and dispose them, how and when he will, as he thinketh best to further his glory, and to edify his elect children. Our care ought rather to be, how we may lead a godly life, and beautify the faith of Christ with good works. We must look, that we be neither ungodly nor hypocrites; but to live virtuously and innocently in his sight, and patiently at his hand to wait for our deliverance. The kingdom of Christ, that is published and offered through the gospel, is not a corporal, but a spiritual kingdom; neither consisteth it in outward things, but in a pure and faithful believing heart: and yet reacheth it throughout the whole world, and amongst all nations. In the hearts of all faithful believers doth Christ reign through his Spirit, and there overcometh he the devil, sin, and death.

And to the intent they should well understand this kingdom, he commandeth them to wait for the Holy Spirit, whom he had promised them; as if he would say: " Now go I to my Father, now enter I into my kingdom, that I may mightily reign upon the earth. This thing ye understand not; but when the Spirit is given you, ye shall perceive it well. All things in heaven and in earth are given into my power. In those that are mine shall I reign, and make them righteous through faith; yea, invincible shall I make them against all enemies: hereof shall ye bear witness, when ye are baptized through the Holy Ghost. This my kingdom shall ye publish in all nations, from one end of the world to another. Thus shall I reign from sea to sea; of the which my kingdom the prophets spake so much before."

Of this kingdom doth Christ take possession through his ascending up to the Father, at whose right hand and in this kingdom he sitteth; reigning much more mightily in his church, and working more effectually in those that be his, than he did before, when he lived yet corporally with them.

Thus taking his leave, he giveth them loving words, comforteth them, and admonisheth them of their office; that they all may be diligent therein, that they continually direct and lift up their hearts into that kingdom; and that they take in hand to bring all men to the same into the obedience of Christ. His blessing he giveth them, saluting them, wishing them good, and praying heartily unto his Father for them.

Thus was he taken from them, and carried into heaven. By the heaven we understand the incomprehensible light in the which God dwelleth, and which no mortal man can attain unto. From thence came Christ unto us; and thither is he gone again, even into the invisible glory and clearness of God. For the eternal Word and Power of God, dwelling in God's incomprehensible light from everlasting, became man, and had his conversation upon earth in all parts, sin except, as a very true man. But when he had fully finished and throughly ended the work that was given him in commission of his heavenly Father, and had obeyed him even unto the death; forasmuch as in all things he had honoured and glorified his Father upon earth, it was convenient that the Father also should glorify his Son. And therefore raised he him from death, and took him up into heaven; not after the Godhead, (for so was he always in heaven,) but after the manhood. For his true human nature, which he took upon him for our sakes, is carried and taken up out of this world into the invisible honour and glory, into the highest incomprehensible, and into the perfect fruition of the Godhead.

In this honour and glory Christ dwelleth and reigneth; and yet amongst those that are his doth he finish and perform all things by his Spirit, having governance in the hearts of the faithful through belief, through love, through patience, and innocency of life.

To the intent now that this kingdom might be erected in the hearts of men, it was necessary that he should give his disciples commission to publish the same, and to prepare men's minds thereunto through the preaching of the gospel. But first he made the minds of his disciples ready and apt to receive the Holy Ghost, whom he afterwards poured into others by them; and therefore he commanded them, until the Spirit appear and open the work, to wait still at Hierusalem; from the which place the kingdom of Christ was afterwards planted in all the world. Of the promise of the Spirit read Isai. xliv. Jere. xxxi. Ezek. xxxvi. Joel ii. John xiv. xvi.

Considering that the mystery of Christ's ascension is great and excellent, and that there is notable power contained therein to those that be faithful believers; the evangelists do therefore describe very perfectly the time, the place, the persons, with all circumstances and assured testimonies thereof. He ascendeth up before his disciples, that they might openly and evidently see it with their eyes: there did appear angels, as messengers and witnesses from heaven, even two of them, that in the mouth of two all truth might be established. The white apparel signifieth the evident glory, into the which Christ is taken up, as a noble, royal, and mighty King and Conqueror, entering into his heavenly kingdom.

Thus the high and glorious King, clothed with our nature, is entered into our royal palace, as one that mindeth faithfully to despatch our matters. He is our own mediator and advocate in the presence of the Father; notwithstanding our sins committed, we have a free entrance unto God by him. Our flesh hath he in himself carried up, and exalted our nature unto the right hand of God the Father. Wherefore we that are bones of his bones, and flesh of his flesh, do justly conceive a comfortable and assured hope, that our mortal bodies shall also be taken up, and have immortal and eternal joy.

The earnest-penny of his Spirit hath he given and left behind him unto us, and contrariwise he hath of us taken an earnest-penny and pledge, namely, our sinful and wicked flesh, which he in himself hath carried up into the kingdom of heaven. Now where the parcel is, there shall also be the whole sum.

By this we that are flesh and blood have a comfortable and assured trust, that in Christ we shall have the possession and inheritance of heaven. Our sins in him are recompensed, heaven in him is opened, in him is the hope of immortal life sealed and made sure unto us; Christ, the victorious and glorious conqueror, is able to defend his church: so that from henceforth no man shall have power to condemn his elect and faithful believers. Rom. viii. Heb. v. vii. viii. x.

That his flesh is withdrawn from us, and taken into heaven, it is our great profit; to the intent that all our devotion and God's service may be directed upwards in the spirit, and that the minds of faithful believers may be drawn from earthly unto heavenly things, even unto the place where Christ sitteth on the right hand of God the Father.

When the disciples saw that their schoolmaster was taken away from them into heaven, they perceived and considered the thing that they knew not before, although Christ had told it them, John vi.; namely, that by the ascension they should receive understanding. Therefore they worshipped Jesus Christ, and according unto his commandment they returned to Hierusalem, where they kept themselves until the time that the Spirit came: neither were they idle, but continued in the holy fellowship and godly exercises, with prayer and devotion, preparing and making themselves ready unto the coming of the Spirit.

By occasion hereof (all niceness, curiosity, and contentious questions, all pride, vain-glory, and fond affections and desires set apart) we ought with upright minds, and with the eyes of faith, to be alway taken up into heaven, and there to have our dwelling, where Christ our head sitteth at the right hand of God, King and Lord of all things, our faithful advocate and mediator. Then shall true godliness increase, then shall virtue blessedly grow and bring forth fruit in us, if we with stedfast faith do consider, that our Lord Jesus Christ died for our sakes, rose again from death, and is exalted at the right hand of God, reigning mightily above all things in heaven, and finishing our salvation, if we in spirit and in the truth worship and honour him as the eternal God; confessing with a true faith, that all power is given unto him of God the Father, that he careth for us, and that for our health's sake he ruleth and shall reign, until all things be brought under his feet. In the meantime he daily in his church purifieth all his members by his Spirit, cleansing them still more and more from all their sins. And when he shall have rooted out all sin in his elect, overcoming death the last enemy, so that God shall be all in all; then shall Christ also give up his kingdom unto God the Father, namely, the mediation for our sins, the purging of the same, defence against the devil, and deliverance from death. For then shall there be no more sin in the elect; so that he shall not need to be mediator for them, to purge from sin, to defend against the devil, or to deliver from death.

O merciful Father, grant us perfectly to know the[1] blessed and glorious kingdom of Christ thy Son: draw up our hearts in such sort, that we with all obedience may yield ourselves into this kingdom, seeing and regarding only those things that are above, and wholly applying ourselves unto this end, that the same heavenly kingdom may be far spread abroad and known unto all men; to the intent, that as for all worldly things, wherein many foolish people set all their salvation, but in vain, men may utterly refuse them, and heartily with body and soul, and with their whole life, may give over themselves perfectly unto the only Lord Jesus Christ, the true God. For thy good pleasure it was, O God, that in him all perfectness should dwell, and that by him all things towards thee should be reconciled and pacified through his blood, whether they be in heaven or in earth. Grant us, O God, unity and brotherly love in thy holy church; kindle our hearts to fervent and devout prayer; make us diligently to watch, and circumspectly to wait for

[1 Old edition, *thy*.]

the coming of thy beloved Son, that we neither be drunken in excess and bodily lust, nor entangled with the snares of this world; but that we, having always the eyes of our heart open, and praying with upright minds, may cheerfully meet our Redeemer, and joy with him for ever. To him be eternal praise and honour. Amen.

[CHAPTER V.]

THE SENDING OF THE HOLY GHOST.

[Acts ii. 1—4.]

WHEN the fifty days were come to an end, they were all with one accord together in one place; and suddenly there came a sound from heaven, as it had been the coming of a mighty wind, and it filled all the house where they sat. And there appeared unto them cloven tongues, like as they had been of fire, and it sat upon each one of them; and they were all filled with the Holy Ghost, and began to speak with other tongues, even as the same Spirit gave them utterance.

_{Acts ii.}

DOCTRINE AND FRUIT.

HERE the evangelist Luke describeth, how that after Christ entered into his glory, the gospel, even the heavenly doctrine and grace, was opened unto the world down from heaven by a glorious and great miracle. For though the law, which is the will of God, and also the gospel, that is his grace, hath from the beginning been always in the world, namely, in the hearts of God's elect children; yet was each one of them at several times gloriously uttered unto the world by manifest and apparent miracle. And like as the Holy Ghost was in the hearts of the faithful believers, (for after the resurrection he gave the Spirit unto the disciples;) even so here he giveth them the Spirit with an open miracle, and with a more perfect working and power. For the Spirit which Christ gave them after his resurrection, when he breathed upon them, was given this day with more perfection; that is to say, his operation and strength declared itself more evidently and more perfectly, and shewed his presence by the visible miracle.

Thus it is here described, how the promises of Christ and of the prophets made as concerning the Holy Ghost were fulfilled, and how the same Holy Ghost, who is the teacher of the truth, the earnest-penny of salvation, the wedding-ring of grace, and joy of the mind, was given. Now when it is said that the Holy Ghost is given unto men, the same may be understood of the gifts and operations of the Holy Ghost; for though God may be comprehended of man's mind, yet can he not be included or shut therein. Nevertheless, his gifts, according to his will and pleasure, are poured and measured into our hearts, unto every one so much as may serve to his welfare and profit.

<small>1 Cor. xii.</small>

Whoso is desirous to know where the Holy Ghost is promised unto faithful believers, let him read Ezech. xxxvi. xxxix. Joel ii. Matt. iii. Now look, what God the Father hath promised by his ministers, the same also doth Christ his Son promise: whereby we may see that the Son hath like power with the Father, and that there is but one only Spirit of them both, as we may read, Luke xii. John vii. xiv. xv. xvi. xx.

But before we come to the sending of the Spirit, we will first substantially and well peruse the story, and look what may be gathered thereof: for here is nothing written or set down in vain.

The evangelist doth here make mention of "the fiftieth day," upon the which this great wonder was done. In the which there lieth hid a notable mystery. The Jews, from the day that they offered the Easter lamb, told fifty days, and upon the fiftieth day was the Feast of Weeks; in the which feast they kept holiday, offering unto God a willing sacrifice of the first-fruits, when they cut them down. We begin to number from the resurrection of Christ, our Easter lamb, who also was offered up. Upon the fiftieth day, when the fruits began now to be ripe and ready to be reaped, the harvest also being great, and the labourers few, then sent God his Spirit to prepare and furnish the disciples, that they from amongst the heathen might gather fruit together unto the Lord. And like as before time, when the children of Israel was departed out of Egypt, the law was given of God

<small>Exod. xii.
Deut. xvi.</small>

<small>Matt. ix.

John iv.</small>

unto the people upon the fiftieth day; even so was it convenient that upon the fiftieth day the Holy Ghost should be given to the disciples; which Holy Ghost is both an interpreter and fulfiller of the law. The place where the Holy Ghost was given is Sion: for there Christ commanded his disciples to wait, and from that place should the law of God, according to the saying of the prophets, proceed forth into the whole world. Therefore like as aforetime the law was given upon mount Sinai, even so was the Spirit given upon mount Sion. Upon Sinai did God at that time with some terrible things declare his might and power, his plague also and vengeance, which should fall upon those that despised his law; and therefore was there such fearfulness through lightnings, thunderings, and other like terrible things. Here there is heard a noise, mighty and vehement, but not horrible and fearful; in the which wind is signified, that the doctrine of the Spirit should speedily and with power break in through the world, and bring fruit; and that no man should be so mighty as to hinder the strength thereof, even as the wind in his course can by no man be kept back. 2 Cor. iii.
Luke xxiv.
Isai. ii.
Micah iv.

Note.

Whereas fiery tongues do appear and are seen, it signifieth the manifold speeches and instruction, which the Spirit giveth to Christ's disciples; the zeal also and ferventness that he worketh in their hearts, making them altogether fire, and kindling them in such sort, that even their words are fervent, and pierce afterwards into the hearts of others. All weakness, fear, and coldness removeth he out of them, so that they are not afraid manfully to step forth before all the people; although not long before they durst not abide, but fled from the Lord. Now they confess him to be the Saviour of all the world, whom they before had denied.

Whereas the tongues were divided, it signifieth the diversity of the gifts of the Spirit. Christ promised them in Mark xvi., that they should "speak with other tongues," or with a new speech or language; which promise is now performed unto them. The tongues of christian men ought to be garnished with gentleness and with the Holy Ghost, that no foul or wanton talk proceed out of their mouth. The tongues that pronounce and confess Christ, the eternal Truth, and his sincere Spirit, must not lie, neither talk any unclean, hurtful, nor venomous thing; for unto all such Eph. iv.
Col. iv.

is the Spirit enemy. Therefore are they not fleshly, but fiery and spiritual tongues; out of the which the fire of the Spirit hath consumed all moisture of worldly and carnal wantonness, and God with his own love hath kindled them. How could the apostles else have been instructors of the whole world, if the Spirit had not taught them the diversity of tongues? O the great wisdom and grace of God, who at all times for our wealth hath set forth and offered unto us poor men his high, spiritual, heavenly things, under corporal and visible tokens! For how might we carnal men else understand godly matters, if they were not exhibited with visible and bodily things? Therefore hath God always this custom, that he represent unto us his high gifts under those tokens, which are most known of us, and likest unto those things which he offereth us; and so with human things he covereth divine and godly things. Not that God is closed or shut in with things of men; but that celestial and heavenly things, set forth unto us by such as be earthly, might be of us the better understood. For else every man of knowledge wotteth well, that the Holy Ghost is not a dove, neither a wind, a tongue, fire, nor water. For God is not a thing corporal, neither a thing that can be felt or comprehended with outward senses. Notwithstanding, things invisible are the better known and perceived of us, when they be set forth and represented by visible things; namely, by such as have some similitude with the invisible and spiritual things; and so far as natural things may set forth heavenly matters, do perfectly describe before our eyes the nature and property of them. Therefore doth the Spirit appear in the form of fiery tongues, and with a sound; that thereby the two principal senses of men might be moved, namely, his hearing and seeing: for the sound toucheth the ears, and the fire moveth the sight. Like as Christ also in the supper with bread and wine, to move the outward senses of men, thought to represent his body and blood. For by bread is signified unto us the true body of Christ, which died for us upon the cross, and by wine the blood that was shed for our sins; which true flesh and blood they that believe do at the supper eat and drink through faith: by the which food and sustenance their souls are upholden to the gracious and eternal life.

Thus with exterior tokens it pleased the wisdom of God

to guide the outward senses of his disciples into the obedience of faith, and under the same to signify and declare the strength and operation of the Holy Ghost. For like as the wind bloweth through the whole earth, piercing, moving, and altering all privy and secret places; even so the Spirit of God goeth through all things, searching all secret corners and inward minds of men: mightily also he worketh in men's hearts, kindling and changing them. He is the clear, pure, and hot fire, that consumeth all filthiness of sin, inspiring men's hearts, and drawing them upward to God.

Without this Spirit may a man work no fruitful thing, yea, think no good thing: for man is nothing but flesh, neither considereth he of himself aught that is spiritual or godly, but only carnal things. Forasmuch now as the wisest and most gracious God knoweth this so to be; whereas he hath made man his creature, to have fruition of himself, he will not suffer him to corrupt in the flesh, but give him his own holy Spirit.

God the Father, through Christ his eternal Word, did shape man out of the mould of the earth, and created him after his own similitude and likeness. Now is God a Spirit; therefore the image of God in man must needs be spiritual: which image in the inward man is such a thing, as partly doth express and declare God that created him.

But when man, being deceived through the devil, fell into sin, and lost this image; then the proportion of God's pure Spirit, in whom his image was printed, was defaced, and the image of God lost his beauty: so that the noble man, who at the first was of God, so fair and goodly fashioned and beautified in similitude of God, became after sin like unto the devil, filthy and shameful, yea, altogether carnal, having nothing more of the Spirit in him, as the scripture in the book of Creation testifieth. Forasmuch now as the miserable man was degenerate from the noble, spiritual, and godly nature, to an unclean, carnal, and devilish disposition, becoming altogether flesh; he was able no more either to think or work any spiritual or godly thing. *Gen. vi.*

All his thoughts and imaginations are carnal, in that he is fallen into eternal death, and hath lost the life of the Spirit: "for the affections and lusts of the flesh are death; but the desires of the Spirit are life and peace. The affec- *Rom. viii.*

tions of the flesh are enmity against God; for the flesh is not subject unto the law of God, neither can be: they therefore which are in the flesh cannot please God." Now when man, who had taken so hurtful a fall, was brought down from life unto death, from the grace of God into his wrath, life might not be given him again but by the Spirit of God, whom man by sin hath lost.

Therefore like as the Father at the beginning had created man, so fashioneth he him again by his Son; who overcometh and destroyeth death, and giveth unto us again the way of immortality. ^{Wisd. i.} "For into a froward soul entereth not the Spirit of God:" therefore is it convenient and necessary, that such foul and corrupt flesh be purged and cleansed again. By Christ the eternal Word were all things created; by him therefore, after the fall, must all things be restored again. For this cause died Christ upon the cross, to banish the sin of the world, and to make satisfaction for it. From death he also riseth again, to give us a certain and assured hope and an undoubted pledge of an immortal and eternal life, and that he hath overcome death and sin for us.

_{John xx.} Immediately after the resurrection, he breatheth upon his disciples, and giveth them the Holy Ghost; to declare that he is the same, who at the beginning created our nature, and sealed it with his Spirit; and that it is even he, who now, in the beginning of a new life, must by his Spirit renew and restore our decayed nature again; that thus Christ, who is the living and "express image of the invisible God," may be fashioned and formed of the new in us. Now cannot Christ the image of God be right proportioned and renewed in us but by the Holy Ghost. Now like as Christ after the resurrection gave his disciples the Spirit, to print into them a new life, whereby they knew and were assured, that he was the fountain and giver of the Spirit; and therefore he said, "All that the Father hath is mine;" item, "All power is given unto me in heaven and in earth;" even so immediately after the same he ascended up into heaven, to declare unto them, that he was the Lord of all things. Out of the high and real throne, where he sitteth at the right hand of God his Father, Christ the eternal King sent down his holy Spirit upon all flesh, that we by him might obtain the old innocency and salvation again; and that the image of God,

(marginal refs: Wisd. i.; John xx.; Heb. i., Col. i., Gal. iv.; John xvi., Matt. xxviii.; Col. iii., Eph. iv.)

stained and defiled by sin, might be restored unto us, and that we thus might become partakers of eternal life. What they be, unto whom God giveth his Spirit, that see we well here; namely, even unto those, that in unity of faith and fervent love are gathered together with one accord; for of all unity he is the fountain and original. In contentious and proud hearts dwelleth not the Holy Ghost: therefore is it meet that we pray:

Come, O Holy Spirit, replenish the hearts of thy faithful believers, and kindle in them the fire of thy love, thou that through manifold tongues hast gathered together all the nations of the heathen in unity of faith. O take all dissension and discord out of thy holy church, and make us to be of one mind in unfeigned love, without the which we cannot please thee.

[Acts ii. 5—11.]

THERE were dwelling at Hierusalem Jews, devout men, out of every nation of them that are under heaven. Now when this was noised about, the multitude came together, and were astonied; because that every man heard them speak with his own language. They wondered all and marvelled, saying amongst themselves: Behold, are not all these which speak of Galilee? And how hear we every man his own tongue, wherein we were born? Partheans, and Medes, and Elemites, and the inhabitants of Mesopotamia, and of Jewry, and of Capadocia, of Pontus and Asia, Phrygia and Pamphylia, of Egypt, and of the parts of Lybia which is besides Syren, and strangers of Rome, Jews and proselytes, Cretes and Arabians; we have heard them speak in our own tongues the great works of God.

DOCTRINE AND FRUIT.

THE eternal Wisdom hath endued all good minds diligently to learn and search the thing wherein they think to find that which they desire: and what can be more worthy to be desired, or more acceptable to the mind of men, than eternal life and salvation, which only consisteth in God the highest good of all? Now was the sacred scripture given by the Holy Ghost, that man thereby might be guided and led unto salvation, and to most excellent felicity. For they that exercise themselves in holy scripture, studying and perusing it, ought thus to do; even to direct themselves and others unto life. Therefore, by the ordinance of God, there hath been ever men in all nations, which to instruct others have applied themselves to the scripture; as among the Jews we find Levi, of whom in the prophet Malachi it is written, that "the law of the truth was in his mouth, and no wickedness in his lips; that he walked before God in peace and equity, and converted many from ungodliness: for the lips of the priests are sure of knowledge, and the law is required at his mouth; for he is a messenger of the Lord of hosts." Thus, as it may well be conjectured, there were at Jerusalem congregations of learned men, that exercised themselves in the holy scripture. For though all wisdom come of God, as the fountain and well, and no man can be learned, whom God himself teacheth not; yet will he not give his grace, Spirit, and knowledge to the idle, slothful, and unthankful, neither to the proud; but unto those that with meekness and fear of God practise themselves in the scripture, and that, applying unto fervent prayer, do not despise the means and gracious gifts granted them of God.

[Mal. ii.]

And if any man will say, that all falsehood and destruction, all erroneous doctrine and discord, were come into the church by such as be learned; let him consider, that the thing which in himself is good, ought not for the abuse's sake to be refused. Remove the abuse, and then the thing is good and profitable. Wine is a profitable and wholesome thing, created of God for the behoof of men, and is never dispraised of any witty man to be evil, because many do abuse it, and is drunken: even so is holy scripture and other profitable sciences to be esteemed as high gifts, although many men, puffed up with pride, blinded in covetousness, and entangled with other affections, have misused the same scriptures.

In the papistry, the universities, colleges, cathedral churches, and monasteries, have highly exalted the pope and his false faith, and by false interpretation of the scripture brought him so far, that the doctrine of the faith and Christ is utterly darkened. Now, whereas lewd learning with false science, with wrong understanding of scripture, have brought such high things, great goods, and plentiful riches to pass, drawing so much people unto themselves; we ought not therefore to cease from reading and exercising of the scripture, but to take upon us to further the true religion and faith of Christ, and to set it forth again with no less diligence than they do theirs. If we will that the true faith of Christ shall grow, continue, and increase, then we must bring the same to pass by true understanding of the scripture, by pure, sound, and wholesome doctrine. With the truth must lies be banished, with sound doctrine must false be rooted out, with the light must darkness be expelled. But how can the true understanding of the scripture, the undoubted, wholesome, and sound doctrine, be had, when men do neither exercise and employ themselves, nor apply their endeavour, study, and diligence therein?

All the charges therefore and expenses, which heretofore have been bestowed upon the unprofitable and noisome learned men, ought now to be converted to godly colleges and studies; to the intent that little seeds, which God hath laid up in young wits, may fruitfully grow, be planted, and brought forth. "If thou seek wisdom, as the gold," saith Salomon, "thou shalt find it." Gold is with great travail and labour digged out of the inward and secret veins of the earth, and of the high hills; it raineth not down upon men's heads: even so must knowledge and wisdom be gotten with great travail and diligence, not with loitering and idleness. But when God giveth us his gifts, we must look that we be not unfaithful in them, but use and bestow them to his glory and edifying of his church. Where godliness cometh to knowledge, or where they two are together in one man, God is highly to be thanked for so excellent a gift and grace, and greatly is such a gift to be had in estimation; but where as pride, heaviness, contention, greediness, and self love, is in a learned man, there is not a more hurtful poison found upon the earth.

O God, thou that of thy grace and fatherly love hast given so good and excellent gifts with singular light of all sciences; grant unto such as be learned a heart and mind, that in all things they may have respect only to thy glory, and that in all their readings, writings, teachings, and doc-

<small>1 Cor. viii.</small> trines they may prefer the same. For "knowledge puffeth a man up, but love edifieth." O suffer not thy holy and excellent gifts to be stained, defiled, and marred, with the filthy dirt of men's affections. Grant that our studies be not heathenish, but godly and christian. Preserve the tender and good youth from wicked and ungodly school-masters; that the pure hearts which thou hast consecrated to be a temple for thee and thy holy Spirit, be not polluted with vice and filthiness.

[Acts ii. 12—21.]

<small>Acts ii.</small> THEY were all amazed, and wondered, saying one to another, What meaneth this? Other mocked, saying: These men are full of new wine. But Peter stept forth with the eleven, and lift up his voice, and said unto them: Ye men of Jewry, and all ye that dwell at Hierusalem, be this known unto you, and with your ears hear my words. For these are not drunken, as ye suppose, seeing it is but the third hour of the day: but this is that which was spoken by the prophet Joel: And it shall be in the last days, saith God, I will pour out of my Spirit in those days, and your sons and your daughters shall prophesy, and your young men shall see visions, and your old men shall dream dreams: and on my servants, and on my handmaids, I will pour out of my Spirit in those days, and they shall prophesy: and I will shew wonders in heaven above, and tokens in the earth beneath, blood, and of fire, and the vapour of smoke; the sun shall be turned into darkness, and the moon into blood, before that great and notable day of the Lord come. And it shall come to pass, that whosoever calleth on the name of the Lord shall be saved.

DOCTRINE AND FRUIT.

When the truth is published in the church of Christ, and the power of God uttereth itself, there be always some simple people, that of good mind seek to know that which they understand not, and therefore they demand questions: unto those the Lord doth gladly open himself. But again there be others, that despise, slander, mock, and abhor all holy things, as in the old and new testament we have many witnesses of the same. Jerem. xx. xxvi. xxxii. John viii. x. xi. Acts xvii. For the natural man understandeth not the things that appertain unto God. And thus do they most of all, which, being puffed up in the wisdom and science of men, have not yet attained to the spirit and right kernel of the scripture: in the sight of which men the wisdom of God, and preaching of the cross of Jesus Christ, is but a derision and foolishness. But blessed are they, that in the singleness of their heart, with pure minds, in meekness, obedience, and in the true fear of God, submit themselves unto his doctrine. From them cannot God hide himself; but openeth their minds, that they may understand the scriptures. For they that of a good mind do here ask the question, "What meaneth this?" are afterwards converted by Peter's preaching. Peter, the fervent disciple of Christ, the faithful shepherd of Christ's sheep, as soon as he receiveth the Spirit, is bold to step forth, and to confess him whom before he had denied. 1 Cor. ii. 1 Cor. i. Matt. xi. Matt. xi. Luke xxiv.

But first he persuadeth that the disciples were not drunken: for if such vice were in the ministers of Christ, and they truly convinced thereof, it should bring unto the gospel and name of Christ great hinderance, stain his doctrine, and make it to be despised and subject. Most diligent therefore ought we to be in keeping us from such vices, whereby our office, ministration, and doctrine might be suspect and set at nought. Yet must we not defer too long in answering such evil reports: for more diligence must we apply in setting forth the name and glory of God, than in defending and maintaining our own estimation.

Thus the apostle Peter, in answering that objection concerning drunkenness, doth shortly pass over, and saith:

"Brethren, these are not drunken, as ye suppose: for why? the time doth not permit; it is yet too early in the morning." Immediately upon the same, he proceedeth forth to admonish them of the excellent graces and gifts, which the God of mercy hath promised before, and now performed them. But this satisfaction concerning drunkenness, and this instruction of the ignorant, is made with all meekness, and yet with sincerity and stedfastness, not lordly or braggingly; although he was highly endued with the Holy Ghost.

Thus we that be ministers of Christ, and teachers of his congregations, ought not by reason of our office or high gifts to take too much upon us, that with bragging or arrogancy we would out-face the weak; but worthily and valiantly, with sincerity and truth of scripture, to instruct such as be ignorant and out of the way. Our mouth is an instrument of the Holy Ghost and of the truth, not of any lightness, bragging, or presumption.

This word "prophesy" is taken not only to tell and shew before of godly and high things, but also to hearken unto the same and to perceive them; and this maketh for the understanding of this place. For the Holy Ghost declareth by Joel, and promiseth also, as he doth by Jeremy, that the knowledge of God should be common in all the world, and that from the least unto the most every one should be instructed in God's knowledge, through the guiding of the Spirit: which knowledge before time was common only to the Jews and scribes, but by Christ is such abundant and plentiful knowledge of God poured out in all the world through his holy Spirit, who worketh in the church until the end; not only in scribes, from whom such high mysteries of God's wisdom are oftentimes hid, but unto simple and unlearned fishers, and to others that in the sight of the world are not esteemed.

Yea, richly poureth he out of his holy Spirit upon all flesh, unto every one his measure, as it best pleaseth him: no man excludeth he from his grace; his knowledge suffereth he to flow over all the earth as a water-flood, unto all those that are his servants and handmaids. This is the dear and excellent treasure, which, instead of it that was given before, by the incarnation of Christ is now offered, that the knowledge of God, which by the Holy Ghost is the preaching of the gospel, is come forth into all the world; whereas before

Joel ii.
Jer. xxxi.

Matt. xi.

1 Cor. xii.
Isai. xi.

it was manifest only amongst the Jews. For after the death of the Lord finished upon the cross, was the gospel published in all the world, by the which preaching the children of God dispersed abroad are gathered together. The Holy Ghost also, who was before in the godly, did by his gifts and operations work much more mightily and strongly after the death and ascension of Christ, than before: by the which Holy Ghost the captivity of the law and ceremonies is taken away, and heavenly freedom given to the children of God. *Ps. lxxvi.* *John xi. Isai. xl.* *Jere. xxxi.*

Forasmuch as to know Christ and his kingdom, it ministereth true godliness and eternal life, Peter in his oration travaileth especially to this end, that the Jews being there present, which held Christ for a wicked doer, and put him to death, might know him to be the true Saviour of the world, and to be risen again from death; and therefore he allegeth the prophecies which in Christ were fulfilled. As if he would say: Behold, Joel told before of the time that these your children should prophesy; now ye see it performed in them. Whereby ye may well perceive, that the kingdom of Messias, which is a spiritual thing, is now begun already. In the which kingdom must be not only Jews, which have the outward temple and ceremonies, but all as call upon the name of the Lord, wheresoever they be in the world. Unto the Jew was promised a Saviour; nevertheless such one as should not only save them, but also the whole world, and whose kingdom should be everlasting; that he also should deliver and bring them, yea, all mankind, from the captivity of the prince of this world. Of these things there were amongst the Jewish people many signs and figures, whereby in bodily and corporal things God did partly set forth these things spiritual: which they also which are spiritual and elect amongst the people of the Jews, understood right well, though darkly; in that they with the eyes of inward faith had a further respect than to gaze only upon the outward corporal things. Thus God the Holy Ghost by visible things led and taught them, (even as a young scholar is first taught by letters and syllables under the schoolmaster,) until the time that the glorious kingdom came, that in Christ the true Messias all things were reformed, and became spiritual.

Thus had the Jews the corporal kingdom of David,

and of other kings; and thus for their sins they were brought unto Babylon into captivity. By the which captivity was figured the grievous bondage and thraldom of mankind under the violent power of the devil. But when they were in captivity at Babylon, God, comforting them by his prophets, promised to bring them thence, and to restore them to their own land; in the which deliverance was figured the redemption of the world by Christ. This custom had all the prophets, that when they told the people beforehand, and promised of God's behalf deliverance out of the captivity before they came into it, they always made mention also of the punishment of the sins that should go before. Prosperity shall come, (said they;) but first there must be an horrible plague for sin, the justice of God must first be satisfied. Thus doth Joel here also: in whom partly we learn, that God will not suffer our sins to pass without punishment; as we see also in the grievous captivity of all mankind, that God will have the sin so worthily satisfied, that even his only-begotten Son, by whom no sin was committed, must therefore die, and by his innocent death pay for our sins. If God now spared not his only-begotten Son, how may we then think that he will suffer our vile and sinful life to pass without punishment? But if we patiently and with good will bear the just punishment of our sins, sent unto us of God; and converting from our sins, do turn us to the gracious Father that beateth us, God undoubtedly shall send us grace, prosperity, and welfare, and help us out of all misery. Once we must either live a godly and innocent life, and throughly amend ourselves; or else sin must be punished, and every unclean thing must in the fire and punishment of God's wrath be consumed. Again, though we were virtuous and godly, yet is God of this nature, that he maketh his chosen to be like-fashioned unto the image of his Son, and by much adversity and trouble he leadeth them unto joy; even as it behoved Christ to suffer, and so to enter into his glory. The punishment of sin is hard, and the judgment of the Lord, as often as he cometh to recompense sin, is sharp; which the prophet partly by bodily things doth describe, as other prophets do also. Isai. xiii. Jerem. xv. Amos viii. "The sun shall be turned into blood, &c.;" and even so is it in the opinion of those, that must bear the judgment of God.

Luke xxiv.

Forasmuch now as the apostle Peter, according as the matter required, did necessarily allege testimony out of the prophet, concerning the Holy Ghost, who is given to the good children of God; he thought also to specify that which was written in the prophet, as touching the punishment of the wicked, that despise the grace of God; giving a warning thereby unto the Jews, to cease from their unbelieving and shameful life; declaring unto them, that if they proceed forth in wickedness, it should happen unto them, as it did before unto their forefathers, unto whom Joel opened the punishment of God. Whereby we must learn, patiently to bear it, and to take it in good part, when our sins are rebuked, our vices spoken against, and we told that the punishment is at hand. For this custom had the apostles in their preaching and declaring of the gospel, that they not only made mention of the grace of God offered unto the world by Christ, but therewithal likewise they threatened sore punishment to those, that either despised such excellent grace, or having knowledge of the truth did cleave unto vice; which thing in the word of Peter is yet more evident.

The gospel also preacheth amendment of life, and not remission of sins only through the blood of Christ. But now at this present time there be many dainty Christians, as certain princes and senates in the countries and cities, whose opinion is, that the grace of the gospel is to be preached, yea, and they permit Christ and his grace gently and worthily to be spoken of. But if the false gods' service, as the honouring of images, and all that is crept in and erected up in the papistry against God's word, be reproved; or if the preacher speaks against their tyranny, unjust acts, their malicious violence and wilfulness, whereby they oppress poor widows and fatherless children, doing right unto no man; or if the preacher touch them on the galled backs for their excessive pomp and pride, for their rioting, whoredom, adultery, gluttony, drunkenness, fighting, and extortion; if such vices, I say, wherein they still lead their lives, be touched to the quick, then is all favour gone; then, 'Burn these preachers,' say they, 'drown them, they be seditious fellows; they will set us together by the ears, and bring the common people in our necks.' But such men should consider, that unto this office of the preacher it belongeth to cry against vice, lest

<small>Isai. lvi. lvii.</small> he be called of God a blind watchman, a dumb dog, and lest
<small>Ezech. iii.</small> all the souls which perish through his silence be required at his hands: their wilfulness, pride, and vain life they should forsake, and reform themselves, and so needed not the preacher to cry out against them. Now considering that the prophets used, as I said before, to make mention of the kingdom of Jesu Christ, and of the calling of the heathen to the grace and knowledge of God, especially in their orations when they speak of captivity, and deliverance from the same; Joel in his prophecy doth also keep that order. For seeing that the Jews were ever still continually a stiff-necked, rebellious, and unbelieving people, unthankful to the grace of God; the Holy Ghost foresaw their rejection, declaring it by the prophets, and that another people, namely, the heathen, should be received in their stead. For inasmuch as they despised the grace of God, which first was offered unto them, it was meet that "the kingdom of God should be taken from them, and given to another nation." Seeing they thought scorn to come to the marriage, and to the royal feast whereunto they were bidden, it behoved others to be called unto the same. Therefore is Peter earnest upon this sentence: "Whosoever calleth upon the name of the Lord shall be saved." As if he would say: 'O ye Jews, brag not of circumcision, of Abraham, of the temple, or of other ceremonies; think not that ye only are the people of God; the time is now come, that God will bestow his grace upon those whom ye esteem to be unclean. God is no accepter of persons, but among all people whoso calleth upon him shall be saved.'

Of this sentence doth Peter now take occasion more manifestly to speak of the kingdom of Christ: for much more pithily and with more evidence doth the apostles describe the kingdom of Christ, than do the prophets. Whoso calleth upon God's name must know God. Now can no man know God but by Christ. Therefore in this little word, "to call upon the name of the Lord," is comprehended the whole sum of the christian faith: like as oftentimes in the prophets be these,[1] "to swear by God," is contained his whole religion. But forasmuch as the Jews knew not Christ, by whom cometh the true knowledge of God, therefore beginneth Peter, and

[1 Perhaps *by* or *in* these.]

declareth with strong arguments, how the name of God is to be called upon; namely, through true faith in Christ, who is the true Messias, the anointed King and Son of God, which was promised in the prophets. This doth Peter prove by the ground of the resurrection of Christ from death, by his ascension into heaven, and by that he now sitteth at the right hand of God, Lord and King of all things. First let us hear the text.

[Acts ii. 22—28.]

YE men of Israel, hear these words: Jesus of Nazareth, a man approved of God among you with miracles, wonders, and signs, which God did by him in the midst of you, as ye yourselves know; him have ye taken by the hands of unrighteous persons, after he was delivered by the determinate counsel and foreknowledge of God, and have crucified and slain him: whom God hath raised up, and loosed the sorrows of death, because it was impossible that he should be holden of it. For David speaketh of him: Aforehand I saw God always before me; for he is on my right hand, that I should not be moved. Therefore did my heart rejoice, and my tongue was glad; moreover also my flesh shall rest in hope; because thou wilt not leave my soul in hell, neither wilt thou suffer thine Holy One to see corruption. Thou hast shewed me the ways of life; thou shalt make me full of joy with thy countenance.

DOCTRINE AND FRUIT.

To the intent now that no man should be offended at the death and cross of Christ, Peter sheweth first, that in the counsel of God it was concluded, foreseen, and determined, that the Son of God, the true Messias, should and must die; and how that the same sacrifice was ordained from the beginning of the world, to be slain and offered up upon the cross for our sins. And that no man should make any stop by reason of his death, Peter therefore declareth that he was no misdoer, which had deserved his death by any transgression; but that he was sent unto us by God the Father, to die for us, whereby we might perceive the love of our Father in heaven. And if they now would think, "Well, if it were so concluded in the counsel of God, then are not we guilty of his death;" he answereth unto the same, and saith: "Unrighteous men brought him thereto, and it is ye yourselves that slew him and crucified him." As if he would say: 'Yea, even so behoved it to be, that the righteousness of God for the sin of mankind might be satisfied. Christ must needs die, to recompense and wash away with his blood the sin of all the world. And yet ye Jews, which have betrayed Christ and brought him to the cross, are not unjustly accused. Ye cannot through the fore-ordinance of God discharge yourselves, that ye be without sin, seeing ye have slain the Saviour of the world, he being guiltless.' By this now we learn, that when we do wrong and evil, we may not excuse ourselves with the free ordinance of God; for it is not God, but the devil and our own wickedness, that provoketh us to sin.

And here we see, that when the grace of God through the gospel is offered unto the world, the sin and vice also wherein the world is entangled, must be spoken of and touched: for no man can be justified, and come to the health of his soul through Christ, which doth not first know and confess his sin and wickedness. How can he be made whole, that will not know his own disease and sickness? Therefore doth Peter set before their eyes their great sin, which they had committed against the innocent Son of God, saying: 'The Innocent and Righteous, whom God had given unto you, have ye slain and crucified; which is a great wickedness and sin. Now go to, on your behalf it was evil done, and grievously offended; but on his behalf it was so ordained before. Therefore at his death, which in the sight of the world was so shameful and vile, ye ought not to be offended, that ye therefore would hold the less of him, or not receive and know him for a Saviour. For if you look upon his former conversation, the same was innocent, pure, and holy; therefore cannot ye doubt but he was sent of God. Besides this, ye have perceived and seen God to be everywhere in his works: for the tokens and wonders which he shewed and declared amongst you, give evident knowledge that God was in him, and wrought in him presently; for no man had been able to do the tokens that he did, unless God had been with him. Which tokens also were spoken of before by the prophets concerning Christ; and by those tokens must ye know and confess, that he is even the true Messias, of whom the prophets spake. Wherefore considering, that by his former doctrine and godly power ye know that he is the true Messias, ye ought not to be offended that he, as an evil doer, was crucified upon the cross: for it was the special determination of God, that Messias should be crucified, according to the foresayings of the prophets. Consider ye also, that the prophets likewise spake of his resurrection from death; by the which ye may well perceive that he is the true Messias.'

Thus earnest is Peter, beating into them the resurrection from the dead, and that out of the scripture. For Christ's resurrection from death is a strong argument to prove his Godhead; as it is taught, Rom. i. John xx.

"Yea, he died," saith Peter, "for our sins, but now he is alive and risen again from death; death hath no more power over him, for he liveth for ever, and his kingdom is everlasting. Yea, unpossible it was, that the Son of God should corrupt in the earth and sepulchre; namely, he that is the firstling risen from the dead, and that from his own godly power." Seeing that these words of Peter concerning the resurrection and life of Christ were little credited among the Jews, he allegeth the 15th psalm of David, who amongst [Psal. xvi.] them was in great reputation. But now might the Jews say or think: "David speaketh these words of himself, and not of Christ." That weapon, therefore, doth Peter take from them, and proveth, that the same words may in no wise be referred unto David; but that David, as a prophet having knowledge of things to come, spake them of Christ, in whom they be now fulfilled; and thus he saith:

[Acts ii. 29—31.]

YE men and brethren, let me freely speak unto you of the patriarch David; for he is both dead and buried, and his sepulchre remaineth with us until this day. Therefore seeing he was a prophet, and knew that God had sworn unto him with an oath, that Christ, as concerning the flesh, should come of the fruits of his loins, and should sit on his seat; he, knowing this before, spake of the resurrection of Christ, that his soul should not be left in hell, neither his flesh should see corruption. This Jesus hath God raised up, whereof we are all witnesses.

DOCTRINE AND FRUIT.

THE prophet David speaketh of one, whose flesh should not corrupt. Now could not he have spoken this of himself, for his flesh corrupted in the sepulchre, which we yet have, and his bones lie yet in the sepulchre: by the which it may well be perceived, that David, as a prophet knowing of things to come, spake of another, which should be born out of his own loins and seed, whom God with a solemn oath had promised to sit upon his seat, and reign after him; not only for a season, but also that his governance, kingdom, and dominion, should be perpetual, and endure for ever. And this king is Christ the true Messias, who as concerning the flesh was born of the seed of David, and is his son.

Ps. lxxxix. 2 Sam. vii.

If this son now of David had after death remained still in death, and not risen from death again, how could he then reign for ever? It is evident therefore, that David out of the Holy Ghost, who had opened this unto him, prophesied it of the resurrection of Christ his Son, the eternal King. For though he as a very man died indeed upon the cross, and was then buried; yet his soul, or life, remained not in death, neither did his body resolve into corruption, as other men's; but on the third day he rose again from death to life. This must we needs testify; for after his resurrection he appeared oft unto us. We saw him, we heard him, we handled him, we did eat and drink with him.

Here we learn, that the saints in the old testament understood and knew by faith the resurrection and eternal kingdom of Christ, seeing they prophesied of it so evidently. Here is also proved, that Christ died in very deed, and yet abode not still in death, forasmuch as he overcame it: also, that the power and virtue of his holy passion and death came not only to the living upon earth, but unto all those that died before him; according as St Peter in his Epistle, and the Article of our Belief, HE DESCENDED INTO HELL, declareth. Whereof in the Catechism upon the Creed there is made mention sufficient[1].

[Acts ii. 33—35.]

SINCE now that he by the right hand of God is exalted, and hath received of the Father the promise of the Holy Ghost; he hath shed forth this gift, which ye now see and hear. For David is not ascended into heaven; but he saith: The Lord said to my Lord, Sit thou on my right hand, till I make thine enemies thy footstool. Psal. cx.

DOCTRINE AND FRUIT.

WE believe that Jesus Christ, our King and Saviour, is not only risen again from death to life, but also is ascended up into heaven, sitteth at the right hand of God, and reigneth for ever. For though he here a season was despised and refused, as the stone of the builders; yet hath the strong hand of God exalted him, and mightily wrought in him. Psal. cxviii. Which thing may well be perceived by this, (as St Peter here valiantly concludeth,) that he sendeth down from on high such an excellent gift of the Holy Ghost upon those that are his. This is a sure evidence, that he mightily reigneth at the right hand of God, and hath all things in his hand; seeing he hath power of the Spirit of God, whom he poureth into the hearts of his, and that sometime in visible manner. For the glorious triumpher, ascending up to heaven Ephes. iv. with great victory, did after the custom of great kings, and let fall his gifts down upon us, and parted them among us, namely, the gifts of the Holy Ghost, whom he as man received of the Father, but after the Godhead he had him

[1 What Catechism is here referred to, is very doubtful.]

alway; for of the Father and of the Son there is one only Spirit.

Neither may this be applied unto David. For though he, as a just friend of God, be saved and come to heaven; yet did not he immediately after death ascend into heaven with body and soul, that he might be reported to sit at the right hand of God. For his words speak of another, whom he calleth his Lord; namely, in the hundreth and ninth psalm he saith: "God the Father said unto my Lord, even the Son, Sit thou on my right hand."

Matt. xxii.
[Psal. cx.]

[Acts ii. 36.]

So therefore let all the house of Jerusalem know for a surety, that God hath made this Jesus, whom ye have crucified, Lord and Messias.

DOCTRINE AND FRUIT.

WITH these words doth Peter conclude his oration, exhorting them not to doubt Jesus Christ to be the same anointed Saviour and King, who of God the Father was first promised, and then given for the deliverance of the people of the Jews and of all nations.

In this conclusion is comprehended the sum of the whole christian faith; namely, that we believe that Jesus, who was born of the virgin Mary, and crucified of the Jews, is the true Christ, that is to say, Messias, even the king that was ordained and anointed of God, to reign for ever over all faithful believers, Lord of the whole world, and Saviour of all such as put their trust in him. This hath God the Father opened and set forth unto us by miracles, by the resurrection, by the ascension, and by the power of the Holy Ghost, that we might believe it, and not doubt thereof. Therefore saith John, "Whoso believeth that Jesus is Christ, the same is born of God."

THE SENDING OF THE HOLY GHOST

[Acts ii. 37—41.]

WHEN they heard this, they were pricked in their hearts, and said unto Peter and to the other apostles: Ye men and brethren, what shall we do? Peter said unto them: Repent of your sins, and be baptized every one of you in the name of Jesus Christ, for the remission of sins; and ye shall receive the gift of the Holy Ghost. For the promise was made unto you, and to your children, and to all that are afar off, even as many as the Lord our God shall call. And with many other words bare he witness, and exhorted them, saying: Save yourselves from this untoward generation. Then they that gladly received his preaching were baptized; and the same day there were added unto them about three thousand souls.

DOCTRINE AND FRUIT.

THIS is the fruit and end which followeth out of the preaching of the word of God, that they whose hearts God toucheth, are so sorry for their sins, that it even pierceth them. For God's word is even a sharp two-edged sword, and entereth through to the depth. Blessed are all they which so read and hear the word of God, that they begin to be ashamed of their sins and wickedness, being repentant and sorry therefore. A blessed and wholesome sorrow is that, which riseth and groweth out of the truth, which is opened unto the heart by the Holy Ghost: which Spirit in the heart giveth hope upon the mercy of God, and driveth away all despair. Then beginneth a man to ask, "What shall I do?" Then inquireth he after the will of God; and such a man that so asketh is easy to be helped. Soon is he healed, that, knowing his disease, would fain be made whole.

Unto such a man doth the faithful minister of Christ give counsel out of the scripture, and sheweth him the fruit of Christ preached and known. He doth not bid him to bestow money on solemnities and dirges, on images, monasteries, or cowls, in buying of pardons; he doth not will to run unto Rome, or to Lauret[1]; but requireth of him the best and most profitable thing of all, namely, amendment and conversion of life. Our minds, our works, and manners must be altered, if we will please God. Whoso saith with his heart, that he believeth in Christ, holding Christ for his Saviour and King, must forsake his evil ways, eschewing evil, and doing good. Jere. vii. xi. Isai. i. Nineve stood still upright, when they took upon them true conversion and amendment. As for Hierusalem, though they offered many sacrifices, and fasted much, it helped not: because there was not true reformation and forsaking of sin, needs must they be destroyed, and miserably perish. To botch or patch the matter it will not help; there is no remedy; we must become godly and virtuous of life. It availeth not to dissemble; God looketh into the heart, which he will have pure and unfeigned. Forasmuch then as we through baptism in the faith of Christ have received Christ, and are marked out for him, having once forgiveness of sins through the grace and gift of Christ, let us be of a virtuous life, walking innocently and in the fear of God. Let us die therefore to the innocency which is restored unto us again through Christ: let us daily remember to hearken and follow the admonishment of the Spirit, which teacheth us all good things. We are they, unto whom God hath promised his grace of the Spirit, yea, and unto our children also, so far as we abide in his covenants. Let us thankfully receive such excellent grace, dear brethren, being ware that we stain not the temple of Jesus Christ and of his holy Spirit with filthiness of the world; that we never make ourselves partakers in the iniquity of wicked and faithless men; but to lead here a pure and clean conversation with a good conscience before God, our most loving Father; and alway lift up our minds unto the place, where Christ our Lord and King reigneth at the right hand of God, from whence he shall come and take us unto himself. At all times therefore ought we to watch and wait for his coming, that we may joyfully receive him, and be partakers with him in eternal bliss.

Col. iii.

Here also we learn, how faithful believers use themselves

[1 Loretto.]

in the outward sacraments. They that, being moved by the inspiration of the Holy Ghost in their hearts, do hear the eternal word preached, giving credit unto it, and gladly receiving it, these do not afterward despise the outward sacraments, which God hath instituted for the welfare of his church, but use the same with all obedience, good-will, and reverence. To use the sacraments without faith profiteth not, but rather hurteth; to be loth to use them declareth a compulsion and unbelief.

For though the water in baptism be an outward thing, and cannot cleanse the soul from sin; yet the faithful do know right well, that Christ, the eternal Wisdom in whom they believe, did not institute it in vain; and therefore will not they contemn or leave unexercised the ordinance of their Head, to whom they as members are incorporated by faith. For they know, that Christ with these outward tokens thought to couple and knit together the members of his holy church in obedience and love one towards another; whereby they knowing one another among themselves, might by such exterior things stir and provoke one another to love and godliness. They know also, that sacraments are evidences of the promise and grace of God, which they after a visible and palpable manner do set forth, declare, and represent unto us. These tokens of grace doth no man use more devoutly and with more reverence, than he that in himself is certified and assured of the gracious favour of God; as we see in Cornelius, in Paul, and in Queen Candace's chamberlain.

What fruit followeth the preaching of the gospel, it is here evidently seen: for in one day at Peter's preaching, by the working of the Holy Ghost, there came three thousand men to the church of God. God suffereth not his word to pass void and unfruitful. Very earnest therefore and diligent ought we to be, and to spare no trouble, cost, and labour, that the pure and sincere gospel, the word of truth, may every where be preached by good and faithful men; not doubting God will give blessed success thereto, that the seed sown by the minister shall bring forth fruit.

[Acts ii. 42.]

AND they continued in the apostles' doctrine, in the fellowship, in the breaking of bread, and in prayers.

DOCTRINE AND FRUIT.

To endure crowneth and rewardeth all works: "whoso endureth unto the end shall be saved;" without continuance may no good thing be brought to end and fruit. Therefore is it now declared, how the word preached in the church of God bringeth fruit, and what the same fruits be, wherein faithful believers do exercise themselves.

Saint Luke mentioneth four things that proceed out of the faith in Christ; for faith is not void nor idle, but worketh without ceasing in them that believe. Therefore here we find a pattern and mirror, how it ought to go in the church of Christ; for where these four things be, there is Christ's church. First, the church of Christ, which is the fellowship of all saints and faithful believers, endureth, abideth, and continueth "in the doctrine of the apostles;" for every thing is preserved with that out of the which it is born. Now is the church of God born first of the word of truth: therefore in the word of truth also must it endure and be kept; daily must it be planted, nourished, and watered with the word and doctrine; the success and the increase doth God give.

<small>John i.
Mark xvi.
Rom. i.</small> The doctrine of the apostles is nothing else but the holy gospel, which the Son of God committed unto them, and which they received of him; which also the prophets before Christ spake of by the Holy Ghost. What gospel was preached by the apostles, it is easy to perceive by the aforesaid sermon of Peter, and of others in the Acts, by the evangelists and epistles of the apostles; namely, that "God so loved the world, that he gave his only-begotten Son for it, that whosoever believeth on him should not perish, but have eternal life." Also, he died for us, rose again from death, ascended up to heaven, and sitteth there at the right hand of God, being king and high priest for ever; in whose name

all knees must bow, and without whom "there is none other name given unto men, in whom we must be saved," than the only name of Jesus, whose blood washeth away our sins, and he is the only perpetual mediation between God and us. 1 John ii.
1 Tim. ii.

In this doctrine continueth the church, being builded upon the sure rock Jesus Christ, and is not moved or driven away by every wind of strange and inconstant doctrine. She Matt.vii. xvi.
Ephes. iv. hearkeneth not to the voice of any other, but of Jesus her shepherd. In the doctrine of the apostles there is no deceit, no guile, no poison. And in this doctrine is found none of those things, which certain years after the apostles were brought in by Romish bishops, as masses, dirges, cloisters, worshipping of idols, setting up of images, buying of pardons, forbidding of this or that meat.

First now, doth faith in Christ bring forth this fruit in the church, namely, in faithful believers, that it draweth them to the doctrine of the truth, by the which they became believers; and in the same it maketh them to continue, that they neither hearken nor give credit to any false erroneous doctrine. For they do very assuredly know, that such doctrines are not wholesome, but venomous and hurtful. But in the gospel of our Saviour Jesus Christ, and in the doctrine of the holy apostles, they are sure to find the truth, which nourisheth and preserveth them unto eternal life. The church of God abhorreth all untruth, for she knoweth it is of the devil; but of the truth is she desirous, for she knoweth that the same cometh of God, and bringeth unto God again.

This evangelical truth and doctrine of the apostles, in the which the church of God and all the members of Christ must continue, hath been of long time, even from the beginning, comprehended in certain articles, which we call the CREED, whereof there is sufficient mention made in the Catechism[1]. Among the true children and servants of God also there is no schism, doubt, nor division, concerning the head and chief articles, in the which they are well and firmly established, fully persuaded, and of one mind and consent.

And whereas there be some men which overreach and go beyond this mark, willing other men, and compelling Chris-

[[1] See above, p. 407.]

tians, as far as in them lieth, thereto, teaching those to be heretics and damned, that cleave to the only doctrine of the apostles; the same cometh and proceedeth of the presumptuous arrogancy of flesh, who esteemeth his own invention more than that which God speaketh: as when they say, that images must be had in churches, that pardons must be bought with money, and such like things, which are not grounded in the doctrine of Christ nor of the apostles, nor mentioned in the articles of the right and true ancient belief, but invented by the fantasy and covetousness of men.

The second thing that must be constantly and inviolably kept in the church of God, is the communion and "fellowship;" namely, that none look unto his own singular profit, that no man seek himself, but that every member, looking one to another what he lacketh, supply the same, helping him and comforting him, and giving him the best counsel he can. This friendly love and loving fellowship ought to be among Christians.

All temporal and outward goods ought to be common among them: not, as some fondly think, that I must defraud another of that which is his, or take it against his will, whether he will or no, or that I should go idly and loitering, eating and consuming that which other men labour and travail for; or to think, that when I do service and am profitable to no man, every man shall give and serve me. Christian love, which groweth out of the belief and doctrine of the gospel, must distribute the goods and make them common; it must not be any man's greedy desire, presumption, nor wilfulness, that shall do it.

All faithful believers are one body. Now, like as in the body one member serveth to the profit and wealth of another, so ought one Christian to help and serve another in love. The eye looketh not to himself only, but unto the whole body; the mouth eateth for the whole body, and for all the other members; the stomach digesteth for all the whole body, and for all the members. Thus ought it to be likewise among the spiritual members of the body of our Saviour Jesus Christ. No man must be wise and learned for himself only; no man ought to be rich for himself; but every man's gifts must serve to the profit one of another, and to the edifying and sustaining of the whole body. Every one is bound to serve the body, according to the gift and measure which the Spirit of God hath distributed unto him.

Among all living creatures, there is none created to a more loving and friendly society and fellowship than man. Hereunto serve all sciences and handicrafts, that men, after a friendly manner agreeing among themselves, may relieve one another's necessity and want, and help to bear one another's burden. Hereunto serve all inward gifts of the mind, as reason, and judgment, will, and remembrance: also the speech given of God unto man, whereby one is known and discerned, and made privy one to another. And therefore is man born into this world without any defence or weapon, bare, naked, and feeble; whereas all other creatures living in this world bring with them every one his weapon and defence. The bear hath his claws and teeth, the horse his hoof, the ox his horns, the hedgehog his pricks, and the serpent his poison, &c. Only man is born smooth and unweaponed, to signify that he must not be mad, furious, and terrible, but mild, loving, and gentle; there must be one mind, one meaning, and one will.

Man also cometh into the world bare, and naked, weak, feeble, and impotent, not able to do any manner of thing to help himself, but must stand unto the courtesy of another: for if he be not helped, relieved, and succoured, he could not choose but perish; there were no remedy. Whereby Almighty God will declare, that there is no man that either may or can live without the help and comfort of another. Thus the poor, wretched, and distressed child, lying upon all four, (whom, if it were not for pity, no man would take up, but let it lie still,) is helped, nourished, and brought up of the mother, nurse, &c. Other folks must cherish it; by other folks' help must it live: for nothing doth it bring with it into this world; it must beg and borrow everything, and therefore it weepeth and crieth.

This teacheth us to do good, to be obedient, loving, and thankful to our parents, and unto those which bring us up and do cherish us, that we recompense them according to our power. By this also we learn to help others, and to have compassion of them when they are in need, remembering and considering, out of what misery and poverty other folks have helped and brought us.

Who is he that is at this present so rich, so mighty, and strong in this world, if he will live, but he must use the help and service of poor and feeble folks, as the husbandman, the miller, the baker, the shepherd, the weaver, &c.? Yea, the higher and greater any man is in office or authority, so much the more must he use and have the help of other people, that are not so great as himself. Therefore doth God set up some so high, that they must make provision and help all those which are under them, seeing that they must have the use of them all. For the poor and they that be under must support and bear up the rich and mighty, as pillars do the house, that they fall not: for without the help and service of such are not they able to live in their dignity and calling one day. Therefore it is ordained of Almighty God in his secret wisdom, that certain countries lack some things, whereof others have sufficient and too much, that one might be sustained by another, and that no man shall be enough to himself.

God hath given unto man remembrance, to the intent that he should never forget the benefits which he from his youth upwards hath received of others, and daily doth receive; without the which he cannot live. And also again remember, and forget not, how and in what manner he ought to behave himself in love, in compassion, in succour, and in faithfulness towards those that have any ways need of his help. To this is he moved when he considereth and pondereth in his thoughts the weakness, feebleness, and necessity of man's corrupt nature, which constraineth us to lack so many things.

Hereof groweth unity, love, and fellowship among men, when we cast and call to our minds thus: either he hath been, or is now, profitable unto us, or he doth good unto ours, of whom we have profit, or hereafter he may do us some good. This to be so, there is not any man that can deny: and whereas we perceive not this, and are not of one mind, friendly, and fellows in love and good-will one towards another, but given unto such variance, dissension, strife, and discord, it cometh through the darkness of our own wicked and froward natures and dispositions.

Forasmuch now as our eyes are so blinded, that we see not God's ordinance and creation in man; our ears are so stopped, that we will not hear the plain and perfect voice of nature; our understanding and remembrance so dull and blunt, that we will not once regard or think any such thing, whereby we might the sooner forsake the division and stiffness of our heart, and in friendly unity and brotherly love to do good one to another; Christ therefore, the restorer of our decayed nature, and the only true and eternal light, came into this world to illuminate and lighten our blind eyes, to cry with his voice unto us that be dumb, and to set that again before our eyes, which we ourselves have made dark and dim. He crieth unto us in his gospel with a loud voice, so that no man can say he hath not heard it. He is the heavenly schoolmaster, the eternal wisdom, the fountain of all knowledge, the only and true teacher, the whole building of his church, the foundation and roof: the beginning and end of all his commandments hath he set and comprehended in only love, exhorting us to love, unity, and friendship, and saying, that "men hereby shall know us to be his disciples, if we love together, and do good one unto another;" and that then we are right and true Christians, when we do love one another, as he hath loved us.

What is a Christian else, but such an one, as being by the grace of Jesus Christ and of his Spirit delivered from the destroyed, poisoned, and wicked nature, is restored again to the original nature and godly disposition, from the which our spiritual enemy the devil had seduced him, taken him prisoner, and overcome him? Thus through Christ is man become the child of God; even he, which through pride, self-love, greediness, envy, hatred, discord, and division, became afore the devil's prisoner. Christ teacheth us love, faithfulness, and friendship; to love our neighbour as ourself, to do good, and help the poor: as in the fifth chapter of Matthew and the seventh verse, and in Luke, the sixth chapter, and in the five and twentieth chapter of Matthew, and in the thirteenth chapter of John, and in the twelfth chapter to the Romans and thirteenth verse, and John in his epistle. The apostles therefore, and faithful believers, at the beginning, as appeareth in the second chapter of the Acts of the Apostles, of very love and ferventness of the Spirit, had all things common, "distributing unto every one according as he had need." And this is the fellowship that is here spoken of, that as oft as the Christians came together, there was collection made and gathered for the relief and sustentation of the poor; whereof it is written in the first epistle to the Corinthians, the eleventh chapter, and fifteenth verse; and also in the second epistle to the Corinthians, the eighth chapter, and ninth verse.

The third thing is the breaking of the bread, the token of the new and everlasting covenant, which Christ upon the cross confirmed with his body and blood. This did the holy apostles and faithful believers use thus after the instruction of Christ. They took the bread; the same was broken, and to every one a portion given, which they did eat, giving thanks unto their heavenly Father, who had purged them from sin through the blood of Jesus Christ his dear Son; and so held they the joyful and glorious memorial of Christ's death.

Thus ought all faithful believers to do likewise: when they come together, as appertaineth, then with the breaking of the bread, and distribution of it among themselves, they must be mindful of the precious death and passion of Jesus Christ, rendering unto him perpetual thanks therefore. For Christ did not institute and ordain this his supper in vain, but thereby to make his church mindful and put them in remembrance of his death; and that over and besides faith, which inwardly liveth in the heart, the outward senses also might have somewhat to stir and draw them unto that, which faith inwardly considereth and looketh upon. These tokens are instituted, to signify and represent unto us high and great things, to gather together and unite the church; that, being dispersed every where over the face of the whole earth, might gather together into one communion and fellowship in Christ, and be made partakers of his promises, and enjoy those comfortable blessings which he hath promised from the beginning, namely, such as be faithful and true believers; and that the exterior and outward sense might from all corporal things be withdrawn to that which is spiritual. For the eyes see the bread, which representeth the body of Christ: they see, as the bread is broken, so was the body of Christ broken upon the cross for our sins; and that as the wine is poured in and out, so was the precious blood of Jesus Christ shed to wash away all our sins. The ears do hear Christ's words spoken by the minister in the person of Jesus Christ; by the which the promise is renewed, by which means those that are his, and of his church, are by a certain feeling and comfort in their souls and consciences refreshed. The taste upon the tongue, the smell in the nose, and likewise the handling, and so each other member in his several office, every one of them hath his delight and operation, in confessing, acknowledging, and doing his service unto faith.

But for what cause our Saviour Christ did specially use bread and wine before any other corporal things, to signify his death and shedding of his blood, it may well and easily be perceived by the nature of faith. With bread is the body fed and sustained, with wine are men's hearts made merry. Forasmuch then as faith, the life of our souls, through the flesh of Christ spiritually eaten is nourished and sustained; and seeing our mind is moistened and refreshed with true and perfect joy through the blood of Christ shed for us; there was nothing more meet, nothing more expedient, nothing more necessary for this sacrament, than bread and wine.

Moreover, through the blood of Christ are all other oblations and sacrifices clean laid aside: and therefore Christ, minding to finish the high sacrifice upon the cross, testified and declared beforehand, that his body being offered up, and his blood shed, should be sufficient to wash away all men's sins, and that from thenceforth there should not need any other sin-offering, in the which there must blood be shed. Therefore would he with evident and plain words testify and say: "This is my body, which is given for you; do this in remembrance of me. This is the cup of the new testament in my blood, which shall be shed for many to the forgiveness of sins." To the intent then that this excellent and worthy propitiation and sacrifice should not [be lost][1] out of their eyes and hearts, he added visible signs, not bare signs, but seals of his covenant, as was the circumcision and passah, and common tokens of love and friendship amongst men, even bread and wine, which have no blood, to declare that all blood for sin is only in Jesus Christ.

Christ's mind was also, in one body to couple and knit together[2] the whole multitude of his church. To signify this,

[[1] A word is here wanting in the original edition.]
[[2] After *together* the old edition repeats *in one body*.]

there[1] was nothing more apt and fit than wine and bread: for like as out of many corns is made one paste and one bread, and like as out of many grapes one wine floweth together; even so by faith and love become they all one body, that eat of one bread and drink of one cup.

And even from the beginning of the world it hath always been the use among men, that with bread and wine they have made and confirmed great friendship and league: and even so Christ with the distributing of the bread among his disciples would establish an everlasting friendship with them.

The fourth thing now in the church of Christ is prayer; namely, as Christ taught them to pray unto the Father of heaven, that the kingdom of his Son might still grow and increase, that his glory might arise and spread itself throughout all the world, that his name might be hallowed, and his will fulfilled, &c.

This is the necessariest thing of all: and if we lack this, in vain are all our good works, in vain are all the honest actions of a civil life, in vain are all godly exercises; nothing prospereth we go about, no oblation is sanctified, all is impurity, that we either do or think. The holy apostle Paul willeth us to pray continually: God granteth not the presence of his Spirit to any thing but unto prayer. Without the presence of God's Spirit, unprofitable is the word preached, unprofitable are the sacraments ministered, unprofitable shall all things be unto us; so that prayer is most requisite. Let us therefore pray unto Almighty God, to increase in us the spirit of prayer, that with our soul and spirit we may pray continually for spiritual gifts, that they may daily increase in us to his glory. Grant this the great giver of all good gifts, for his mercy sake! To whom be all honour, glory, power, dominion, and thanks, for ever and ever. Amen.

[[1] Old edition, *that there.*]

A PRAYER.

O MERCIFUL God, preserve our hearts from pride, from vain-glory, and from shameful covetousness: give us grace to abide in thy holy vocation, and to be thankful for thy grace; that the fall of thy apostle being always before our eyes, we may walk in thy fear before thee. For if we stand, we must take heed that we fall not, neither despise those that as yet do not stand. Make us to continue [in] thy grace; for nothing have we, saving only that which we have received of thee. And if of weakness we fall, put thy hand under us, O Lord, and suffer us not to despair in sin; but cause us with repentance and sorrow for our offence to resort unto thee. O keep us, that we neither despair, nor betray thy dearly beloved Son, whom thou through thy gospel dost send unto us; for without him is no safeguard, but eternal death and damnation. From which keep us, good Lord, for thy mercies' sake. Amen.

FINIS.

Glossary

This glossary gives words and phrases that are likely to cause difficulty to modern readers. Within the book, the Parker Society editor also added footnotes defining expressions that were obsolete in the 19th century.

affiance	trust or faith.
again	in return (back again).
approved of God	proven, shown, or attested by God.
away with(al)	put up with or get along with.
bewray, verb	to divulge secrets; to discredit a person by exposing his secrets or sins; more generally, to reveal, make known, show.
captain	leader.
certify (someone)	make (a person) certain or sure (*of* a matter); to assure, inform certainly.
Christ his sheep	Christ's sheep.
church militant	members of Christ who are yet living in this earth and doing battle with the world, the flesh, and the devil pursuant to their baptismal vows (as opposed to those who have died and are now at rest).
comfort, verb	The old meaning included strengthening a person's spirit or resolve as well as providing solace.
comfortable	able to give comfort, comforting.
commodity	benefit, convenience, advantage, or interest.
conceit	according to the context: notion, opinion, sometimes frame of mind or disposition.

conditions	characteristics.
contentation	willing acceptance.
convenient	befitting, proper.
conversation	life, manner of life, way of living.
crack, verb	boast, sometimes with sense of scorn toward others. Past form 'crake.'
dainty	particular about comfort and luxury.
despise, verb	hate, scorn, or hold in contempt; more weakly, neglect or ignore.
despite	contemptuous and injurious attitude or action.
dizzard	idiotic; as a noun, idiot.
doctrine	in some contexts, a lesson or piece of instruction.
dubitation	uncertainty, hesitation.
Easter	Passover. See also 'passah.'
entreating	treatment.
fain	in "would fain": would gladly, would like to.
fly, verb	flee, escape away.
force not	care not, have no concern for.
froward	habitually contrary, rebellious. More generally, evilly inclined.
fumishness	irascibility, inclination to fume.
furnish, verb	supply, provide, prepare; sometimes, adorn.
gear	according to the context: (1) doctrine; in depreciatory sense, stuff and nonsense (2) apparatus, equipment (3) armour, arms (see also 'harness' and 'ordnance').
ghostly	spiritual.
godly	divine, as in "godly power" or "godly wisdom."
hale, verb	pull, drag.

GLOSSARY

happen of course	happen as a matter of course.
harness	defensive armour or equipment, military accoutrement. See also 'ordnance' and 'gear.'
health	salvation.
Helias	Elijah.
Hierusalem	Jerusalem.
holiday	holy day.
honesty	decency, whence *honest* or decent.
hurley-burlies	commotions, tumults, uproars.
inconvenience	according to the context: disagreement or strife; sometimes absurdity.
indurate	hardened.
Jewry (also spelled Jury)	depending on the context, Judea in ancient Rome, or more generally Israel or Judah; also the Jewish people collectively.
keep, verb	guard, protect, watch over.
lovers	loving friends.
lust, noun or verb	wish or desire.
lusty, lustily	according to the context: willing, strong, valiant, vigorous, desirous. Also pleasing (as in "lusty to the eyes"). Whence *lustily*: willingly, valiantly, etc.
meat	food, sustenance.
meddle (with), verb	to concern or occupy oneself with or in a matter. The sense of undue interference was not always present in older use.
naughty	according to the context: worthless, morally bad, or blameworthy.
noise, verb	tell widely as a report or rumour.
noisome	harmful, noxious; more weakly, annoying.

notify (to), verb	tell, inform.
nurture	upbringing or education.
open, verb	according to the context: declare, reveal, disclose, or show.
ordnance	armour, weapons, and military supplies. See also 'harness' and 'gear.'
original	origin, fount, or source.
passah	Passover. See also 'Easter.'
pelf	rubbish, frippery. Also riches; in depreciative sense, ill-gotten goods or riches as a corrupting influence.
prevent, verb	go before.
prince	high ruler.
publish, verb	declare widely, make known abroad.
save, verb	in some contexts, safeguard.
scholars	students.
science	knowledge; also a field of study.
sentence	judgement or meaning.
shifting	wily maneuvering.
stomach	used like 'heart' or 'breast' to indicate the inward seat of emotion, feelings, or secret thoughts.
sweep-stake	in "make sweep-stake": remove totally; i.e., sweep away.
target	a shield or buckler to ward off blows.
tell, verb	count (past form 'told' = counted).
temptation(s)	in some contexts, trial(s).
token	sign.
trow, verb	trust, believe. In "I trow (you)" = I trust, suppose, think, believe.

GLOSSARY

trusty	depending on the context, either trustworthy or trusting.
tutor	guardian, protector.
ugsome	horrible, loathsome.
unspeakable, unoutspeakable	indescribable, inexpressible.
utter, verb	reveal by deed or declare by word.
wealth	well-being, welfare.
Whitsunday	Pentecost.
witty	wise or prudent.
wot, verb	know.
wroth	deep anger or resentment.

www.ingramcontent.com/pod-product-compliance
Lightning Source LLC
Chambersburg PA
CBHW020904080526
44589CB00011B/432